RETURN

HOW TO DRAW YOUR CHILD BACK TO THE CHURCH

BRANDON VOGT

SECOND EDITION

WORD
on FIRE

Word on Fire, Park Ridge, IL 60068
© 2021 by Word on Fire Catholic Ministries
Printed in the United States of America
All rights reserved.

Design and layout by Cassie Pease.

While all stories in this book are true, some names and identifying information
have been changed to protect the privacy of the individuals involved.
Also, while all stories are based on real experiences, some have been
merged or generalized to represent common themes.

First Edition published 2015 by Numinous Books.
Second Edition 2021.
24 23 22 21   1 2 3 4

ISBN: 978-1-943243-74-7

Library of Congress Control Number: 2020925473

https://wordonfire.org/return

ENDORSEMENTS

"Every Catholic parent needs this book. It demolishes the myths about why young people leave the Church and lays out a wonderful (and very practical) step-by-step plan for helping them come back to the faith."

— **Trent Horn**, staff apologist for Catholic Answers

"*Return* is the resource that parents of fallen-away children have been waiting for: it combines powerful spiritual insights with practical tips that you can begin applying right now. It's like a bootcamp for spiritual warriors who are about to go out on a great search-and-rescue mission."

— **Jennifer Fulwiler**, blogger and author of *Something Other Than God*

"Brandon Vogt's *Return* offers practical and realistic ways to bring lost souls home. And I should know: I was one of those kids who left the Church for over ten years. *Return* hits home for me. It reveals not just why people are drifting from the Church but how to get them back into the fold of Christ. It's a true treasure for our times."

— **Leah Darrow**, Catholic speaker, author, and founder of Lux University

"Everywhere I go I meet parents who are troubled because their children no longer practice the faith. Finally, here is a practical guide to doing something about that. It's time we took this problem seriously, and *Return* can help with that."

— **Matthew Kelly**, founder of Dynamic Catholic

"*Return* is a resource that is desperately needed by today's Catholic families. This terrific new resource is full of practical, supportive, and affirming answers. A 'must have' for every Catholic home, parish, and library!"

— **Lisa M. Hendey**, author of *The Grace of Yes*

"The number one question I am asked frequently is, 'How can we get our son or daughter back to the Catholic Church?' This grieves the hearts of millions of parents. Finally, someone has given us sound tools, prayers, and wisdom on this vital issue. Brandon has once again created an inspirational book to help us bring loved ones home to Jesus and His holy Church!"

— **Tom Peterson**, founder of Catholics Come Home

"What greater gift could any parent want for their fallen-away Catholic child than to help them get back in touch with God's grace? Brandon Vogt's new book, *Return*, offers more than just practical wisdom and timeless advice, it is a roadmap of evangelization for Catholic parents of fallen-away Catholics. Buy this book. Read this book. Do what this book says. Then see what great gift God has for your family!"

— **Marcel LeJeune**, author and founder of Catholic Missionary Disciples

"Well-researched and realistic, Brandon Vogt's *Return* is not just hope-filled, but superbly hope-filling. A resounding answer to many Catholic parents' most ardent prayers."

— **Dr. Stephen Bullivant**, Director of the Benedict XVI Centre for Religion and Society at St. Mary's University

"One of the most common questions I get as the director of St. Paul Street Evangelization is, 'How can I bring my son or daughter back to the Church?' I hear it all the time. Every Catholic I know has at least one close family member who has drifted away from the Church. Brandon Vogt's *Return* is an excellent answer to that question. He does a great job laying the foundation and sharing the best tips and practical strategies. Buy this book if you want to help your child come back."

— **Steve Dawson**, founder of St. Paul Street Evangelization

"The LORD says . . .

Stop your crying and wipe away your tears.

All that you have done for your children will not
go unrewarded. . . .

There is hope for your future;

your children will come back home.

I, the LORD, have spoken."

–JEREMIAH 31:16–17 (GNT)

For all those who have drifted away
and those preparing to draw them back

TABLE OF CONTENTS

PART I – UNDERSTANDING THE PROBLEM

PART II – THE GAME PLAN

PART III – THE BIG OBJECTIONS

FOREWORD

by Bishop Robert Barron

The Church faces many challenges today, but I am convinced that the most pressing concern, at least in America, is the attrition of our own people. Thirteen percent of Americans identify as former Catholics, and for every one convert to the Catholic faith, more than six people leave. One-third of people raised Catholic no longer identify as Catholic today, and attendance at the Mass, identified by the Second Vatican Council as "the source and summit of the Christian life," continues to fall, with only a paltry 24% in the pews on any given Sunday. The statistics get worse among younger generations. One-third of the Millennial generation now claims no religious affiliation, and only 16% identify as Catholic.

It's easy to gloss over these numbers and justify a false sense of security. Admittedly, the overall Catholic population has remained relatively stable, but this is mostly a result of immigration, of faithful new immigrants replacing the Catholics who leave. But obviously this is not a sustainable or desirable trend. Even among immigrants, as cultural assimilation takes hold of second and third generations, they leave the Church at rates similar to the general Catholic population. As many evangelists have observed, "God has no grandchildren." Each generation must meet Christ and the Church for the first time, not relying on mere cultural ambience or ethnic identification.

But while God may not have grandchildren, people do. If you're reading this excellent book by Brandon Vogt, chances are high that you're a parent or grandparent, worrying that your child has drifted away from the faith. In the face of apparent failure and heartbreak, you're asking yourself, *What went wrong? Did I do enough? What more could I have done? Is there anything I can do now? How does one repair a broken relationship with Christ and the Church?*

To these many questions, Brandon Vogt's *Return* offers tremendous and desperately needed help. Every parent or grandparent with a fallen-away child needs to read this book. You'll find concrete advice and practical strategies. Rather than opting for despair, Brandon calls for creativity and courage, new approaches imbued with the liveliness of the New Evangelization. *Return* includes one of the best summations of Catholic attrition, coupled with keen insights as to why people dismiss the Church's faith. He doesn't cast aspersions or blame, and he avoids the scapegoating that marks some approaches to this problem. Instead he focuses on the solution, using a positive emphasis on what parents can say and do to respond to their child's objections, rebuild relationships, and ultimately draw them back to the Church.

Return offers no magic-bullet guarantee that your child will come back. But you will find a complete game plan to create the best possible environment to reintroduce your child to Christ and his Church.

I have worked alongside Brandon Vogt for some time now in the fields of the Lord's work. His dedication to the cause of evangelization is exemplary. He is a pioneering missionary disciple, whose sense of joy for the Gospel is contagious and reassuring. Therefore, if your son or daughter has left the faith, I encourage you not to give up hope and to learn from his advice in this book. *Return* will serve as an essential resource for the Church's evangelization efforts and a true game-changer for desperate parents everywhere.

— **Bishop Robert Barron**
Auxiliary Bishop of Los Angeles and Founder of Word on Fire

INTRODUCTION

John's family was enjoying a nice, quiet dinner together, sitting around the table discussing his first semester at college. The conversation was great until his mother, Dianne, casually wondered which parish he was attending at school.

John hesitated, then said, "Well, to tell you the truth, I haven't really been to church in a while. It's hard in college—I have class, and sports, and activities, and I'm so busy. I went to Mass a few times when I first got there but then I skipped one or two Sundays. Over time, I guess I just stopped going. I actually haven't been in a while . . ."

"Oh," his mother replied, gulping nervously. "Hmm. I'm a little surprised. You went to church every Sunday growing up; we raised you Catholic. It's really important that you . . ."

"Mom, it's okay," John interrupted. "To be honest, I'm not sure I really see the point anymore. I mean, I appreciated church growing up. I'm really glad we all went. It shaped me and helped me to become a good person. But after meeting new people at college, and really thinking about God and faith for the first time, I realized that I'm not sure if I really believe it myself. I just kind of accepted it because that's what you guys believed. I went to church because that's what we did as a family, and that's what everyone believed growing up. But I'm not sure I believe it all anymore, and I feel that if I go to church now, I'd just be a hypocrite."

Dianne's heart sank. Her throat tightened. She looked at her husband for support, but neither knew what to say. A few moments passed before she murmured out a reply:

"Wow, I'm . . . not even sure how to respond. I just thought by sending you to Catholic schools . . ."

"Really, it's okay, Mom," John interrupted. "It's not a big deal. None of my college friends go to church and they're all really good people—nice, generous, open-minded, tolerant. Like I said, I think it was good that I went to church growing up and Catholic school, and I'm happy that you and Dad get a lot out of it, but I just don't see the need anymore. Maybe one day when I have kids, I'll come back so they can be raised with good morals, but I'm fine without it for now."

If you're a Catholic parent in the United States, and if the statistics hold true, this isn't a far-fetched scenario for you. It's real and familiar. Chances are at least one of your children has drifted away from the Church and, at least right now, shows no signs of coming back.

And it's not just your family. The Catholic Church is hemorrhaging young people.

Half of young Americans who were raised Catholic no longer identify as Catholic today. Roughly eight in ten (79%) who shed their faith leave before age twenty-three.

Some drift away as teenagers while searching for their own identity. Some have been hurt by people in the Church. Others slide into lifestyles that conflict with Church teaching. Many go off to college, connect with non-Christians or skeptical professors, and slowly lose their faith. Some move into the world, start a family, and get swept up in work, hobbies, and family life, losing their faith in the shuffle. There are lots of stories, but most of them share the same outcome: young people fleeing the Church.

The parable of the prodigal son is being reenacted every day in homes across the country as millions of mothers and fathers wait for their children to come home to the Church. It is being relived in the eye-rolls and shrugs of children who don't care about God, and in the tears, pain, and frustration of the broken dreams and cries of "Where did we go wrong?"

Few experiences cause more despair than having a child leave the Church. Parents become deeply concerned about what will happen to their child after death if he continues to reject the faith. How will God judge him? How will God judge us? Will we all be together for eternity?

Others worry about how the situation will impact family relationships. Will it change how the family celebrates holidays and special occasions? Will it cause divisions in the family? Will the child begin to distance himself? One mother laments, "My son and his wife will not attend family First Communions or confirmations because they don't want their child exposed to Catholic rituals. It has driven a wedge through the core of our family."

If the grief wasn't enough, many parents also experience guilt and shame, thinking they are to blame for their children drifting away. "All of this is so humiliating," one mother admitted. "We were always known as the perfect Catholic family. I can just hear people saying, 'Well, I guess they weren't as good as we thought they were.'"

Most parents feel helpless. They're desperate to draw their child back to the Church, but they don't know what to do.

Over the last several years, I've encountered this situation many, many times. I've spoken with thousands of Catholics around the country at large conferences, small parish groups, and everything in between. After each talk I give, there's usually a question-and-answer session. Inevitably, no matter the topic of my talk, the most common question I hear is some version of this: "My child has left the faith and I'm devastated. What should I do?"

For a long time, many Church leaders suggested we just play the waiting game. "Oh, take heart, your child will come back," they encouraged. "Just wait until they get married or have children." But as we'll see later in this book, that's just no longer the case. Today, very few young adults who drift away end up coming back solely because of marriage or children.

The passive wait-and-see game is no longer an option. We need a different strategy, something more attuned to reality. We need to understand the landscape and the real reasons why our young people drift away. Then, once we understand the problem, we need a game plan to bring them home.

That's precisely what this book will give you. I spent over a year planning and researching this book, talking with experts and chatting with hundreds of parents and young people who have left and returned to the Church. I wanted to figure out exactly what works, and then share it with the millions of parents who are desperate for help. In this book, you'll discover the best practical strategies for drawing your child back—no fluff, no spiritual platitudes, just real, proven strategies that work.

Imagine the joy of seeing your child next to you at Mass again, not just sitting there disinterestedly but excitedly praying and worshipping the

Lord. Picture the bliss of having deep conversations about God and the faith. Imagine the satisfaction of knowing your child is in a thriving, personal relationship with Jesus in his Church, and is a committed disciple who will spend all eternity with you and the heavenly Father, and all his saints and angels.

Those are not just fantasies. They are real possibilities, and this book will put you on the path toward fulfilling them.

A few quick notes before we dive in. First, the language. You'll notice throughout the book that I frequently refer to "your child." This isn't because your son or daughter is an adolescent or teenager (though perhaps that's true)—they might be college-aged, or even a young adult. But I use the word *child* because that's the place they still hold in your heart. We're talking about your *child*, your own flesh and blood, a person you would do anything for and sacrifice whatever was necessary to bring back to the Church. In this book, I also use the masculine pronoun *he* because I wanted to avoid the confusing shifts between *he* and *she* and the burdensome *them* to describe individuals. But the advice in this book applies equally well to sons or daughters. Lastly, I use the term *former Catholic*, which is how many people think of themselves after drifting from the Church, even though such people are not—and can never become—former Catholics as far as Christ and the Church are concerned. The Church never regards her children as having left the family, no matter what they do or how distant they drift, even if they themselves no longer regard themselves as belonging. But with that in mind, for the sake of clarity, we'll use the term *former Catholic* to describe those who no longer actively practice their Catholic faith.

Another thing worth noting is that this isn't a guide to *keeping* your kids Catholic. Lots of other resources help instill a deep and lasting faith in your children while they're young. These are desperately needed. But the question we're focusing on here, and likely the question you're asking is What do I do *after* my child has already left? You may wish you had responded differently while he was young, but that ship has sailed. You don't need to keep it docked; you need to steer it home. Thankfully, that's what you'll learn in this book.

Third, this book doesn't propose a magic formula. I wish there was a simple, plug-and-play formula that was guaranteed to lead your child back to the Church, no matter his situation. You just plug in the child, follow the steps, and *voila!* He's back. But alas, we're dealing with real people and many variables—you, your child, personal beliefs, free will. I can't guarantee that the steps in this book will *definitely* lead your child back to the Church. But I can promise these strategies will create the *best possible environment* to facilitate his return. They will increase the odds dramatically.

Fourth, this isn't a quick fix. You probably won't finish this book and see your child heading for the confessional the next day (though anything is possible with God!). As you'll discover later, this journey could take months or even years to reach its goal. Conversion is a slow process. In most cases, a child drifts from the Church over a long period of time, and what took months to occur usually takes months to reverse. So commit right now to being in this for the long run. If you're looking for a convert-your-child-quick scheme, this isn't it. But if you want solid tools that work, even if they take time, you're holding the right book.

I should say one final thing. You might be tempted to skip ahead in the book. In fact, you may have already skimmed the Table of Contents and jumped to an intriguing chapter. But it's really important that you read the sections in order since they build on one another. So, for example, if you skip Part I and move straight to the "Game Plan," you'll learn how to draw your child back before really understanding *why* he left in the first place. That's like a doctor diving into surgery before he diagnoses what's wrong with the patient—it's bad and potentially harmful. So be sure to read the chapters slowly, in order. Trust me, it's worth it.

So now you have a choice to make: Are you ready? Do you want to finally make progress with your child? Do you want to help him reverse course and find his way back to the Church?

If so, then now is the time. Now is the time for him to encounter Jesus anew. Now is the time for him to rediscover his faith. Now is the time for him to receive all the gifts God has for him in his Church.

Now is the time for him to return.

PART I
Understanding the Problem

"The most significant challenge facing the Catholic Church today is the attrition of our own people."

— BISHOP ROBERT BARRON

CHAPTER 1
Why Are They Leaving?

If there's one thing about which any parent of wayward children should take solace, it's that you're not alone. The statistics surrounding those who leave are not just dire. They signal a religious epidemic.

Reliable data shows that half (50% exactly) of young Americans who were raised Catholic no longer call themselves Catholic today. Think about what that means. Over the last twenty to thirty years, half of the babies you've seen baptized, half of the children you've seen confirmed, and half of the kids in your parish youth group have left the Church. If you're a parent with multiple children, it's a fairly sure bet that at least one has drifted away.

But that 50% statistic only concerns religious *identification*, not practice. Although just 50% of young people raised in the Church still identify as Catholic, that doesn't mean they all attend Mass or have a personal and dynamic faith. Researchers at Notre Dame found that when we gauge young people by that more stringent criteria, the number sinks to shocking lows: just 7% of young people raised in the Church still actively practice their faith today, meaning they still attend Mass weekly, pray a few times a week, and say their faith is "extremely" or "very" important to them. So only half of our young people are still "Catholic" but among those, a huge majority aren't seriously living out their faith.

So when does the breakdown occur? A recent Pew Research Center study showed that eight in ten (79%) who drift away from faith leave before age twenty-three. These aren't middle-aged Americans, fed up with the Church or disgruntled because of changes at Vatican II. They're disenchanted teenagers and young adults. They attend high schools and colleges, they're on social media every day, but there's one place they're not: in church.

This problem extends across many ethnicities and regions. For instance, although 55% of Hispanic adults are Catholic, a stunning one in four Hispanics in America are now *former* Catholics. Soon, the majority of US

Catholics will be Hispanic but the majority of Hispanics will no longer be Catholic.

When we parents and leaders hear these statistics, our first reaction is likely shock and despair. And because we're natural problem solvers, our next inclination is probably to ask, Why? Why are children leaving? What's pulling or pushing them away?

The hard reality is that there's no one answer. Pope Benedict XVI was once asked, "How many ways are there to God?" and he said, "As many as there are people." Similarly, G.K. Chesterton, a famous convert to Catholicism, said, "The Church is a house with a hundred gates; and no two men enter at exactly the same angle."

If people *enter* the Church through different routes, they certainly leave through just as many—if not more. The most recent Pew religious land-scape survey found that for every person who becomes Catholic, roughly 6.5 leave the Church. That ratio of loss-to-gain was the worst of any religious or nonreligious group. It means that for each person coming in the front door of the Church, six or seven leave through the back. We might paraphrase Chesterton to say, "The Church is a house with a hundred gates and people are rushing out of each one!"

But again, what's causing people to exit? Some leave for personal reasons. They had a bad experience with a priest or fellow Catholic, they became too busy for Mass, or they just find church boring. Others leave for moral reasons. They disagree with the Church's sexual teachings or they think Catholics are too judgmental. Still more leave for theological reasons. They think Catholics don't place enough emphasis on Jesus or the Bible, or they weren't being spiritually fed, or maybe they just stopped believing in God altogether.

We must be careful not to assume everyone leaves for the same reasons. Having spoken with hundreds of former Catholics, many of whom have returned to the Church, I can say from personal experience that assuming their reasons for leaving can have harmful consequences. For example, a friend of mine was beginning to doubt that the Eucharist really was the Body and Blood of Christ, and so he stopped going to Mass. But when his mother found out he was no longer attending, she dismissively suggested he was actually just lazy and wanted to sleep in on Sunday mornings. The sting of that barb took many months to heal.

Of course, as a parent, you're not worried as much about national statistics as you are about your own child. You want to know why *your* child left. Later in the book, you'll learn how to set up conversations to pull this information into the light. You'll discover how to dig past the surface-level reasons your child might give, which often mask deeper issues and concerns.

But before we get there, let's first take a 30,000-foot view of the situation to see the most common reasons why people leave in general. We'll look at data from large surveys of thousands of former Catholics, and we'll also discover common misunderstandings about God and the Church. Later, you'll discover exactly how to answer these objections. But for now, we just want to learn *what* the objections are and why they cause people to leave.

As you continue reading, focus on detecting *your* child in one or more of the descriptions. Understanding the "big picture" of why people leave the Church can equip you to handle your child's particular reasons.

The Most Common Reasons Why People Leave the Church

The Diocese of Springfield, Illinois, knew they had a problem. Catholics were leaving the Church in droves and they weren't sure why. So, in 2014, the diocese partnered with researchers at Benedictine University to commission a large survey of lapsed and former Catholics to ask them a simple question: Why did you leave?

Many businesses use this "exit survey" technique to poll former customers or employees. But few church groups have considered the approach. Instead of assuming or imagining why they left, why not just ask them?

The survey was admittedly not perfect. It didn't use random sampling, and the respondents skewed older. It was not completely representative since, as we learned, most people who leave the Church do so while they're young. But the results still paint a helpful picture of why many Catholics abandon the Church today.

Here were the most common reasons people gave (the percentage indicates the number of respondents who said the factor played a role in their departure):

- Spiritual needs not met (68%)
- Lost interest (67%)
- Too many money requests (56%)
- No longer believe (48%)
- Dissatisfaction with atmosphere (47%)
- Too ritualistic (38%)
- Too formal (36%)
- Music not enjoyable (36%)

How many of those reasons do you think rubbed *your* child the wrong way? Maybe your child doesn't personally feel put off by donation requests, but did he lose interest or fail to have his spiritual needs met?

A few years before the Diocese of Springfield conducted its exit surveys, the Pew Forum on Religion and Public Life released a much larger study. Instead of a few hundred people, it involved tens of thousands of respondents, and was both scientific and representative. Titled "Faith in Flux: Changes in Religious Affiliation in the U.S.," it revealed many of the same insights as the Springfield survey.

Here were the most common reasons people gave for leaving the Catholic Church:

- Just gradually drifted away from the religion (71%)
- Stopped believing in the religion's teachings (65%)
- Spiritual needs not being met (43%)
- Unhappy with teachings about the Bible (29%)
- Dissatisfaction with atmosphere at worship services (26%)
- Dissatisfied with clergy at congregation (18%)
- Found a religion they liked more (10%)

Between the Springfield and Pew surveys, we learn that there are two main groupings: people leave the Catholic Church because they drift away slowly and unintentionally, or they leave for specific, spiritual/theological reasons.

The Diocese of Trenton, New Jersey, found similar conclusions in a survey they commissioned in 2012. Like the Diocese of Springfield, they wanted to know why Catholics were leaving their parishes, so they interviewed nearly three hundred non-churchgoing Catholics to find out. Interestingly, about a quarter said they had separated themselves from the parish but still considered themselves to be Catholic. One respondent wrote, "I separated my family from the Catholic Church and turned to an alternate religion for a while and then returned knowing I had the right religion but the wrong people running it." Several chose to specify that they separated themselves from "the hierarchy." Many sociologists have noted that the millennial generation (those born between the early 1980s and the early 2000s) are especially skeptical about institutions and authorities, and so they naturally grate against the hierarchical Catholic Church. In many cases, young people have no problem with Jesus but many problems with the Church.

A common theme in the Trenton survey was how the lack of community pushed people away. "As much as I wanted to get involved and expand my faith," said one respondent, "there were no clear avenues to do that. So, it was just a place to attend Mass. And because attending Mass was a guilt-ridden obligation, I was always alone in a crowd where I knew no one and no one knew me." Another said, "I did not experience community in the sense that I knew people just from going to church. The ones I knew, I knew them outside of church. No one misses the fact that we stopped going. No one has called from the parish, even though we were regular attendees and envelope users!"

The Church's Sexual Teachings

While lots of young people drift away unintentionally, or for spiritual reasons, many rebel against the Church's sexual teachings, primarily those on homosexuality, abortion, contraception, divorce, and cohabitation. Recently, a teacher at a Catholic university handed out note cards on the first day of class. She asked her students to write down their answers to this question: "What do Christians believe?" A few of the answers, though not many, predictably centered around Jesus, Baptism, and salvation. But she was shocked that almost every single card referenced homosexuality or abortion (and many listed both). Most references were negative. One student responded, "I know Christians don't like gay people or women, but that's all I ever learned in Christian school. I don't know what else to list."

Those students aren't alone. Another recent Pew study found that among former Catholics who are now unaffiliated with any religion, 56% said they were unhappy with teachings on abortion and homosexuality; 48% were unhappy with teachings on birth control; 39% were unhappy with how the Church treated women; and 33% were unhappy with teachings on divorce and remarriage. A group of University of Notre Dame researchers found that despite distinctive and strong Catholic Church teachings against abortion, birth control, capital punishment, suicide, and divorce, the views of Catholic young adults on these issues "are nearly indistinguishable" from their non-Catholic counterparts.

What does this mean? It means the Church's sexual teachings are leading many young people to leave and stay away from the Church. To give just one common example, for many young people Catholicism is no longer a serious option simply because they assume the Catholic Church condemns same-sex-attracted people. Since most of them have friends who identify as gay or lesbian, they feel they have to make a choice between the Catholic Church and those friends. And the friends almost always win.

Later in this book, we'll see how this is a false choice. The Catholic Church doesn't condemn same-sex-attracted people but instead lifts up their dignity, even while recognizing the disorder of sexual acts outside of marriage. You'll learn how to delicately discuss this and the other sexual issues later.

But the point to realize now is that these obstacles may have played a large role in your child leaving the Church *and* may be great barriers to him returning.

A Warped View of God

Most of the issues we've discussed so far are spiritual and moral. We've seen how people drift away because they aren't spiritually fed or because they disagree with the Church's sexual teachings. But a different problem, one that accentuates the others, is the way many young people misunderstand God.

Several studies over the last two decades have confirmed that most young people in America, churched and unchurched, believe in what sociologists Christian Smith and Melinda Lundquist Denton have called "moralistic therapeutic deism." It's so critical to understand this misguided view about God, because it's likely this is a main reason your child resists the Catholic Church.

The authors sum up this "moralistic therapeutic deism" view in five statements:

1. A God exists who created and ordered the world and watches over human life on earth. This is where we get the "deism" part. Catholicism is a form of *theism*, meaning it holds a personal God who continually interacts with his creation. Followers of *deism*, however, believe that God set the world in motion but rarely involves himself in daily affairs. He's like a watchmaker who places all the gears and springs and starts the watch, but then sits back as it runs on its own. Your child probably sees God this way—distant, uninvolved, and pleased to let the world just tick along. More than half (54%) of nominally Catholic young adults believe in God but think he is not personal, which is essentially deism. And if your child believes in deism more than theism, it's no surprise he has no personal connection to God or the Church. Thus, one of your first tasks is to make faith personal for him.

2. God wants people to be good, nice, and fair to each other, as taught in the Bible and by most world religions. This is the "moralistic" part. It assumes the goal of religion is simply to be nice to others. If you ask your fallen-away child, "What's the point of religion?" he'll likely offer some form of that answer: religion is about becoming a good person. This, of course, is a far cry from the core of Christianity, which is centered on knowing, loving, and imitating Jesus Christ, who is God incarnate. True Christianity is about Christ's death and Resurrection, his forgiveness of our sins, and his reconciling all creation into a new and glorious kingdom, which begins through his Church. Reducing that breathtaking vision to "just being nice" is like suggesting the Sistine Chapel is about "just some colors."

It's important to recognize this misperception because chances are, when you try to help your child "return to church" or "get right with God," they'll see those pursuits through a moralistic lens. They'll assume you're mainly interested in changing their *behavior* rather than drawing them into a dynamic relationship with God. This is why leading with moral commands can often harm your child's chances of returning. But we'll get to that later. For now, the key insight is that becoming a disciple of Jesus Christ *leads* to becoming a good person, but that's not all it involves. True religion can't be reduced to morals.

3. The central goal of life is to be happy and to feel good about oneself. This is the "therapeutic" part. It holds that the most important thing in life is to be happy and emotionally stable. C.S. Lewis gives voice to this view when he says, "What would really satisfy us would be a God who said of anything we happened to like doing, 'What does it matter so long as they are contented?' We want, in fact, not so much a Father in heaven as a grandfather in heaven—a senile benevolence who, as they say, 'liked to see the young people enjoying themselves' and whose plan for the universe was simply that it might be truly said at the end of each day 'a good time was had by all.'" On this view, God becomes a sort of cosmic therapist whose main goal is not to upset our feelings or bring us discomfort. Yet as Pope Benedict XVI affirmed, "We were not created for an easy life, but for great things, for goodness." True Christianity leads to more than happy feelings, although they may come. Instead, it offers everlasting joy. As we all know, that sort of deep joy sometimes involves difficulty, pain, and discomfort along the way— you know this especially as a parent. Thus, the goal of life is not to feel good about ourselves; it's to find joy in knowing and loving God.

4. God does not need to be particularly involved in one's life except when God is needed to resolve a problem. This is where each of the above three parts fit together. If we combine the deistic view of God with his therapeutic role, we assume God exists to solve our problems. Need help studying for test? Ask for God's assistance. Receive a bad diagnosis? Time to turn to "the big guy." Strapped for money? Ask God to send some funds your way. To be clear, these requests are not bad in themselves. In fact, we're encouraged to bring our greatest needs to God. Jesus says, "Come to me, all you who labor and are burdened, and I will give you rest" (Matt. 11:28). The problem arises when the *only* times we turn to God are when we need help, when "asking" becomes our only form of prayer.

Imagine if you had a friend and the only time you ever talked to him was when you needed a favor—and only huge favors. That's not real friendship. Any relationship predicated *only* on begging is not a mutual relationship.

5. **Good people go to heaven when they die.** Finally, this part assumes that we earn our way to heaven simply by being good people. It's the effect of reducing religion down to morality. Decent people are automatically saved because of their decency and since every person is essentially decent, pretty much everyone will be saved (except maybe Hitler and Judas). You can only lose salvation by doing something really, really bad like mass murder, and then not saying you're sorry. On this view, we earn our own salvation by doing nice things and avoiding really, really bad things.

So, look back over these five characteristics. Do you think they describe the way your child sees God? Do they describe the way *you* see God? In either case, you'll learn in the coming chapters how to reorient this perspective. But the point is clear: if someone has a dramatically warped view about God, that's the first thing we need to address before helping him to return to God out of love.

The Ultimate Reason Why Anyone Leaves the Church

We've now covered several common reasons why young people leave the Church, and chances are at least one will strongly resonate with your child's situation. However, consider a boat untethered from the dock, drifting out to sea. We can observe factors that *pull* the boat out (e.g., the wind and waves) but also factors that allowed the boat to leave in the first place—namely, that it was not properly tethered to the dock, or anchored. Most young people who leave the Church are easily pulled away because they have nothing anchoring them to stay.

To put it simply, the ultimate reason people leave the faith is because they're not rooted in a living encounter with Jesus in the Church. If they consistently encounter the Lord in the Church, then despite all the problems, frustrations, scandals, and pain they may suffer and observe, they would nevertheless echo St. Peter's reply to Jesus when he asked whether the disciples would leave him: "Master, to whom shall we go?" (John 6:68).

Catholics have a specific term for the act of helping people encounter Jesus: *evangelization.* To *evangelize* means to announce the Good News of Jesus raised from the dead and help others to personally encounter him.

But over the last several decades, we've done a poor job at that. As many Church leaders have pointed out, most people raised in the Church are baptized. Many are catechized. But few are evangelized. Most have moved through institutional and sacramental funnels, but they have not truly encountered the Lord Jesus in a personal, profound way.

If we want to prevent our children from leaving the Church, and if we want to win them back after they've drifted, we need to create what Pope Francis calls a "culture of encounter," which unites young people to Jesus *through* his Church, not in spite of it.

The whole second part of this book will show you how to do that. But before we get there, let's focus on another important question. We now have a good sense of why young people leave the Church. But when they leave, where are they going?

CHAPTER 2
Where Are They Going?

It's the major religious story of the past twenty-five years: the meteoric rise of the "nones." These are people who check the "none" box on religious surveys, signaling they don't associate themselves with any religious tradition. Sociologists often group the "nones" alongside smaller nonbelieving groups such as atheists (who don't believe in God) and agnostics (who are not sure whether God exists) to create the broad category of the "religiously unaffiliated."

From 2007 to 2014, the percentage of religiously unaffiliated Americans soared from 16% to 23%. That 7% gain, which represents around 19 million people, was more than five times higher than the gain of any other group. What does that mean? It means the "nones" are taking over—and fast.

This is bad news for all religious groups, but especially Catholics, since we're suffering the greatest losses to the "nones." Among the nonreligious, 21% were raised in an unaffiliated home, while 28% were raised Catholic—more than any other tradition. That means if you bump into the average unaffiliated adult, he's more likely to have been raised Catholic than anything else.

The percentage of those who identify as "nones" is even higher among young people. In 2014, the median age of the entire US population was forty-six. The median age of Catholics was forty-nine. The median age of the unaffiliated? Just thirty-six.

When we focus only on millennials, those born between the early 1980s and the early 2000s, roughly 35% identify as religiously unaffiliated compared to just 16% who identify as Catholic. In other words, young people are now *twice* as likely to say they have no religion than to identify as Catholic.

Now, I don't want to overwhelm you with statistics. So let's pause, step back, and focus on the big picture that all these statistics point toward. Here it is:

If you raised your child Catholic, there's a roughly 50% chance he left the Church before turning thirty. And if he did so, he likely became unaffiliated, no longer identifying with any religion.

However, it's important to note that unaffiliated isn't the only label former Catholics settle on. According to the Pew Research Center, here's a breakdown of where they end up.

Where Do Former Catholics End Up?

Unaffiliated (49%)

We discussed the unaffiliated above, so we don't need to spend much more time on them. This is a broad group that includes about half the Catholics who leave the Church. It's also diverse, encompassing many categories of unbelief or quasi-belief: active seekers, the "spiritual but not religious" crowd, agnostics, and hardcore atheists. Some of their traits may surprise you:

- 68% say that they "believe in God or a universal spirit" (30% say that they are "absolutely certain" of this)
- 37% say that they are "spiritual but not religious"
- 21% report that they pray daily
- 18% consider themselves "a religious person"
- 14% say that "religion is very important in their life," despite not committing to a particular tradition
- 12% identify as "atheists"

Many parents worry that "unaffiliated" means "atheist." They think that if their child leaves his religion behind, he also turns his back on God. But that's not often the case. In fact, nearly seven-in-ten unaffiliateds still believe in God. Many of them also pray daily and consider religion important in their lives.

So even if your child no longer identifies as Catholic and would answer "none" if you asked which religion he identifies with, there's a decent chance he still has some traces of faith. This is important and will be helpful later on as you learn to tap into those religious vestiges in order to draw him back.

Evangelical (25%)

In his book *Search and Rescue*, Catholic apologist Patrick Madrid shares the story of a young man named Rick. Rick was raised in a good Catholic home, and his parents took him to Mass every Sunday. They taught him his prayers, drove him to altar-boy practice, and made sure he attended CCD classes. His parents scrimped and budgeted so he could attend a Catholic high school, where they assumed he would remain Catholic. But after he went off to college, they discovered he had become friendly with a large, dynamic group of Evangelical Protestant students who met every week for Bible study.

Madrid asks you to imagine yourself as Rick's parents: "At first, you were happy to see him remaining interested in religious issues, so you didn't give it much thought when he began quoting Bible verses when he came home on weekends. . . . [But] eventually, you noticed his vocabulary changing. He started saying things like 'The Lord spoke to my heart about this' and 'Praise God about that.' . . . Before long, he broke the news to you that he's no longer a Catholic. He left, he explained, because his Evangelical friends convinced him that the Catholic Church is unbiblical and that her traditions are man-made and her doctrines are false."

If your son is like Rick, Madrid counsels, you shouldn't despair. "Even though Rick may think he has already discovered the answers in his new church, he still wants, deep down, to grapple with what the Catholic Church claims to be true. Believe it or not, that makes it easier to bring him back to the Church."

Typically, people who leave the Church to join an Evangelical or non-denominational community display a deep spiritual hunger, a strong appreciation for the Bible, a dynamic prayer life, and are heavily involved in activities, ministries, and small groups. These are all good things that can translate easily back to the Catholic Church.

Mainline Protestant (13%)

The mainline Protestant communities, which include Methodists, Lutherans, Anglicans, and Presbyterians, draw a significant number of Catholics away from the Church, often through a mixed marriage. Catholics marrying a mainline Protestant will frequently change religions shortly before or after the wedding to satisfy their spouse and achieve religious harmony in the home.

However, as the general size of mainline Protestant communities continues to plummet, this group is shrinking as well. The share of mainline Protestant Americans dropped from 18% in 2007 to 14% in 2014.

For former Catholics, mainline communities often serve as stepping-stones down the path toward becoming unaffiliated. Many people who leave the Catholic Church for a mainline Protestant denomination find that after a few years they've stopped attending church altogether.

Other (13%)

This last destination includes a broad and eclectic range of religious groups. Some who end up here become Mormons or Jehovah's Witnesses. Both groups are known for their masterful evangelism, going door-to-door and park-to-park to find new converts. They offer warm, tight-knit communities that make it easy to stay once you've been draw in. It's not uncommon for Catholics to be sucked into one of these groups, especially if they don't know their faith too well or if they marry someone who is part of the community.

Six Main Types of Fallen-Away Catholics

Most of the data above, while helpful, concerns religious identification. In other words, it deals with the answers people give to the question, "What religion do you hold?" But that data doesn't tell the whole story, since it doesn't look behind the label to the real thoughts and personalities of the drifters.

So let's turn now to some of the most common profiles of former Catholics. These profiles don't perfectly align with the labels in the last section. For example, you can find "shruggers" (which I'll explain in a moment) who still identify as Catholic, and others who become Evangelical. While the labels above draw outlines of those who have drifted, the descriptions below color those outlines in.

See if you recognize your child in one or more of these descriptions.

Cultural Catholics

I focus on this one first because people in this group straddle the line between being in the Church and having drifted away. Though it contains a wide spectrum of beliefs and practices, it usually includes those for whom "Catholic" is more of a cultural, ethnic, or familial label than a personally meaningful identity that shapes their lives. They still might come to Mass because of family, but they aren't personally connected to God or the sacraments. (People in this group are sometimes negatively referred to as "C&E Christians" since they rarely show up outside of Christmas and Easter.)

Cultural Catholics often still identify as "Catholic." Thus, they don't technically count as "unaffiliateds" or "nones." But for all intents and purposes, they've drifted from the Church. Their bodies sometimes show up in Mass, but their minds and hearts are far away. They float on the margins, often with much disinterest, confusion, and not a little dissent.

Almost every survey confirms that *most* self-identifying Catholics in America fit this description, meaning most US Catholics are "cultural Catholics."

A perfect example is Rob, who was interviewed during a large study on young adults and religion. When the interviewer asked about his religion, he said "Catholic," but when the interviewer asked what he meant by that, he said, "I believe in God and basically I celebrate Christmas."

Rachel offers a similar view. Although she drifted away from church in college and hasn't been to Mass in eight years, she says, "I don't necessarily feel like I've 'left' the church so much as taking a decent sized hiatus. I still identify as Catholic. I simply don't practice anymore."

So what's the problem with "cultural Catholicism"? The problem is that it masks a lifeless and decaying faith life. Few "cultural Catholics" have a living, personal relationship with Jesus in his Church, but worse, they don't *realize* they're missing out because they think the label and occasional church attendance is enough.

With an atheist, you at least have someone who *knows* they aren't Catholic. Therefore, becoming a fully active Catholic requires a significant, intentional shift in their life. But "cultural Catholics" already think of

17

themselves as Catholic. It's much harder to convince them that by attending Mass sporadically or living against the Church's teaching, they're in fact missing out on the fullness of Catholic life.

On the other hand, as sociologist Christian Smith notes, "cultural Catholics" sometimes stand a better chance of actually returning to the Church than estranged Catholics, because, "while they disagree with the Church on some points, they are not generally hostile toward the faith, but rather see it as a positive source of family identity and togetherness."

"Cultural Catholicism" isn't an insurmountable problem, and we'll see later how to help this type return to a full and thriving life of discipleship.

The Shruggers

One mother wrote to me saying, "My oldest son left the Church because of complacency. I asked if he was mad about anything the Church teaches and he said, 'No.' I think it is just general laziness. He works in a restaurant/bar and getting up early on Sunday is difficult."

Bishop Robert Barron describes this young man's attitude as indicative of the "meh" culture, an allusion to the ambivalent response many young people give toward faith—"meh" or "whatever," usually alongside a shrug of their shoulders (thus the other label sociologists apply to this group: the "shruggers").

Molly Oshatz, a Catholic who once identified as a "meh" young adult herself, writes about this growing trend. "Forty-four percent of the respondents to a 2011 Baylor University study reported spending no time whatsoever seeking 'eternal wisdom,' and 19 percent replied that 'it's useless to search for purpose.' In the same year, Lifeway, an evangelical research agency, found that 46 percent of those it surveyed never wondered whether or not they will go to heaven, and 28 percent reported that finding a deeper purpose in life wasn't a priority for them." In other words, when it comes to God and the Big Questions of life, many young people today aren't just confused—they don't even care.

This religious indifference inevitably leads to the belief that *no* religion matters at all, or that religion is akin to a sort of recreational hobby—something like quilting or coin-collecting. A "shrugger" may say, "If you're into religion, that's great for you, but I prefer sports or reading (or sleeping) instead."

How do they develop this "meh" attitude? Sometimes it's rooted in the desire to appear open-minded, a valued trait among young people today. But as G.K. Chesterton observed, open-mindedness is not a virtue in itself—it's a pit stop on the way to finding truth. "The object of opening the mind, as of opening the mouth," he wrote, "is to shut it again on something solid." To shrug off religion in the name of "open-mindedness" is a sign of stagnancy, not progress.

Others develop their "meh" attitude through lethargy. The lazy seeker wanders around aimlessly, neither committing to a particular religion nor even believing such a commitment is worth making. Meaning of life? Eternal joy? The value of faith? Meh. This indecision, of course, eventually becomes a decision to oppose *all* religions—an "I don't care" now becomes an "I reject all" at death. Frank Sheed and Maisie Ward, two prominent evangelists in twentieth-century England, agreed that such a position is, literally, insane: "A man may investigate the claims of religion and accept them; he may investigate those claims and reject them; and in both cases he is acting like a sane man. But a man who simply ignores the whole thing is acting like a fool."

If your child is a "shrugger," your main task will be to convince him that the Big Questions of life matter, that it's worth seeking answers about God, morals, and meaning. He needs to see what the convert C.S. Lewis came to realize, that "Christianity is a statement which, if false, is of *no* importance, and, if true, of infinite importance. The one thing it cannot be is moderately important." Similarly, when it comes to the person at the center of Christianity, Lewis notes that "Jesus produced mainly three effects: hatred, terror, adoration. There was no trace of people expressing mild approval."

In the second part of this book, you'll learn how to transform your child's indifferent shrugs into genuine interest, but for now just know that the key involves presenting the stark truth of Jesus and Christianity in a way that demands he make a choice. The Big Questions of life, including those of Christianity, must be answered; they can't be ignored forever.

The "Spiritual But Not Religious"

This group still falls under the "unaffiliated" label, but they are quite different from other subsets of the unaffiliated. Typically, they reject religion, liturgy, doctrines, and dogmas, but they still believe in God or a higher power, still pray, and still seek experiences of God.

Many of the "spiritual but not religious" claim they don't need to go to church because they can find God anywhere—in a beautiful sunset, through movies and music, during yoga, or while gazing on mountains or the ocean waves. Stephen, who grew up Catholic but no longer attends Mass, explains, "I can go on a 40-mile bike ride and get as much from it as I can from going to church. Nature to me is what God is all about. It's a renewal."

These people naturally see the Mass through the frame of feelings and experience. They think the Mass is fundamentally designed to evoke feelings of wonder and awe, and to generate religious sensations. While those are some of the effects of Mass, and a reverently celebrated liturgy can and should do all those things, the Mass is about something much more, as we'll come to see. It's about a real encounter with the living God through Word and sacrament, an encounter that simply can't be matched by a bike trip or mountain vista.

Moral Movers

Jason was a typical Catholic growing up. His family regularly attended Mass, and he went through Catholic schools, but nothing really stuck. When he got to college, he stopped attending church. There he met Jessica, a beautiful young woman, and they quickly fell in love. After graduating, Jason and Jessica decided to move in together. As marriage came on the horizon, Jason thought about possibly returning to the Church to celebrate their wedding in his local parish. But when he inquired about that possibility, his living situation became a problem. The priest suggested that before they get married, Jason and Jessica live apart or at least cease their sexual relations. Jason balked at the idea and decided if that was really the Catholic Church's position, then returning to the Church was no longer an option.

Like Jason, many people leave the Church (and stay away) because of her moral teachings on topics such as contraception, abortion, homosexuality, or divorce and remarriage. These people aren't necessarily evil or egotistical. They typically pursue what they think are truly good things—love, sexual intimacy, personal freedom. They just think the Church is misguided in her teachings. However, in my experience, most of these people have very distorted ideas about what the Church teaches and why.

Drawing a "moral mover" back to the Church can be tricky. If your child's moral hang-up involved a one-time decision, such as an abortion, perhaps one that occurred many years ago, that rift can be healed rather easily through the sacrament of Confession. But if your "moral mover" is involved in a more continuous practice, such as a homosexual or cohabiting relationship, the journey back to the Church may be more challenging (though not impossible). We'll handle these particular cases later in the book, providing a roadmap for each of them.

Religious Switchers

A large percentage of former Catholics end up switching to another faith, usually to an Evangelical or nondenominational Protestant tradition. They often do so for spiritual reasons. One of the biggest complaints made by former Catholics is that they "weren't being spiritually fed" in their Catholic parish. Others switch because their spouse has a different faith and they want to preserve religious harmony.

"Switchers take a wide range of personal journeys to end up in a different religious group from the one in which they began," explains researcher Christian Smith. "However, it does seem that personal connections to others outside of the Catholic faith and a dissatisfaction with the Catholic Church in general or a home parish in particular are factors that contribute to a lot of switching."

Bringing "switchers" back can be both easier and harder than helping other types of former Catholics. On the positive side, "switchers" generally have a real passion for faith, as well as specific reasons why they left. Unlike the "cultural Catholics" or "shruggers," they actually know why they're not fully Catholic. That makes it easier for you to home in on their primary hang ups.

But on the other hand, the reason why "switchers" leave can often be strong and deeply felt, which can be challenging. For example, if your child became Mormon to satisfy a Mormon spouse, convincing him to return to the Catholic Church isn't just an intellectual appeal—you're asking him to potentially upset the harmony of his marriage. Later we'll learn how to deal with these prickly sorts of issues and help religious "switchers" revert back to the Church.

Skeptics

Although atheists (3%) and agnostics (4%) make up a relatively small part of the population, I'm constantly surprised by the many stories I hear of young people leaving Catholicism for one or the other. The number of atheists and agnostics, often grouped together as "skeptics," continues to expand rapidly. Their numbers have doubled over the last decade, in no small part due to Catholics: 12% of former Catholics identify as atheist and 16% as agnostic.

Why the sudden surge of skepticism? It was fueled, in part, by polemical books written by the so-called "New Atheists" during the early 2000s. This group included writers such as Richard Dawkins (*The God Delusion*), Christopher Hitchens (*God Is Not Great*), and Sam Harris (*Letter to a Christian Nation*), each of whom wrote bestselling books denouncing God. Their books were characteristically harsh and full of mockery and insults toward religious people and were meant to dissuade Christians by depicting their faith as violent, irrational, and even dangerous. Although the New Atheist rhetoric has been exposed as more heat than substance, young people across the world have gravitated to it, especially on college campuses. Chances are high that if your child has come out as an atheist, he has read one of these books.

Many parents despair when learning their child no longer believes in God. It might seem the child is as far away from faith as possible, and that it's impossible for him to return to the Church. Yet in my experience working with thousands of atheists through my Catholic-atheist dialogue website StrangeNotions.com, I've discovered that many atheists are closer to the Church than we might assume.

Why? Two reasons. First, they're generally open-minded and are willing to investigate the God question through reading and dialogue. This is great for Catholics hoping to win them back to the truth. Second, atheists are typically passionate about the question of God, even if they answer it negatively. Sometimes it's easier to win an atheist back to faith than someone who just doesn't care (like the "cultural Catholics" or "shruggers"). Atheists, even if they don't believe in God, at least acknowledge that the question is worth considering and discussing.

* * *

As we saw in the last chapter, there isn't just one type of "fallen-away Catholic." Every person, and every journey away from the Church, is unique. Hopefully among these different destinations and types, you've been able to develop a clearer picture of where your child may be, religiously and mentally. If not, don't worry. Later in the book, you'll learn how to elicit these exact answers, directly from your child.

Now, though, after wrapping our heads around the general problem, we'll turn to five big myths about fallen-away Catholics that prevent many parents from helping their children return.

CHAPTER 3
The Five Big Myths About Fallen-Away Catholics

"**M**y son is totally gone," Dianne explained. "I love him, and I really hope he'll see the light one day, but there's absolutely no way he'll ever come back to the Church. It's hopeless."

Many parents feel this borderline despair. They look at how far their children have drifted, and they can't see any possible way they would return to the Church. Their children show zero interest in religious things, or they've developed such strong feelings against the Church that it would take a miracle for them to come back.

But what I've learned time and again, talking with many parents and young adults, is that this is one of the most common and devastating myths. No child is hopeless, and there is *always* a path back to the Church. How do we know? Because your child is ultimately in God's hands, who loves him even more than you do. He wants him back more than you do, and in his providence, he can do anything.

But when we believe this myth that there's no hope, we become jaded and frozen. We think, "The situation's hopeless. There's nothing I can do, so I won't even try."

That myth is just one of many, and each of them can seriously prevent you from making headway with your child. In this chapter, we'll carefully expose each of these myths, clearing our line of sight so we can better see how to facilitate your child's return.

MYTH #1: "They'll come back eventually once they get married or have kids."

TRUTH: As young adults increasingly delay marriage and having children, the odds are low they'll return because of those events.

For many young adults, "taking a break from religion" is a normal part of emerging adult life. They complete the initial sacraments (Baptism, First

Communion, and Confirmation), jump through the major "hoops" of Catholic religious education, and then settle down and pack away their religion until, perhaps, marriage and children come along. It's not that young people drift passively down this path. According to Notre Dame sociologists, "Some youth seem to *expect* to be religiously inactive during their pre-marriage, emerging adult years." Many parents who are baby boomers or Generation Xers traveled this path, and their children naturally expect to follow suit.

But will marriage and children really bring them back? At least statistically, the answer seems to be "probably not." One reason is that young people are delaying marriage longer than ever before. Our culture presumes that you should put off marriage so you can focus on your education and career first. As a millennial, I can confirm this is pretty much what all of my young adult peers believe. Consequently, the average marrying age for both men and women has soared over the past several decades. In 1960, the median age for first marriage was twenty-three for men and twenty for women; it's now twenty-nine and twenty-seven, respectively. Researchers at the National Marriage Project at the University of Virginia conclude, "Culturally, young adults have increasingly come to see marriage as a 'capstone' rather than a 'cornerstone'—that is, something they do after they have all their other ducks in a row, rather than a foundation for launching into adulthood and parenthood."

How does that affect our mission of drawing them back to the Church? Well, the longer they delay marriage, the longer they stay away from the Church. Worse, even when they do get married, they're less likely to get married in the Catholic Church—especially if the couple is already living together or has been married before. Most couples choose to get married elsewhere, and therefore marriage does not serve as an opportunity to draw them back.

A second problem is that even after getting married, young people may not have children right away—or at all. Birth rates for US women in their twenties dropped more than 15% between 2007 and 2012, and the 2013 data from the Centers for Disease Control and Prevention (CDC) revealed that for every 1,000 US women of childbearing age, there were just 58.2 births in

2019—the lowest birthrate in recorded American history. But doesn't that just mean young women are having babies *later* in life? Researchers from Princeton analyzed the CDC data and cast doubt on the notion of a "baby rebound." They found that women in their early twenties are likely to forgo births *altogether*, not just postpone them. So, if young people today are not having babies, or at least waiting a long time to have them, it's increasingly unlikely that they'll return to have their children baptized or raised in the Church.

What does all this mean? Marriage and childbearing are no longer reliable magnets to pull people back to the Church. We can't count on them, assuming they'll magically do all the work for us. Their pull has diminished to the point where, for many young adults, we have to assume that neither life moment—marriage or children—will exercise any significant draw back to the Church.

MYTH #2: "I took them to Mass and sent them to Catholic schools—that should have been enough, right?"

TRUTH: Simply moving through Catholic institutions doesn't ensure that a young person encounters the Lord or develops a strong, personal faith.

Lisa, a mother of two fallen-away Catholics, gave voice to this myth: "Perhaps we were too strict with the mechanics of the faith. We helped our children practice our faith by going to Mass, but they never developed their own personal relationship with Jesus. That was the missing piece that I was unable to pass on since I didn't have my own reconversion until later in life (you can't give what you don't have). Lacking a personal relationship with Jesus, I tried to compensate by pushing the rules, rituals, and rites of Catholicism onto my kids. Now, even though my adult daughters are otherwise very moral in their behaviors, they do not practice their faith. The rituals without the relationship were not worth keeping."

Throughout the nineteenth and twentieth centuries, American Catholicism flourished through institutions. In most cases, children moved smoothly through our religious systems. They were born in Catholic hospitals, attended Catholics schools, participated in religious education classes, and enrolled in Catholic colleges. Most emerged as strong Catholics on the other side.

But that's rarely the case anymore.

We can't assume today, despite the valiant effort of many pastors, educators, and ministry leaders, that when a child moves through our institutions, he will develop a genuine friendship with Jesus Christ.

In their book, *Young Catholic America: Emerging Adults In, Out of, and Gone from the Church,* researchers at Notre Dame found "there is no significant direct effect of attending a Catholic school on increased religiousness in emerging adulthood." Even when the researchers controlled for students' family background, Catholic high schools had "little to no independent influence five years later on those who attended them."

A recent Pew Forum study arrived at a similar conclusion. "Former Catholics who are now unaffiliated are just as likely as lifelong Catholics to have participated in religious institutions and practices such as religious education classes (68% and 71%, respectively) and religious youth groups (32% for both groups)." In other words, sadly, participating in church, attending religious education classes, and joining a parish youth group seem to have little to no effect on whether young people sustain their faith into adulthood.

That's not entirely the fault of our institutions. The problem is that we're expecting the institutions to bear the *entire* burden of evangelizing our children, something they were never meant to do. The Church has been very clear about this. In the *Catechism of the Catholic Church,* we learn that the most responsible party for forming our children is not the parishes or schools, but the parents. "Through the grace of the sacrament of marriage," the *Catechism* says, "parents receive the responsibility and privilege of evangelizing their children. Parents should initiate their children at an early age into the mysteries of the faith of which they are the 'first heralds' for their children. They should associate them from their tenderest years with the life of the Church. A wholesome family life can foster interior dispositions that are a genuine preparation for a living faith and remain a support for it throughout one's life."

All of this holds for attending Mass too. Just as putting your children in Catholic schools isn't enough, so bringing them to Mass, even consistently, isn't enough, by itself, to instill a deep and lasting faith. The sacraments aren't magic. If your child received the Eucharist without adequate formation, or was confirmed without the proper disposition, there's a good chance he may not have cooperated with the grace flowing from those sacraments.

But here's the good news: once your child *does* have the proper disposition, which this book will help guide him toward, the results will be incredible. The sacraments will profoundly transform his life.

MYTH #3: "They left because of me. It's all my fault!"
TRUTH: There are almost always multiple causes, and it's not all your fault.

Ronda's son left the Church at age sixteen and didn't return until he was thirty-two. As with many parents, she felt buried under an avalanche of regret and guilt. "I remember wrestling with tormenting thoughts such as, 'I should have seen this coming' or 'I could have taken more time with him' or 'I ought to have known . . .' or 'If only I had . . .' I was not perfect in my parenting. None of us are. By the time we have it figured out, our kids are out the door. Imperfection does not make for a bad parent. Beating yourself up with the shoulds and haves and ought tos will drain you of the energy you need to see this through. Mostly I would advise, just don't go there. Set those thoughts aside for another day, and when that day comes push them on into the next. There is nothing you can do about the past, but there is a whole lot you can do about today."

Not only is it a myth to believe that you're solely responsible for your child denouncing God or leaving the Church or drifting away—it can be utterly devastating. I've seen many parents become spiritually paralyzed through such guilt.

There is no doubt that we have a powerful influence over our children. Good parenting has an impact, as does bad parenting. But having an *influence* is not the same as having *control*. Every person has free will, which means that even if we provide the ideal atmosphere for faith to take root, our child may still reject it. You could take your child to Mass, enroll him in Catholic schools, facilitate moving religious experiences, provide him with the best answers to his questions, and offer a compelling witness of holiness. Yet even after all that, your child may still choose another path. The gift of free will requires that he has the option.

You can't make the decision for your children. As my friend Bert Ghezzi counsels, "We can drag loved ones to places where we think the Holy Spirit might strike, but we cannot climb into their skins and manipulate their free wills. Their faith decisions are between them and God—which means if they do drop out, we cannot legitimately be held responsible for that decision."

Now of course this doesn't mean we parents are completely blameless when a child leaves the faith. Certainly, none of us are perfect parents, which means we likely contributed something, if only a little, to our child's drifting away. But you are not *completely* responsible for the decision—it likely involved several factors outside of your control—and even more importantly, you *can* play a key role in drawing him back.

Coming to grips with this reality is hard but liberating. Once you realize that the only thing you can do as a parent is to facilitate the best environment for your child to know and love God, you can focus on that goal rather than stressing out about how your child responds to your overtures. Let the layers of self-blame and guilt peel off of you as you redirect your focus to helping your child return.

It's likely this shift in perspective will also help your child. If you blame yourself for your child leaving the faith, that may become clear to your child and give him an easy excuse. Your child might think, "Hmm. I can either take responsibility for my own bad moral and religious decisions, or I can blame you, my parent. Okay, I choose you." What child wouldn't alleviate his own responsibility, and put the blame on you? But if your child senses you no longer hold yourself accountable for his religious decisions, the jig is up. What he does from that point forward is a reflection of *his* decisions and actions, not yours. You giving up responsibility places the burden where it belongs—on him.

Ultimately, the main way to move past this myth is to detach yourself from your children and their religious decisions. This doesn't mean you aren't interested or involved, but it means you won't let his choices shape your own identity and self-evaluation. "If being the parent of your children is your core identity, you're on shaky ground," writes Carol Barnier, herself both a former prodigal and the parent of several teenage children. "If every time they stumble, you find yourself questioning your own value, you're on shaky ground. If every time they make a serious mistake, you find yourself sinking into an isolated depression, you're on shaky ground. If *anything* your kids do has the power to lead you to believe you are worthless, you're on shaky ground. Our kids are not meant to be our center. The one identity that is sound, true, and unshakable is that *you* are a precious child of God."

**MYTH #4: "They won't listen to me; it's just impossible
to have a discussion about faith."**
TRUTH: Your first goal should be to listen to *them*, not talk at them.
Through listening, conversations will start to bear fruit.

For many parents, their child's departure from the Church is doubly tragic, first because the child has turned his back on the faith, but second because he's not open to discussing why. This leaves parents in a bind. They want to discuss the matter with their children and help change their minds. But their children shut down the conversation before it can even begin. Even a mention of "God" or "Church" or "Catholicism" can trigger a heated reaction.

Thankfully, as we'll learn in the next chapter, there are several ways to open up a fruitful dialogue even when doing so seems impossible. The most important tactic, though, is to stop talking *at* your child about the faith and to start listening to his opinions and feelings. For instance, instead of nagging your child about why it's so important for him to start going to Mass again, ask why he's decided to stop going. Instead of inquiring why he no longer believes in God, ask what changed his mind. If he takes issue with the Church's teaching on contraception, homosexuality, or divorce, ask what bothers him most about it.

Leading with questions and an attitude of listening can open up even the most closed-hearted young person to conversation. We'll cover this more later in the book and learn specific tips and strategies.

MYTH #5: "It's hopeless. No matter what happens, my child is never coming back to the Church."
TRUTH: It's never hopeless. God will never give up on your child and neither should you.

One thing you must know, deep in your bones and with absolute certainty, is that God will *never* give up on your child. Nobody wants to see your child return to the faith and be saved more than God does. St. Augustine affirmed that God loves each of us as if there were only one of us to love. He loves your child infinitely; his love, concern, and desire have no limits.

So be sure of one thing: God will *never* stop pursuing your child. Which means there is always hope.

Remember Jesus' parable of the prodigal son. A reckless child deserts his father, fleeing to the first-century equivalent of Las Vegas. He squanders all of his money on wild living. But despite getting all the pleasure he can acquire, it isn't enough. He still isn't satisfied. Coming to his senses, he realizes that true happiness comes not from money or sex or parties but from love, the very love he had rejected. So he decides to return to his father, in shame and sorrow, to apologize for his rash decisions and to beg his father to hire him as a servant.

But before the son has a chance to apologize, his father spots him in the distance and *runs* toward him. When the father reaches his son, he doesn't excoriate him or issue a list of requirements that must be met in order to welcome him back—he throws his arms around him and kisses him. Instead of letting his son apologize, the father turns to his servants and says, "Quickly bring the finest robe and put it on him; put a ring on his finger and sandals on his feet. Take the fattened calf and slaughter it. Then let us celebrate with a feast, because this son of mine was dead, and has come to life again; he was lost, and has been found" (Luke 15:22–24).

The point of the parable is clear. No matter how far your child has drifted from God or the Church, no matter what sort of promiscuity or problems or darkness he has fallen into, God is yearning to embrace him. The Lord isn't just waiting disinterestedly for your child to return. He is pacing the horizon, preparing to rush toward your child at even the smallest sign of openness. God will *never* give up on your child.

Remember, too, what we learned in the last chapter, that even if your child has drifted away from the Church, it doesn't mean he has stopped believing in God. Statistics show that most former Catholics, including many of the unaffiliated, still love God, pray, and are open to spiritual things. So even if on the surface it looks like your child has renounced faith altogether, he may just be wrestling with moral issues or questions surrounding the Catholic Church.

From our dim and incomplete view, trapped as we are within the limits of space and time, it may seem impossible that your child would ever consider returning to the Church. It may require a *huge* change in his thinking, his actions, and his lifestyle. But knowing there's always hope can reassure us even when the path forward is unclear.

And I should add that by the time you finish this book, you won't be feeling hopeless anyway! The tools and strategies you'll discover in parts two and three of this book will give you a clear path for drawing your child back. As you close the last page, you'll feel confident, excited, and hopeful.

So commit right now to getting rid of the discouraging idea that there's no hope—there is always hope, and you will soon know it well.

* * *

At this point in your reading, you should have a much better sense of why young people leave the Church, where they go when they leave, and some of the most dangerous assumptions you can make about them—namely, the myths that tend to derail any progress. It's now time to move to the second part of the book, when we'll take this helpful understanding of the problem and begin to solve it.

PART II
The Game Plan

"A goal without a plan is just a wish."

— ANTOINE DE SAINT-EXUPERY

CHAPTER 4
The Basics

I hope after reading through the first few chapters of this book, you have a clearer picture of what your child is likely thinking. I hope you also feel lighter, having busted the most common myths. Letting go of incorrect assumptions can be freeing and change your outlook.

But now, you're likely itching for action. The better you understand the problem, the more urgently you want to fix it. That's what this second part is about.

Over the next several chapters, you'll carefully craft a game plan for drawing your child back to the Church. The plan involves several elements, some of which you may already be doing, but much of which will be new. Don't get overwhelmed. There is a lot here. Take it in slowly and know that you don't have to implement it all overnight.

But before we dive into the specific tips, there's one thing we have to establish: *you* are the key. No tool or strategy can replace the fact that, by nature of being your child's parent, you're already the most important factor in this equation. No tip, strategy, or tool can substitute the role you play.

You are the key.

Notre Dame professor Christian Smith affirms that "sociological studies around the turn of the twenty-first century have shown that the single most important measurable factor for determining the religious and spiritual lives of teenagers and young adults is the religious faith, commitments, and practices of their parents." Whether parents realize it or not, Smith continues, "[They] are the most important pastors that any youth will ever have."

Why? Because "close relationships to religious adults . . . serve as valuable reference points of belief and participation, and make attending Mass rewarding and meaningful." However, the researchers continue, "most crucial are the commitment, intentionality, examples, and encouragement of Catholic *parents*."

One young man confessed, "I left the Catholic Church at the age of 19, not to join another church but because I ceased to believe. I returned to the Church ten years later because I saw the way faith helped my family and friends through some very tough times. My own life seemed empty. I wanted the peace that seemed to come from their faith in God."

You are the key.

That may seem challenging at first, because it means you can't just sit idly on the sidelines, hoping someone will step in and do everything for you. There's a chance your child might connect with another friend or mentor who helps bring him back to the Church, and indeed this is an important factor that we'll come back to later. But you can't count on that. *You're* the main factor, which means *you* have to pursue your child.

Now, I'll be blunt: this isn't easy. It's much easier to brush aside your child's drifting. It's more comfortable and certainly makes family events more bearable. But while ignoring his unbelief might make holidays easier, it won't help his eternity. So, before we dive into the rest of the game plan, commit to your role. Resolve that you'll do everything you can to radiate "commitment, intentionality, examples, and encouragement" to your child.

But to get there, we'll begin by first recognizing what *not* to do. You're likely desperate to help lead your child back to the Church. But that desperation can sometimes lead you to pursue the right goal with the wrong methods. So let's look at five strategies you should *not* pursue. Each of these mistakes will create a wall between your child and his return.

Five Mistakes That Will Almost Certainly Keep Your Child Away

1. Force him to go to Mass.

"Ugh! If I could only get him to start going to Mass again!" Maria complained to me, lamenting her teenage son. "It doesn't matter what I do—beg, plead, command, cry—none of it works. On a few occasions I was able to force him to go by threatening to lock his cell phone data or cut his allowance, but even then he just sat in the pew and clearly didn't want to be there."

Here's a crucial and likely surprising tip:

Stop forcing your child to attend Mass. Now, to be clear, I'm talking about older children and young adults here. Obviously, you should take young children to Mass. That's your religious duty as a parent.

But for older children, in their late teenage years or early twenties, forcing Mass often makes the child *less* attracted to religious things. This is because the Mass was never intended to evangelize the uninterested. Mass is the *last* step on the evangelization journey, not the first. It's the final destination, the fruit and consequence of a personal relationship with Jesus Christ, not the cause of it. To draw your child back to Christ and the Church, you therefore have to lay down other building blocks first.

A priest recently observed to me, "If someone comes to Mass, unwilling and unprepared, he's in great danger of spiritual sickness. As long as our agenda is simply to get people to Mass—if that's all we're trying to do, without any intermediary steps—we're likely making them sicker, from a spiritual perspective."

That idea may seem discomforting, but it goes back to St. Paul, in his First Letter to the Corinthians. There he wrote, "A person should examine himself, and so eat the bread and drink the cup. For anyone who eats and drinks without discerning the body, eats and drinks judgment on himself. That is why many among you are ill and infirm, and a considerable number are dying" (1 Cor. 11:28–30).

Paul was alluding to physical pains the Corinthian people had suffered as a result of not celebrating the Mass with proper reverence, and specifically not recognizing the Real Presence of Jesus in the Eucharist. In our day, it's rare that God strikes down someone with sickness or death just for dozing off at Mass or for casually receiving the Blessed Sacrament. But if we come to Mass unprepared, unfocused, or unwilling to participate, then we could suffer serious *spiritual* effects. Instead of uniting us to God, the Mass could *harm* that relationship and cause greater distance.

Of course, most parents don't intend this. When they force their child to attend Mass, they're acting out of good intentions, thinking that since Jesus is present at Mass in a special way, they should do everything possible to get their child there. This desire is encouraged by our surrounding Protestant culture, for which the Sunday worship service is viewed as a gateway to full participation in Christian life. When our Protestant brothers and sisters want to lead a fallen-away friend back to the Lord, their first move is to bring him to church. Once there, they know he will find a warm reception, a relevant and powerful message, and an invitation to join a small-group community. In other words, if the path of discipleship is a funnel, Protestants place the church service at the top of the funnel, at the beginning, while Catholics place the Mass at the bottom, at the end of the funnel. That's a critical difference, and it explains why forcing people to go to Mass often backfires.

So the next time you're tempted to push and goad your older child to attend Mass, even when you know he's deeply resistant, pull back a bit. Don't force him. Plant other seeds first.

In the coming chapters, you'll learn various strategies to draw your child back to the Eucharist, ones that build a strong spiritual foundation first so that he *wants* to go to Mass instead of being forced to go.

2. Criticize his lifestyle.

Abraham Piper, who drifted away from church as a teen, has some good advice for parents of children who make bad moral decisions: don't lead with moral disapproval. "If he's struggling to believe in Jesus, there is little significance in his admitting that it's wrong to get wasted, for instance. You want to protect him, yes, but his most dangerous problem is unbelief—not partying. No matter how your child's behavior proves his unbelief, always be sure to focus more on his heart's sickness than its symptoms."

Beginning with moral commandments is often a nonstarter for young people. If the first thing your child hears is "stop doing that" or "change your life" or "break off that relationship," he will quickly tune you out. You'll never have a chance to make a more persuasive case for his return to God and his Church. This doesn't mean you should just watch silently and passively as your child makes bad decisions. Instead, it means your first approach should be marked by gentleness and patience, not criticism.

Pope Francis has spoken often against this hyper-moralizing approach. In his first big interview as pope, he explained how introducing someone to Jesus Christ *before* getting to the moral requirements that flow from that encounter is the best strategy:

"The most important thing is the first proclamation: Jesus Christ has saved you. . . . Proclamation in a missionary style focuses on the essentials, on the necessary things: this is also what fascinates and attracts more, what makes the heart burn, as it did for the disciples at Emmaus. We have to find a new balance; otherwise even the moral edifice of the church is likely to fall like a house of cards, losing the freshness and fragrance of the Gospel. The proposal of the Gospel must be more simple, profound, radiant. It is from this proposition that the moral consequences then flow. . . . The proclamation of the saving love of God comes before moral and religious imperatives. Today sometimes it seems that the opposite order is prevailing."

Remember from an earlier chapter that most young people today believe in something called "moralistic therapeutic deism," which places a strong focus on the dos and don'ts of faith (hence the "moralistic" dimension). But as a parent, your goal is not simply moral improvement or behavior modification. Your goal is *reversion*, to draw your child into a thriving relationship with Jesus in his Church. Once you do that, the moral changes will inevitably follow.

But let's be frank: this isn't easy. It will involve biting your tongue many times when you feel the urge to rebuke your child, knowing that will likely drive him farther away. Yet the scar tissue will be worth it!

That said, sometimes moral rebuke *is* necessary for a child to begin his return to the Church. Wayward children sometimes need someone to snap them out of their moral confusion and say, "These decisions are destroying your life" or "You can be so much more if you choose a different path." But it's often better when that correction isn't the first thing they hear and, ideally, when it comes from a trusted friend, mentor, or significant other, rather than a parent. Your relationship with your wayward child is likely already tenuous and should be protected at all costs. Don't risk it by leading with a strong rebuke.

3. Nag him.

Many parents nag, badger, and hound their children—even far into their adult lives—to get them to attend church more often or change their lifestyle. Nagging almost never works and, in fact, it usually has the opposite effect. Many people purposely stay away from the Catholic Church simply because their parents constantly nag them about religion.

So commit right now to putting away questions like "Why are you doing this to us?" or "When are you going to stop being so lazy and come back to church?" It's almost impossible to have your child fully feel your pain, to know how desperately you want him to return to the Church. So it's not worth wasting your energies on nagging him or sending him on a guilt trip.

Even worse than general nagging, though, is passive-aggressive nagging. Sarah, a young adult who had stopped going to Mass, said, "I can't stand it when my mom gets on me about church but I hate it even more when she does it by making little comments, or sighs, or when she clucks her tongue. She goes on and on about how my sister goes to Mass and the feeling I get is that she's somehow a better daughter. Ugh! It just bugs me so much. It's worse than if she just came out and said what she thought instead of pretending she was trying to help."

Other young people are dismayed when their parents constantly forward over-the-top religious or political emails. "My parents *and* my grandparents send me at least one ridiculous e-mail a day either claiming the country is being overtaken by the devil and we're all going to hell, or that this or that politician is the incarnation of evil. I wish they would just stop. It's not helping their cause at all—it makes me think their religion is even crazier than I already believe." There can be value in sending your child helpful articles, links, and videos—we'll cover this later—but if you're not careful, it can come across as aggressive proselytizing.

Pope St. John Paul II, perhaps the most effective evangelist of the twentieth century, summed up a better, alternative strategy. He said simply, "The Church proposes; she imposes nothing." Parents who successfully draw their children back to the Church don't nag or force religion on their children. Instead they invite them, gently and respectfully, through warm conversation and unconditional love. Don't complain about your child's deficiencies; invite him to something better. Propose, but don't impose.

4. Dismiss his objections.

It was Nick's first semester at college when one of his new friends said something derogatory about Christianity. The rest of the group laughed, but John stayed silent. One of the guys noticed. "Wait, you're not super religious, are you?" his friend asked. "Well, I don't know," John replied. "I grew up Catholic and my parents are pretty religious, but I'm not sure where I stand." Immediately his friend responded, "Well, I used to believe in God, too, but that was before I discovered there is just no evidence for God. Christianity is just like every other myth or fairy tale. I prefer science and things that are true, rather than made up stories." He recommended John read a few atheist books, and pretty soon John agreed with his take.

Later that year, when John came home for a visit, he shared his many experiences at college. But at some point, the discussion turned to their local home parish, and that caused his mother to ask, "Oh, by the way, John, have you found a parish up there?" John paused for a moment, swallowing hard. Then he replied, "Well, to be honest, I'm not sure I believe in God anymore. I just don't see any evidence."

John's mother immediately snapped back, "Oh. Wow! You don't actually believe that, do you? That's ridiculous. Of *course* there's evidence. Where do you think the world came from? Who do you think made you? How could you possibly deny that God exists?"

John was shocked. He expected his mom to be disappointed, but he didn't expect her to just flippantly dismiss his objections. He wasn't sure he actually *believed* the objections—he was actually just parroting what he heard from friends and atheist books. But the fact that his mother so casually rejected it made him think she didn't respect him at all. Rather than helping him overcome a serious period of doubt, she instead solidified his departure, making him dig in his heels even more.

Many parents aren't lucky enough to have their child explain why he has drifted away from God. So, if you're able to discover *why* your child has left the Church, don't dismiss the objection. It may sound silly to you, but it's meaningful to him. Take it seriously, no matter how ludicrous you think it sounds. The more respect you grant your child's concerns, the more open he'll be to your responses.

5. Assume you can change him.

As we learned earlier, both leaving the Church and coming back involve many different variables—you, your child, friends, personal beliefs, and free will. You can exercise some influence over your child's decisions, even a significant amount, which is what this book will help you do. But the ultimate decision is his to make.

This leads to one of the hardest but most important truths: you must let go of trying to change him. This is a hard truth to hear. Most of us want to control our own destinies. But when it comes to your child's faith decisions, it's ultimately out of your hands.

Jesus told a parable about a sower who scattered seeds on the ground (see Matt. 13:3–9). Some fell on the path and the birds ate it up. Some fell on rocky ground and it failed to grow. Some fell among thorns, which choked the plants. But some seed fell on good soil and produced an enormous crop.

What was the lesson of his parable? That we can't control when, how, or *whether* our seeds will produce fruit. All we can do is scatter our seeds of prayer, conversation, and love, and beg God to ensure the seeds fall on good ground. Yet it's ultimately out of our control.

This doesn't mean you should stop caring about the outcome, or that you've given up on your child. It simply means that you've put God in control of the results instead of yourself. It means you acknowledge that you can't make decisions for your child, that the outcome is only partially in your hands. Many parents find this deeply liberating. Instead of manipulating their children so they return to Mass, they instead entrust them to God, follow the strategies outlined in this book, and turn the results over to the Holy Spirit.

The Five Thresholds Your Child Needs to Cross

The most common way Catholics measure spiritual progress, or the degree to which someone is "devout," is by gauging sacramental steps. As a child progresses from Baptism, to First Reconciliation, to First Communion, to Confirmation, he presumably moves into a deeper life of discipleship as a fully formed Catholic.

Except as we all know, this rarely happens.

Huge numbers of those who follow the sacramental steps still end up drifting away from the Church, as is perhaps true with your own child. Simply moving through the sacramental funnel is no guarantee that your child will emerge having experienced a genuine encounter with the Lord Jesus and a real conversion of life.

Sherry Weddell, in her book *Forming Intentional Disciples: The Path to Knowing and Following Jesus*, offers a much better way to measure spiritual maturation. Building on a framework proposed by two Evangelical ministers, Weddell offers what she calls the "thresholds of conversion," which every person must cross in order to become a true disciple of Jesus Christ.

As we briefly examine the thresholds below, ask yourself two questions. First, which threshold am I currently at? Second, which one best describes my child?

1. Initial Trust

This is the most basic stage of conversion and requires trusting or having a positive association with Jesus Christ, the Church, a Catholic believer, or something identifiably Catholic. Many people never make it to this stage, harboring lifelong grudges and suspicions toward anything that has to do with Catholicism. This includes not a few people who have been personally hurt by Catholics, either physically or emotionally. But if you can lead your child to at least hold a positive view of God, the Church, or Catholics, even if they don't buy into the whole thing and even if they still disagree with some core Catholic teachings, you've helped them cross this first threshold and prepare for the next one.

2. Spiritual Curiosity

Here your child finds himself intrigued by Jesus, his life, his teachings, or some aspect of the Catholic faith. Again, he doesn't have to agree with it yet. He just has a curiosity that ranges from mere interest about a new possibility to a strong fascination. Your child is not yet open to personal change. His curiosity is passive, almost as something happening *to* him rather than *through* him, yet it is more than mere trust.

3. Spiritual Openness

At this threshold, your child acknowledges to himself, and perhaps to God, that he is open to the possibility of personal change. Moving from the second threshold to this one is a significant step. In fact, Weddell affirms, "This is one of the most difficult transitions for a postmodern nonbeliever." Note that this step involves merely *openness* to change. It doesn't require that your child is particularly *committed* to changing his life yet. People who are open are simply admitting the possibility.

4. Spiritual Seeking

The key shift that happens at this threshold is that your child moves from a passive openness to an active search. He senses something drawing him closer to God and the Church, and he wants to respond to that call. At this stage, the seeker is engaged in an urgent spiritual quest, seeking to know whether he can commit to Christ in his Church. This threshold typically includes a heavy dose of personal study—reading Catholic books or articles, listening to podcasts, or watching YouTube videos and films. The spiritual seeker is wrestling with their difficulties and doubts about Catholicism and wants to know the truth. He wants to know what the Catholic Church teaches and why.

5. Intentional Discipleship

Using biblical language, this is the decision to "drop one's nets," just like the Apostles did when deciding to follow Jesus. It involves a conscious commitment to follow Christ in the midst of his Church as a genuine disciple. This commitment naturally leads your child to reorder his life to align with Jesus' promised way of happiness. They return to the sacraments, attend Mass regularly, strive for holiness, and cultivate their interior life.

Keep in mind that these thresholds don't necessarily parallel the sacramental progression. For instance, many people who were raised in Catholic schools and received all their early sacraments still have never advanced past the first threshold, initial trust. They still lack a positive association with Jesus Christ or the Church.

Others, despite never receiving any religious preparation, have already passed through multiple thresholds. It's even possible that someone could reach the threshold of intentional discipleship without even being baptized! (This doesn't mean the sacraments are inconsequential to your child's conversion or reversion. They're crucial, and we'll focus on several of them throughout this book. But as we've seen a little already, if your child is not properly disposed to receive them, he's in danger of real spiritual harm.)

Many of us oscillate among these thresholds during our life. We might live as an intentional disciple for many years before lethargy or a personal crisis sends us drifting back down a threshold or two. That's okay. The goal is for all of us—including both you and your child—to become intentional disciples. Don't be discouraged if the process involves two steps forward and one step back.

After learning about these thresholds, and diagnosing which one you and your child are each at, the next question to ask is this: What can I do to help my child reach the next threshold? If he lacks even a basic trust of religious things, how can I begin to build that foundation? If he's already spiritually seeking, how can I feed that interest with good Catholic resources and conversation?

If you don't have a clear vision yet for how to help your child to the next threshold, don't worry. But let that question reverberate in your mind throughout this book. At its core, this book is designed to help move your child through these thresholds of conversion, taking him from wherever he is now all the way to intentional discipleship.

Help Him Find the Treasure

At the end of the day, your child's real problem is not apathy or rebellion or sex or cussing or laziness or promiscuity. The real problem is that your child doesn't see Jesus clearly. "The best thing you can do for rebellious children is to show him Christ," writes Abraham Piper, himself a former rebellious teenager. "It won't be simple or immediate, but the sins in his life that distress you and destroy him will begin to disappear only when he sees Jesus more as he actually is."

The whole purpose of the game plan we're about to explore is to help your child encounter the Lord, to personally know and love him. This can't be stressed enough. No strategy for reaching your child will have any lasting effect if the underlying goal isn't to help him see Jesus clearly and befriend him personally.

But if this is the goal, then it means we're not just preoccupied with making your child a nicer person. We're not just trying to give him a cleaner haircut, gentler speech, or more modest clothes. And our goal is not just to soothe our own consciences so we can sleep better knowing that our child has returned to the Church.

Your goal is to give your child all the gifts that Jesus offers through his Church and to save him from the harrowing slavery of sin and death.

Once your child experiences the wonder, freedom, and grace of Jesus Christ, he'll have a whole new conception of satisfaction. It will be totally redefined. He will replace the money, praise, power, or pleasure that he is now chasing and find his satisfaction in Christ. And when that happens, all the other positive changes you desire will follow like dominoes tumbling one after another.

But Jesus is the first domino. He's not just one among many; he's the main domino. If your child never encounters Jesus, the other changes will be unlikely. Or at best, you'll have succeeded in modifying a few of his behaviors, but you won't have affected his soul.

So as we now move into the actual game plan and wrestle with how to implement it with your own child, let this driving thought echo over and over in your mind: *My goal is to show my child Christ. My goal is to show my child Christ.*

Jesus tells a parable about a man who finds a great treasure buried in a field, and out of joy, he sells everything he has to buy the field (Matt. 13:44). But note the order of those events. The man doesn't first buy the field—he first finds the treasure. And in that lies the secret to drawing your child back to the Church.

You first need to help your child find the treasure—Jesus, the pearl of great price—and only then will he "buy the field," only then will he buy into the way of life offered by the Church.

Every step of the way, through each tactic and strategy, through every move you make to draw your child back to the Church, this is your mission:

Show your child Christ, the Treasure of Life.

CHAPTER 5
Pray, Fast, and Sacrifice

O n one occasion, when Jesus was on Mount Tabor with Peter, James, and John, the other Apostles encountered a boy plagued by an evil spirit. They tried all the tactics they knew, but nothing worked. Later, the disciples asked Jesus, "Why could we not drive it out?" Jesus answered, "This kind does not go out except by prayer and fasting" (Matt. 17:21, NKJV).

Whenever he teaches, Jesus assumes that prayer and fasting are normal parts of the Christian life. For example, in his famous Sermon on the Mount, he says, "*When* you pray. . ." and "*When* you fast. . ." (Matt. 6:6,16, emphasis added). He doesn't say "*If* you pray. . ." or "*If* you fast. . ." He assumes those are normal practices in the Christian life.

Prayer, fasting, and sacrifice are especially needed in your mission to draw your child back to the Church. And one story illustrates this vividly.

How One Mother's Prayer Birthed a Saint

You know the pattern. A smart and gifted boy leaves home for school. He makes new friends. They spend most of their time partying, chasing girls, and embracing new philosophies. The son becomes drawn to a trendy religious cult. Eventually, he moves in with his girlfriend, and they have a child without being married. The boy's mother can only sit by in despair, heartbroken over his choices and seemingly helpless. The only thing she can do is pray.

That's the story of many Catholics today—and maybe *your* own story. Parents think they're alone in facing these sorts of troubles, but this pattern isn't a new one. It stretches back across centuries, and in the case above, even more than a millennium. In fact, the story above is actually the fourth-century story of St. Monica and her young wayward son, Augustine.

Monica was raised as a Christian, but she married someone from a different faith. In her case, the husband, Patricius, was an atheist politician. They had three sons together, but their marriage was rocky. Patricius was a violent man and regularly abused her. He was also unfaithful to her throughout their marriage. But Monica remained patient. Other wives with marriage problems came to her for advice, and she became a source of comfort for anyone suffering through difficult marriages. She served Patricius with selfless love and devotion, and she prayed for him every day. Eventually, her prayers bore fruit. A year before Patricius died, he converted to Catholicism—due mostly to Monica's prayers and powerful example.

Although the conversion of Monica's husband pleased her indescribably, she still worried about one of her sons, Augustine. Though brilliant and gifted, he spent most of his time carousing the streets with friends, living promiscuously, and seeking to advance his career. He even fathered a son out of wedlock. Yet Monica refused to give up on her son, just as she was committed to her husband. She prayed daily and intensely for Augustine, fasted for his sake, and begged God to help him return to faith. When Augustine traveled to Rome and Milan for his education, Monica followed him and continued praying.

While in Milan, she met Ambrose, the local bishop who would later be canonized a saint. Ambrose became a spiritual guide to her. He noted her restless longing for her son and the hours she spent praying for him. He promised her, "Surely the son of so many tears will not perish." His prediction was right, although it took several years to reach fulfillment.

Augustine and Ambrose struck up a friendship, and the bishop led Augustine to become curious about Christianity. Ambrose was the first high-level Christian thinker Augustine had met. As a result of their many back-and-forth dialogues, Augustine finally decided to convert to the faith. Ambrose baptized the thirty-two-year-old Augustine, who would eventually grow into one of the most influential thinkers in Western history, and one of the greatest saints in the Catholic Church.

After Augustine's baptism, Monica could hardly contain her enthusiasm. She and her son began sharing beautiful conversations about God and heaven. As she lay on her deathbed, content at having seen both her husband

and her son come to share her faith, she felt her whole life had been fulfilled. Today, the Church celebrates the feasts of St. Monica and St. Augustine right after each other on the liturgical calendar, with Monica on August 27 and Augustine on August 28.

St. Monica exemplifies the power of a praying parent. She wasn't able to convince Augustine with words. In fact, whenever she tried to talk to her son about religion, he brushed her away. But through her daily, committed intercession, persisting over fifteen years, Augustine was able to journey into the Church.

What can we learn from Monica's example? First, don't stop praying for your child. When Monica complained that Augustine would not listen to her admonitions, Ambrose urged her, "Speak less to Augustine about God and more to God about Augustine." She took his advice and never gave up, even when things looked dim. Eventually, her tenacity paid off.

It reminds us of Jesus' parable of the persistent widow. In the Gospel of Luke, Jesus tells of a widow who was upset that a judge refused to hear her case. The woman kept coming to the judge with her request, over and over, until he finally relented, saying, "While it is true that I neither fear God nor respect any human being, because this widow keeps bothering me I shall deliver a just decision for her lest she finally come and strike me." Jesus interpreted the parable this way: "Pay attention to what the dishonest judge says. Will not God then secure the rights of his chosen ones who call out to him day and night? Will he be slow to answer them?" (Luke 18:1–8). In other words, God loves persistent prayer. He never tires of your requests, even if you bring the same needs to him every day.

Joan Hamill knows that from experience. Joan prayed weekly for fifteen years for different family members to return to the Church. "I prayed for St. Monica to intercede for our family members," says Hamill. "As a result, I had two brothers come back to the Church as well as my sister and brother-in-law."

So don't give up praying for your child. Like St. Monica and the persistent widow, have confidence that God will reward your perseverance. The more resilient your prayer, the more likely God will answer it.

The second thing we can learn from St. Monica is to not just pray for our child—we should also pray for an "Ambrose" to step into our child's life. Perhaps there is just too much baggage between you and your child that your child will no longer hear truth from your lips. That's understandable. The strategies in this book will help melt some of that frigid tension, but in the meantime, pray that God will bring someone else into his path, someone with just the right combination of personality, interests, intelligence, and heart. Just as Ambrose stepped in to help Augustine, so you might need someone to nudge your child along.

(Also, keep in mind that while you're praying for someone to step into *your* child's life, other parents are praying the same thing for *their* child's life. And you may be that person! Even if your child tunes you out, don't be closed off to using the tips in this book to help *other* children return to the Church. You could be the Ambrose for someone else's Augustine!)

The third takeaway is that we can ask St. Monica's intercession for our child. A recent survey asked Catholic parents, "When you pray, how often do you pray to or ask the intercession of . . ." and then listed several options. By far, the most common responses were "God the Father" (74% prayed to him always or most of the time), "God the Son, Jesus Christ" (59%), and "God the Holy Spirit" (45%). But what was the *least* common response? The saints. Only one-in-five Catholic parents regularly asked the saints' intercession. That means the overwhelming majority of Catholic parents are missing out on some of the greatest spiritual support we have.

For Catholics, the saints are not dead and gone. For instance, St. Monica didn't cease to exist when she died in 387. Her body may have ceased to function, and her soul departed, but she remains alive in Christ, residing with him in heaven for all eternity. And because the Church is one indivisible body (see 1 Cor. 12:12), which neither death nor life can break apart (see Rom. 8:38–39), we can still connect with those holy men and women who have already passed into the next life and ask for their prayers.

Among all the saints in heaven, few know the gut-wrenching pain of a wayward child more than St. Monica. So reach out to her and ask her to pray for your child, just as she did for Augustine. If her prayers worked for

Augustine, they can work for your child too! We regularly ask our friends on earth to pray for us, and we can do the same with the saints. In fact, the saints' prayers are generally *more* powerful than ours here on earth since they are closer to the mind and heart of God—they're already in heaven! So next time you pray, perhaps offer a short request to St. Monica such as this:

"St. Monica, I need your prayers. You know exactly how I'm feeling because you once felt it yourself. I'm hurting, hopeless, and near despair. I desperately want my child to return to Christ and his Church, but I can't do it alone. I need God's help, and I need your help. Please join me in begging the Lord's powerful grace to flow into my child's life. Ask the Lord Jesus to soften his heart, prepare a path for his conversion, and activate the Holy Spirit in his life. Amen."

The Most Important Way to Spend Your Time

Even after hearing St. Monica's story, some parents still aren't convinced. "Well, that's a beautiful story and I'm glad it worked out for her," they think. "But I doubt my prayers would do much."

That makes me think of a story Bishop Barron once told me. He was visiting a college campus in Arizona where FOCUS missionaries had served for a few months. FOCUS, the Fellowship of Catholic University Students, is a large national evangelization ministry that sends recent college graduates to universities across the country. The young missionaries pledge two years of their life to praying for and evangelizing students on campus. It's become one of the most effective outreaches in the country.

During Bishop Barron's visit, he asked how things were going at their new outpost. One of the missionaries responded, "Well, when we first got here, we decided to identify the most influential student on campus and then pray for his conversion. The most influential person here is the quarterback of the football team, so we've been eagerly praying for him."

"Oh," Bishop Barron replied. "How's that working out?"

"Well," the student responded, "We've been praying for him every single day, by name, for three or four months now. And though we haven't gotten him yet, we have his roommate and his girlfriend. They've both come into the Catholic Church. We figure it's only a matter of time before God wins him over too."

This story highlights the importance of strategic evangelization. But it also affirms the grounding power of prayer. FOCUS missionaries on every campus place a strong emphasis on prayer, because they've seen it work time and again. It's not just a pious duty to them; it's one of their most important tools.

But many of us lack that sort of confidence in prayer. We might mutter a few Our Fathers or Hail Marys, or offer a quick prayer for safety every now and then, but we have trouble believing that prayer can do something as significant as leading to someone's conversion.

The survey of Catholic parents I mentioned above also asked about their prayer habits, and it found that only one in three Catholic parents prays at least once per day. When asked why they didn't pray more often, parents were most likely to give the following reasons: busy schedule or lack of time (51%), having missed Mass (39%), or that prayer just did not cross their mind (39%).

Again, few of us *really* believe that prayer has the power to shape the world in big ways. If we did believe that, then how come we don't pray more often? Sure we have jobs, families, and responsibilities, but if we really believed that our prayers could move the heart of God and bring about massive changes in the world, why wouldn't we pray regularly and make it our top priority?

The most common answer in the survey—one that, admittedly, most of us would probably give—is that we're just too busy.

What If I'm Too Busy to Pray?

Imagine if an NBA player said, "I don't have time for practice and conditioning. My schedule is just too full with filming commercials, doing interviews, and signing autographs." We would rightly say, "You're crazy! If you don't practice, soon none of that other stuff will matter." The same goes for prayer. If we skip out on prayer, our entire spiritual life is compromised, and when that happens, all areas of life tumble with it.

St. Francis de Sales, an incredibly busy evangelist, taught, "If you don't have time for prayer, you don't have time for anything. . . . Half an hour's prayer each day is essential, except when you are busy. Then a full hour is needed." Being too busy to pray is precisely the reason we need to pray *more*. It means our priorities are out of alignment.

Here's an unchangeable fact: you will never just *have* time for prayer; you must *make* time. Ask yourself, *Isn't my child worth that time? Isn't my child worth committing five to ten minutes a day to praying for him to return to the Church?* Right now, determine the best five-to-ten-minute slot that you can commit to every day. For many people, that's at the beginning of the day. For others, it's right after lunch or before going to bed. But whenever it is, make it a routine and commit to it. You might even schedule it into your calendar and have your phone send you an alert or message when it's time.

Even after you initially commit to prayer, though, the battle isn't over. One priest I know says, "You want firsthand proof that there are dark spiritual powers at work? Simply commit to praying for ten minutes, every day, and watch how the whole world conspires against you fulfilling that."

Chances are, you'll commit to regular prayer, show up for a few days, but after a while, you'll begin to wonder, *Is this really working?* What if we don't feel like we're making any headway? We pray for our child over and over and nothing seems to change. At this point, we want to remember a fact that all the spiritual masters affirm—namely, that prayer usually works behind the scenes, through imperceptible movements and invisible effects. Peter Kreeft writes, "If God showed us all the differences all our prayers made to all the lives they affected, down through the generations, we'd never be able to get up off our knees again for the rest of our lives."

For now, at least on this side of heaven, we can't see all the ways our prayers are shaping us and our children. But we must push on and keep praying, confident that they are making a real difference.

Four Powerful Ways to Pray for Your Child

One problem many parents face, especially if they were raised only on rote prayers in church or school, is that they struggle with what to *do* during prayer. They worry that they don't know what to say to God. That's all right. St. Josemaría Escrivá said, "You don't know how to pray? Put yourself in the presence of God, and as soon as you have said, 'Lord, I don't know how to pray!' you can be sure you've already begun."

You might begin your time with a traditional prayer. For example, one simple Our Father can open up deeper prayer. As St. André Bessette affirms, "When you say to God, 'Our Father,' he has his ear right next to your lips." The Hail Mary is also potent. A priest friend of mind likes to point out that "one Hail Mary brought Jesus to earth (Luke 1:26–38). What could it do for you?"

After beginning with traditional rote prayers, you might then move into more spontaneous prayer. Jesus taught his followers to refer to God as "Abba," which is an affectionate term for "Father." God is your loving Father who wills all good things for you and your child. Talk to him. Lay out your concerns, feelings, and angst. Don't hold back. With confidence, beg him to draw your child back into his family, the Church. This sort of authentic, unfiltered prayer is extremely pleasing to God, as it would be to any loving father.

In addition to the prayer tips above, many Catholics rely on four other tools and methods.

First is the Rosary. During the Rosary, we reflect on the life of Christ and ask for his Mother's intercession. The Bible teaches that the Blessed Mother has been crowned the Queen of Heaven (see Rev. 12). She sits at the right hand of her Son in heaven and can be a powerful advocate for you. She knows well the agonizing pain of seeing her child suffer, and can commiserate with your pain. As you pray the Rosary, ask her to share your worries and to intercede on your behalf. Along those lines, you might commit to praying the Rosary every day for one month for the conversion of your child and see what happens.

Second, many parents find great power in praying novenas. A novena is a short series of prayers, usually prayed once a day over a nine-day period, that is aimed at a certain goal or intention. For instance, you might pray a novena to St. Thérèse of Lisieux, the young saint who died at just twenty-four-years old, asking her to intercede for your own young-adult child. Each day you would ask for a specific gift for your child—good friends, the Holy Spirit, the grace of conversion, etc. The website PrayMoreNovenas.com makes this easy by sending you a novena prayer each morning, straight to your email inbox.

A third way to pray for your child is to spend one hour each week in front of the Blessed Sacrament, asking Christ to move in your child's life. The great preacher Archbishop Fulton J. Sheen famously completed a "Holy Hour" every day during his sixty-year priesthood, without exception. Despite a grueling schedule and persistent travel, he never missed spending an hour with the Lord, even if it meant finding a chapel in the middle of the night. Near the end of his life, Sheen reflected on its importance to his life: "It is impossible for me to explain how helpful the Holy Hour has been in preserving my vocation. . . . The Holy Hour became like an oxygen tank to revive the breath of the Holy Spirit in the midst of the foul and fetid atmosphere of the world. Even when it seemed so unprofitable and lacking in spiritual intimacy, I still had the sensation of being at least like a dog at the master's door, ready in case he called me."

Fourth, you might try the Chaplet of Divine Mercy. This prayer was revealed by Jesus to St. Faustina Kowalska, a favorite saint of St. John Paul II, who was given visions and messages from Jesus Christ. In her *Diary*, she explains that Jesus asked that the Feast of Divine Mercy, known today as Divine Mercy Sunday, be established and preceded by a novena dedicated to the Divine Mercy. Our Lord told St. Faustina, "I desire that during these nine days you bring souls to the fountain of my mercy, that they may draw . . . strength and refreshment and whatever grace they need in the hardships of life." On the fifth day of the novena, the prayer is specially dedicated to "the souls of those who have separated themselves from the Church." Jesus affirmed to Faustina, "The prayer most pleasing to me is prayer for the conversion of sinners. Know, my daughter, that this prayer is always heard and always answered."

Whatever type of prayer you choose, the most important thing is, as Nike says, "Just do it." Just show up and open your heart to God. He loves your child more than you can fathom and wants him to return even more than you do. Entrust your child to God and remind God that you're counting on him, that you're completely relying on his grace and providence to bring your child home.

It Takes a Village to Pray for a Child

Rhonda, a New Hampshire mother of three, can testify to the power of praying for fallen-away children. "When my youngest daughter was fifteen," Rhonda said, "she announced to me one day, very calmly, that she didn't know if she believed in God or not. We spoke for quite a while, but needless to say, I was very concerned. She had always been our hardest child, somewhat of a rebel."

Rhonda's daughter had begun staying out late with friends, let her grades drop, and did everything she could to skip going to Mass each Sunday. One day, Rhonda heard about a healing service at her parish. She had always been skeptical about such things, but something urged her to go anyway. So Rhonda went, prayed, and asked others to prayer for her drifting daughter.

"In just a matter of months," Rhonda recalls, "my daughter turned her entire life around. She once again became an honor student, kept all the house rules, loved going to Mass, and even got a job. It was amazing. She began to sing in the folk group at Mass, as she is very musically gifted. You would never have known it was the same girl."

Today, Rhonda's daughter is married with children and is raising her own family in the Catholic faith. As Rhonda says, "Prayer is a powerful gift."

Many parishes host special services focused on praying for former Catholic loved ones. For example, St. Mary Magdalen Parish in Altamonte Springs, Florida, offers a "Teardrops" service where parents are invited to write their children's name on a card, place it on the altar, and together pray for the fallen-away children in the community. The teardrops motif alludes to the many tears shed by St. Monica for Augustine. Just as those tears helped bring Augustine back, so the parents at St. Mary Magdalen believe their prayerful "teardrops" will help their children.

Another parish hosts an event where hundreds of people write the names of their prodigal children on small cards and bring them to the foot of the cross for prayer. The leaders stand and pray for each of those named, and then the stewards collect all of the names, place them into baskets, and carry the baskets to the exits. After the prayer service, as people leave, they're invited to take a card from the basket and to pray for someone else's prodigal in addition to their own.

It's significant that the names are placed at the foot of the cross. The cross of Christ is a place of apparent defeat and turmoil. It's where Jesus' mother knelt and wept as her son faced excruciating torture. But it's also the place of unassailable victory. It's where Jesus overcame the darkness of the world and brought hope where none seemed to exist. There is no better home for parents of children who have left the Church than the cross of Jesus Christ, and when a community of faith gathers around the cross to pray, great power emerges.

If your parish doesn't already offer a service like those described above, consider asking your pastor or someone on the staff to get it started—or maybe coordinate it yourself!

How and Why to Fast for Your Child

Many parents understand the benefit of prayer, even if they don't pray as much as they would like. But there are two other fruitful practices many parents ignore that can amplify the effects of prayer significantly. These admittedly require a bit more resolve, however. The first is fasting, and the second is offering up sacrifices.

In general, Roman Catholics know about fasting. Most "give up" something for Lent, often chocolate, TV, alcohol, or social media. They also abstain from meat on Fridays during Lent and commit to eating only one full meal on Ash Wednesday and Good Friday. But compared to members of other religious traditions, these commitments are relatively light. For example, during the celebration of Ramadan, which lasts about a month, Muslims fast from all eating, drinking (including water), and sexual activity from sunrise until sunset. Even among other Christians, there are typically stricter fasting rules. The Eastern Orthodox give up all meat, dairy, and eggs during Lent, during the forty days before Christmas, and also have two other fasting periods in preparation for the Feast of Saints Peter and Paul and the Dormition (Assumption) of Mary. Beyond these four fasting seasons, the Orthodox also fast *every* Wednesday and Friday during the year!

But what's the point of all this fasting? It's certainly not to lose weight or look better for swimsuit season. For religious people, the purpose of fasting is to detach ourselves from the world and draw closer to God—and also to deepen the power of our intercessory prayer.

Here are a few basic principles to consider while fasting for your children:

Fast for the right purpose: When it comes to fasting, motivation matters. There are many reasons why you might give up food, such as losing weight, cleansing your body, preparing for surgery, or impressing others with your pious discipline. Christian fasting is different. Its purpose isn't to look or feel better. The purpose is to orient our minds and hearts more completely toward God.

Fast humbly: Fasting was very common in Jesus' day. However, it was often done pompously and publicly, in order to gain admiration. Many of the religious leaders liked to exaggerate their sacrifice, dirtying their faces and making it apparent to everyone when they were fasting. But Jesus discourages this. He teaches that when we fast, we should look and act normal, while inwardly seeking the face of God. The reward for this hidden fasting is far greater than the temporary ego boost you get from public displays.

Fast from nonfood items: Although most people choose to fast from edible things, it doesn't have to be food. In fact, fasting from nonfood items can often be more spiritually beneficial. Ask yourself this question: What things or activities am I most attached to? Perhaps it's binge-watching too many shows on Netflix, spending too much time on Facebook, or checking your cell phone too often. Maybe you need to fast from sarcasm or complaining or gossiping. Whatever the case, don't restrict your fasting to food.

Fast from things you enjoy: Fasting is typically helpful only if you actually enjoy whatever you're giving up. If you can't stand social media, for instance, then giving up Facebook for a week probably won't have much effect.

Fast in small doses: St. Thérèse of Lisieux, one of the Church's most popular saints, is not remembered for any grand spiritual accomplishments in her life. She's honored for developing a simple, ordinary path to God, focused on doing small things with great love—what she called the Little Way. That's a great attitude for fasting. We may get burned out if we try to fast too much, too soon. For instance, a friend of mine, who didn't have much self-control to begin with, decided he wanted to heroically sacrifice all meat and dairy throughout the entire season of Lent. He gave in after less than a week. It was just too much for him. He would have been far more successful just giving up one food item and then progressing from there, maybe adding a second food item the next week. Consider ways that you can fast in small doses. You might simply choose to go without dessert. Or when you're at a fast-food restaurant, you might choose to *downsize* your meal rather than upsizing it. Or you might take the stairs next time rather than the elevator, or park in the farthest spot away from the entrance. Remember, small doses.

Fast specifically for your child: Giving something up, or skipping a meal or two, is only part of the equation. To apply the spiritual benefit resulting from fasting you need to specifically unite that sacrifice to your child's needs. This can involve saying a simple prayer during times of longing. For instance, if you're fasting from food, whenever you hear your stomach rumble, say a prayer such as, "God, I'm choosing to skip lunch today for the sake of my son. You know his needs and love him even more than I do. Please give him the grace he needs to return to you in your Church." It also helps to keep reminding yourself while fasting, "I'm doing this for my child."

Fasting is one of the most powerful—and underused—spiritual disciplines, and today, few Catholics turn to it outside of Lent. But if you commit to making "small fasts with great love," it can really help your child.

Offer Up Your Sufferings

In the early days of his time as a pastor, St. John Vianney had one all-consuming desire: to help his parishioners become holy. Although many pastors, then and now, would undoubtedly share that mission, St. John was utterly committed do it, willing to do whatever was necessary to attain it. He spent several all-night vigils in his chapel, praying: "My God, grant me the conversion of my parish; I am willing to suffer all my life whatsoever it may please thee to lay upon me; yes, even for a hundred years I am prepared to endure the sharpest pains, only let my people be converted."

This may sound crazy to the outside world. Someone inviting suffering on himself? Most of us do everything we can to *avoid* pain and suffering—or even a little discomfort. But as Catholics, we know that our suffering is not pointless. If we let it, it can be redemptive, offered up to God as a sacrifice for the sake of others. Even if suffering is not inherently good, it can produce good if we endure it, allow it to purify us, and transform it into a sacrifice.

St. John Vianney had plenty of opportunities to "offer up" his sufferings. When he arrived at his parish in 1818, there were only sixty households and about two hundred people. Few of his parishioners were literate and most were indifferent to their faith. Almost nobody cared what this new priest had to say. Even though he would spend up to seven hours writing his homilies and spend all day Saturday practicing and memorizing them for the Sunday Mass, he faced what we might diplomatically call a "difficult" crowd of listeners. They entered late and left early, banging the loud door each time. They whispered to each other throughout his homily and yawned noisily. Some parishioners even mocked the priest's voice and mannerisms. But that still didn't shake the pastor's commitment: "When I preach, I speak to people who are either deaf or asleep, but when I pray, I speak to the God who is not deaf."

Even with this heroic degree of sacrifice, it took a long while to see any change. Besides their deplorable behavior at Mass, John's parishioners accused him of debauchery, wrote songs to taunt him, threw mud, and hung crude posters on his rectory door. They sent hateful letters to his bishop about him. One woman even falsely accused him of fathering her child. His response to all this vehemence? "We must pray for them."

Jesus said, "Whoever wishes to come after me must deny himself, take up his cross, and follow me" (Matt. 16:24). For many parents, that means picking up the difficult cross of your child leaving the Church—but then carrying that cross on his behalf. We must not flee the crosses in our lives. Just as Jesus accepted beatings, torture, and ultimately death on our behalf, offering his sacrifices for our sake, so we must channel our much smaller pains and sufferings for the sake of our children.

What does this look like in practice? Each time you face a difficult situation at home or work, pray, "Lord, I offer this to you for the sake of my child." Each time you suffer a small cut, or perhaps a sore throat, bear it willingly and say, "Lord, I offer this sacrifice to you for my son or daughter."

To be clear, this isn't an attempt to manipulate God. We can't force God's hand by demanding he offer grace to our children in return for our good works. Grace is, by definition, an unmerited gift. But in God's spiritual economy, he always meets sacrifice with grace. When we make small sacrifices for the sake of our children, new grace flows out in abundance, grace that we can apply to our children through prayer.

Rely on the Holy Spirit

The Holy Spirit is unquestionably the greatest gift Jesus left us before ascending to heaven. As the third person of the Trinity, the Holy Spirit is the divine soul of the Church and the power behind all our spiritual endeavors. Simply put, you can't do *anything* to help your child return without cooperating with the Holy Spirit.

He is your greatest ally in this mission. He came into your life at Baptism, but if you're like most Catholics, you haven't fully received all of the "fruits" of his presence. The Bible lists several that he wants to produce in you: love, joy, peace, patience, kindness, generosity, faithfulness, gentleness, self-control (see Gal. 5:22–23). Read those again slowly. Do you want to acquire those behaviors? Would they be helpful in your mission? Would you have greater success with your child if you were more joyful, had more patience, or if you exuded more kindness and love? If so, call on the Holy Spirit to take control of your life. Tell him, right now, in your own words, that you want him to form those fruits in your life.

The Holy Spirit, if you ask him, will be your confidant and guide in this mission, and he'll carry most of the burden. Working in you, he will provide you the right words to say, at the right moments, and will soften your heart. Working in your child, he will slowly prepare the way of your child's conversion, raking away rocky barriers and planting seeds of grace that the Spirit will later water and grow.

Without the Holy Spirit, our tips and strategies have a very limited chance of success. Sure, you might be able to manipulate your child through a well-placed question or phrase, but unless the Holy Spirit has already been stirring in his heart, your child will likely be resistant.

Therefore, keeping in mind the value of all the other types of prayer and fasting we've discussed, the most important prayer is this: that the Holy Spirit come into your life and into your child's life, in order to "prepare the way of the LORD" (Isa. 40:3).

Prayer, fasting, and sacrificing for your child are bedrock disciplines that will undergird the rest of your game plan. But we're still not ready yet to approach your child directly. Before that happens, you need to make sure that you're well prepared.

CHAPTER 6
Equip Yourself

"I don't want them to know I'm Catholic," I thought. "If they do, they'll probably challenge my faith and I won't know how to respond. Or they'll ask me difficult questions and I won't have the answers. I'd rather they just not know about my conversion."

That's how I felt around friends in college after converting to Catholicism. Though I'm ashamed to admit it, I was young and new to the faith, and I was worried about discussing it with others. Whenever my conversion came up in conversation, I would clam up or become tongue-tied. And when I *did* try to explain or defend my faith, I felt I did more harm than good.

Maybe you feel like that too. Maybe you love your faith deeply. You never miss Mass. You say your prayers. God is real and alive to you. But still, you hardly feel equipped to share your faith with other people, much less your own child. Like me after my conversion, you're worried people will ask you difficult questions and you won't have a response.

That's how I felt for a long while—for more than a year after I became Catholic. But as I learned more about my faith, that attitude slowly changed. I began reading good Catholic books that explained God and the Church in ways I could understand and articulate. I found resources that pointed to Bible verses or historical references that backed up the Church's teachings, which was helpful when my Protestant friends pressed me. I also found a good Catholic study Bible and devoured it. It had several notes and explanations from Catholic theologians, clearing up confusing passages.

Then I discovered the *Catechism of the Catholic Church*, which for me was like finding a veritable gold mine. Here, in one single book, I discovered what Pope St. John Paul II called a "sure norm" for understanding and teaching the faith. It was like an all-inclusive guide to all things Catholic. The more I studied it, the more I knew. And the more I knew, the more confident I became in sharing my faith with others.

These books helped me see *why* Catholics believe what they do. Of course, the *what* was important. But I needed the *why* just as much. When discussing your faith with your child, chances are what they really want to know is *why*—why do Catholics believe this or do that, and more importantly, *why* should I care?

Even after all that reading, what I didn't know still far outweighed what I had learned. But I felt confident I could hold my own with any skeptic or seeker who had substantive questions about Catholicism. Over the past several years, I've dialogued with hundreds of people about the Church and have helped many of them find satisfying answers to their questions, thanks in no small part to the time I spent studying the Bible, the *Catechism*, and other helpful resources.

Looking back, I unknowingly fell upon a secret that many Catholic parents miss when trying to draw their children back:

You can't give what you don't have.

You may be excited about sharing the faith with your child. But enthusiasm and goodwill won't get you very far. You need to *know* your faith and be able to explain it.

It's certainly possible that you can help them even if you have little more than a basic understanding—God will use whatever you give to him. But the more you know, and the better you know it, the more effective you'll be. And the less likely you'll misinform your child and make it harder for him to return.

We all know this is the case in other areas. For example, if you want to fascinate your child with baseball or music or quantum mechanics, good luck trying to do that without being familiar with the subject yourself. If you've never tossed a baseball or studied music, and if you haven't opened a science book since high school, you probably won't be of much help. But when you have a working knowledge of the subject you're sharing, your passion will shine through and you'll dramatically improve your chances of transmitting that passion to your child.

Want your child to take Catholicism seriously? Want him to become as passionate about God as you are? After praying and fasting for your child, the next step is to equip yourself.

This is a demand straight from St. Peter, the first pope, who said, "Always be ready to give an explanation to anyone who asks you for a reason for your hope" (1 Pet. 3:15).

But how do you do that? You must learn your faith. This doesn't mean you have to be able to answer every question or soothe every concern. As we'll learn in a moment, sometimes a humble "I don't know" is more effective than a bumbled attempt to answer every challenge. But in general, the stronger you grasp your own faith, the more confident, passionate, and effective you'll be at drawing your child back to the Church.

To begin with, you need to become familiar with two particular books.

The Two Go-To Sources

"Reading has made many saints," wrote St. Josemaría Escrivá; and he was right. Books have affected the lives of Christians up and down the centuries. Books have tremendous power to change our lives. There are hundreds of good Catholic books available today, but two stand out as indispensable.

The Bible

First, and most obvious, is the Bible. It's been called the "best known and least read" book in the world, which is sad but probably true—at least for Catholics. If you're like most faithful Catholics, you probably have a Bible in your house, but that doesn't mean you read it regularly. While Protestant Christians are generally known for their deep devotion to Scripture, Catholics, regrettably, have a less-than-stellar reputation.

Thankfully, that's changing. Over the last few decades, the Catholic Church has experienced a biblical renaissance, in no small part due to the Second Vatican Council's call for renewed Scripture study, along with the pontificate of Pope Benedict XVI. Having a pope who doubled as one of the world's premier biblical scholars helped to revive the Church's focus on the Bible. Today, the Catholic Church is blessed with an abundance of biblical experts who are writing books, giving talks, producing study programs, and raising the Church's biblical literacy by leaps and bounds.

Of course, Catholicism has *always* been a Bible-based religion. Since the early centuries of Christianity, the Bible was compiled by Catholics, copied by Catholics, and spread by Catholics. The Bible is a Catholic book. But Catholic men and women haven't always given it the attention it deserves. Sure, we hear large parts of the Bible proclaimed within the Mass, but few of us are personally familiar with the stories, teachings, and overarching themes of Sacred Scripture.

So how do we become more conversant with the Bible? The simplest way is to start reading it consistently, in small doses. This sounds easy, but it usually doesn't happen without a firm commitment. So, right now, as you're reading this chapter, commit to reading the Bible for ten minutes every day. That's it—just ten minutes. You can surely do that. Many Catholics prefer to read in the mornings, right after they wake up. It gets their day off on the right foot, setting a good tone. Fr. Larry Richards, a well-known speaker and Bible advocate, encourages Catholics to operate on the "No Bible, no breakfast" principle. He says whenever he asks people whether they read their Bible, they answer, "Well, I *try*, Father . . ." "Oh, come on," he replies. "Nobody *tries* to eat breakfast. They just do it!" They don't forget to eat breakfast or watch as the meal casually slips down their to-do list. Food is a top priority. That's why Fr. Larry suggests you not eat breakfast until you've read the Bible for ten minutes. Make that your own policy. Prioritize the Bible over food and you're almost guaranteed not to miss it.

Reading the Bible just ten minutes a day can change your life. Begin with one of the Gospels, such as Matthew or Mark, and gradually make your way through the New Testament. As you read, stop every now and then to reflect on the person of Jesus. Pray to him, ask him to speak to you, and invite the Holy Spirit to show you how to apply the passage you just read to your own life. Slowly, over time, you'll not only become familiar with the contours of the Scriptures and of Jesus' life and teachings, but those passages will begin to shape your mind and heart. They'll also bring to birth in you a new confidence and zeal to share what you've discovered. Jesus will become real to you, more than just a historical figure. You'll encounter him as someone alive and deeply alluring.

One word of caution: many people find the Bible confusing, even the New Testament, if they start reading in isolation, without any context. Therefore, it's a good idea to find a helpful study Bible, one with notes and commentary alongside the passages. In my view, the best option is the *Word on Fire Bible* series (full disclosure: I serve as general editor for this series). The *Word on Fire Bible* not only brings together a wealth of commentary from the greatest theologians, poets, and artists from 2,000 years of Church history, but it's produced in a breathtakingly beautiful format. Beyond that, you also might consider the *Ignatius Catholic Study Bible: New Testament* (Ignatius Press, 2010) and *The Navarre Bible: New Testament Expanded Edition* (Scepter, 2008). Both feature the entire New Testament along with quotes and insights from saints, popes, Church Fathers, and contemporary Catholic theologians.

In terms of books that will help you understand Scripture, I recommend *Walking with God: A Journey through the Bible* by Tim Gray and Jeff Cavins (Ascension Press, 2010), which opens up the larger story of Scripture so you can understand how individual books and passages fit into God's overarching plan for the world. Other good Catholic books on Scripture include Peter Kreeft's *You Can Understand the Bible: A Practical and Illuminating Guide to Each Book in the Bible* (Ignatius Press, 2005), which offers helpful introductions and summaries to each book of the Bible, and *The Bible Compass: A Catholic's Guide to Navigating the Scriptures* by Edward Sri (Ascension Press, 2009), which answers many common questions about the Bible.

But whatever you choose, the key is to commit, right now, to reading the Bible for ten minutes a day. Then find a good Catholic study Bible, and consider picking up at least one book that helps you better understand the Scriptures.

Catechism of the Catholic Church

For many years, if someone asked a Catholic, "What does the Catholic Church believe about [insert subject]?", it could be difficult to find the answer. Although you could turn to a broad range of creeds and local catechism books, there wasn't a single, up-to-date book that collected all Church teaching in one place. That all changed in 1992 when Pope John Paul II pro-mulgated the *Catechism of the Catholic Church*. Several years in the making, the project became the first authoritative book since the sixteenth century to bring together all of the Church's teaching in one volume. It was especial-ly welcome because of its beautiful language. Whereas previous collections were more juridical and formal, dryly listing out hundreds of doctrines, the new *Catechism* is written in a more explanatory, almost poetic essay style. It's rich and easy to understand.

As with the Bible, the *Catechism* is indispensable, and if you commit just five to ten minutes per day reading the *Catechism*, within a short time you'll have a masterful understanding of not only *what* the Church teaches but *why*. In fact, at just five to ten minutes per day, you'll get through the entire *Catechism* in less than a year. It may seem like an intimidating book—some editions have over seven hundred pages—but when you read it in small dos-es, you'll progress through the whole thing fast.

Within the *Catechism* you'll find clear, helpful explanations of the most prominent—and even the more controversial—Catholic teachings. If your child doesn't understand why Catholics venerate Mary, or pray to the saints, or confess their sins to a priest, or reject artificial contraception, you'll find what you need in the *Catechism*.

Many editions come with detailed indexes in the back, organized both by subject and biblical verse. So if you or your child needs to know what the Church teaches about a particular topic, such as heaven, or how the Church understands a passage of the Bible, such as Matthew 16:18, you can turn to the index and find every reference within the *Catechism*.

Read Good Catholic Books

The Bible and the *Catechism* should be the first books you turn to, but not the last. Today, we're blessed to have many great Catholic books to help grow your faith. Don't feel like you have to read all of them. You really just need at least one general book on Catholicism, and then perhaps one or two more dealing with the specific questions, doubts, or objections your child is struggling with. In term of general books, here are some of my favorite "must-reads":

Catholicism: A Journey to the Heart of the Faith by Bishop Robert Barron (Image Books, 2011)—One of the clearest, most beautiful explanations of the Catholic faith from today's premier evangelist. Bishop Barron uses stories, art, architecture, music, history, the saints, and more to unveil the genius and beauty of Catholicism. It's the first book I would recommend to someone asking the question, "What's Catholicism all about?"

Fundamentals of the Faith: Essays in Christian Apologetics by Peter Kreeft (Ignatius Press, 1988)—With wit and charm, Kreeft considers all the fundamental elements of Christianity and Catholicism, explaining, defending, and showing their relevance today. This takes you down the whole path, from the existence of God all the way through comparative religions, prayer, and the nature of the Church.

Essential Catholic Survival Guide by the Catholic Answers Staff (Catholic Answers, 2005)—Compiles seventy of the best articles and tracts from Catholic Answers, the world's leading apologetics ministry, into one cohesive, comprehensive book that can be used by anyone, anytime, anywhere to defend the Catholic faith. It covers questions and misconceptions dealing with the Church, the pope, Mary, the saints, the sacraments, morality, non-Catholic Christians, and more.

What to Say and How to Say It: Discuss Your Catholic Faith with Clarity and Confidence by Brandon Vogt (Ave Maria Press, 2020)—A clear guide on how to discuss the most difficult, hot-button issues with friends and family, topics such as atheism, same-sex marriage, transgenderism, the Eucharist, and more.

In terms of books that drill down into a particular objection or stumbling block your child may have, here are my favorites:

Abortion—*Persuasive Pro-Life: How to Talk About Our Culture's Toughest Issue* by Trent Horn (Catholic Answers, 2014)

Annulments—*Annulments and the Catholic Church: Straight Answers to Tough Questions* by Edward Peters (Ascension Press, 2010)

Atheism—*Answering Atheism: How to Make the Case for God with Logic and Charity* by Trent Horn (Catholic Answers, 2013)

Bible—*The Bible Compass: A Catholic's Guide to Navigating the Scriptures* by Edward Sri (Ascension Press, 2009)

Confession—*Lord, Have Mercy: The Healing Power of Confession* by Scott Hahn (Image, 2003)

Contraception—*The Contraception Deception: Catholic Teaching on Birth Control* by Patrick Coffin (Emmaus Road, 2018)

Death—*Love Is Stronger Than Death* by Peter Kreeft (Ignatius Press, 1992)

Divorce—*Divorced. Catholic. Now What?* by Lisa Duffy (Journey of Hope, 2007)

Early Church—*The Fathers Know Best: Your Essential Guide to the Teachings of the Early Church* by Jimmy Akin (Catholic Answers, 2010)

Eucharist—*Jesus and the Jewish Roots of the Eucharist: Unlocking the Secrets of the Last Supper* by Dr. Brant Pitre (Image, 2011)

Evil and Suffering—*Making Sense Out of Suffering* by Peter Kreeft (Servant, 1986)

Jesus—*Jesus Shock* by Peter Kreeft (Beacon Publishing, 2012)

Heaven—*Heaven: The Heart's Deepest Longing* by Peter Kreeft (Ignatius Press, 1989)

History—*Seven Lies about Catholic History: Infamous Myths about the Church's Past and How to Answer Them* by Diane Moczar (TAN Books, 2010)

Homosexuality—*Made for Love: Same-Sex Attraction and the Catholic Church* by Fr. Michael Schmitz (Ignatius Press, 2017)

Mary—*Behold Your Mother: A Biblical and Historical Defense of the Marian Doctrines* by Tim Staples (Catholic Answers, 2015)

Mass—*The Lamb's Supper: The Mass as Heaven on Earth* by Scott Hahn (Doubleday, 1999)

Pope—*Pope Fiction: Answers to 30 Myths and Misconceptions about the Papacy* by Patrick Madrid (Basilica Press, 1999)

Pornography—*Delivered: True Stories of Men and Women Who Turned from Porn to Purity* by Matt Fradd (Catholic Answers, 2014)

Protestantism—*The Protestant's Dilemma: How the Reformation's Shocking Consequences Point to the Truth of Catholicism* by Devin Rose (Catholic Answers, 2014)

Sacred Tradition—*By What Authority? An Evangelical Discovers Catholic Tradition* by Mark Shea (Ignatius Press, 2013)

Saints—*Any Friend of God Is a Friend of Mine: A Biblical and Historical Explanation of the Catholic Doctrine of the Communion of Saints* by Patrick Madrid (Basilica Press, 1996)

Salvation—*The Drama of Salvation: How God Rescues You from Your Sins and Delivers You to Eternal Life* by Jimmy Akin (Catholic Answers, 2015)

Same-Sex Marriage—*Getting the Marriage Conversation Right: A Guide for Effective Dialogue* by William B. May (Emmaus Road, 2012)

Science and Faith—*Faith, Science, and Reason: Theology on the Cutting Edge* by Christopher Baglow (Midwest Theological Forum, 2009)

Sexuality—*Good News About Sex and Marriage: Answers to Your Honest Questions About Catholic Teaching* by Christopher West (Servant, 2004)

Suffering—*Making Sense Out of Suffering* by Peter Kreeft (Servant, 1986)

Transgenderism—*When Harry Became Sally: Responding to the Transgender Moment* by Ryan T. Anderson (Encounter Books, 2018)

All of the books above can be found at your local Catholic bookstore or through online bookstores. In fact, you can find used copies of many of them for just a few pennies online.

Read them at your own pace, but do read them! If you commit to reading just one good Catholic book every one to two months, you'll quickly become an expert at explaining and defending your faith. You'll be amazed at how much that will help when you finally open a dialogue with your child.

Know Where to Find the Answers You Need

Reading good books will give you a wealth of knowledge. But what if your child stumps you? Parents often come to me and say, "My child asked me a question about [difficult Catholic topic], and I have no idea how to answer him. What should I say?" I almost always give the same advice: "Go visit Catholic.com and in the search box at the top of the page, enter the topic or question. You'll immediately find several helpful resources."

Catholic.com is run by the Catholic Answers apostolate, which specializes in helping Catholics explain and defend the faith. They have hundreds of articles, videos, tracts, books, and podcasts available through their website and the search box ties it all together. Their website is truly one of the most valuable Catholic tools online. Catholic Answers even keeps track of the most-searched terms, and they ensure they have plenty of resources for those issues. (In case you're wondering, their most popular search is "Purgatory.")

So if your child stumps you with a question or challenge, you'll be able to say, "Hmm. That's a great question and I don't know the answer. Let me get back to you." Then visit Catholic.com, use the search box, find the answers you need, and then go back to your child. (Later in this book we'll learn how to dialogue and share these answers. For now, though, we're just learning where to find them.)

Besides the Catholic Answers website, the internet offers many other tools. For example, websites such as StrangeNotions.com, which I founded, are especially helpful if your child is an atheist or agnostic. The website features articles on God's existence, morality, science, philosophy, and more. It features over thirty expert contributors and hundreds of articles that are nicely categorized and tagged.

You'll also enjoy WordOnFire.org, the hub for Bishop Robert Barron's online ministry, which contains thousands of videos and articles, many of them tying faith into popular movies, books, and current events. If you and your child go see a new movie, for example, check and see if Bishop Barron has a YouTube commentary on it. If so, share the YouTube video with your child—it's an easy, nonthreatening way to share your faith and open a discussion.

Of course, the entire Bible and *Catechism of the Catholic Church* are available online through the Vatican's website, Vatican.va. One helpful trick is to visit Google and then type "[topic/question] Catholic Catechism" in the search box. The results will then point you to the exact section in the

Catechism that focuses on the topic or question you're interested in. (Swap out "Catechism" for "Bible" to accomplish the same thing with the Scriptures.)

With this handful of websites, you'll quickly be able to find all the answers you need. Remember, you don't have to *know* all the answers that your child might ask about God or the Church. You just have to know where to find them.

Be Able to Answer the Most Important Question

G.K. Chesterton, one of the most famous journalists in twentieth-century England, shocked the world when he announced his conversion to the Catholic Church in 1922. His intellectual peers asked in confusion, "Why did you become Catholic?" Chesterton gave different answers to this question, depending on the occasion, but one time he said, "The difficulty of explaining 'why I am a Catholic' is that there are ten thousand reasons all amounting to one reason: that Catholicism is true."

Like Chesterton, you need to equip yourself to answer that most important question, the one that ultimately lies behind each of the minor disagreements and doubts your child may have: Why should I be Catholic? In the end, your child has drifted away from the Church because he has found no satisfying answer to that one question.

But many Catholics have never seriously considered that question, especially those who were baptized and raised in the Church. If someone stopped you on the street today and asked, "Why are you Catholic?", what would you say? Take a moment and reflect. How would you answer? Would you talk about the positive ways your faith has shaped your life and how it brings you peace, comfort, and security? Would you explain that you're Catholic simply because your family was Catholic and raised you that way? Would you reference the Eucharist, Confession, or the other sacraments?

Some answers are better than others. For example, being Catholic simply because that's how you were raised is a poor reason. If your faith is rooted in nothing more than family custom, it's in serious danger of withering, and it won't be attractive to anyone else. This is why so many young people leave the Church when they go off to college. Growing up, they only went to Mass because their family did. But after they move away, they lose that anchor and begin to drift.

A much better answer to the "Why are you Catholic?" question is the one Chesterton gave: "I'm Catholic because it's true." In other words, "I'm Catholic because I believe that everything the Catholic Church professes in its creed is true. I believe God exists. I believe he created the world out of love and providentially cares for it. I believe God became man in Jesus Christ, and that he was crucified, died, and rose from the dead. I believe Jesus established the Catholic Church, giving it the authority to teach, heal, and govern in his name. And I believe that at the end of time, God will resurrect our bodies and welcome the faithful into everlasting joy."

It's important to equip yourself with the answer to this question. You need to know why you're Catholic, and you need to be able to succinctly explain that to your child. If you're not sure how to do that, I recommend my own book, *Why I Am Catholic (And You Should Be Too)* (Ave Maria Press, 2017).

Your child may be intrigued by your answer to the "Why be Catholic?" question, but he'll likely be more responsive to personal evidence of how God and the Church have positively shaped your life. That's why you need to know more than just that answer—you need to know and share your own story.

Know Your Story

Walk into the average Evangelical church today and you'll inevitably find a strong emphasis on testimony. For instance, many Baptist churches expect each member to explain how and when they were "saved" before they're formally welcomed into the community.

The story usually involves three parts. First, the dark and weary time before conversion. Second, the moment of conversion, which typically involved praying the "sinner's prayer" and submitting their lives to Christ. Third, the joy and fulfillment found in a new friendship with God. For Protestants, learning and sharing one's testimony is a rite of passage, because it's an incredibly powerful tool. Evangelicals know that non-Christians are more attracted to stories than lectures and are usually more compelled by personal sharing than abstract argument.

Unfortunately, Catholics don't generally place this same emphasis on testimonies. We often fall prey to the belief that religion is personal and private—nobody wants to hear *our* story or what *we* think. One's faith is a personal decision predicated on their own tastes, thoughts, and preferences.

In reality, though, your story, your account of how God has worked in your life, is an extremely potent tool to bring your child back to the Church. Why? Because while all stories are powerful, in your child's mind, *your story* is especially meaningful.

Now, maybe you find it hard to articulate how God has worked in your life, or perhaps his influence has been a little cloudy. That's okay. The important thing is to start intentionally reflecting on these topics. The more you look for these moments, the more evident they'll be.

But eventually you'll want to know how to give a two to three minute account of your conversion story—of how you met Jesus and came to love and follow him.

When compiling and practicing your testimony, a few guidelines will help. Shaun McAfee, a convert from Protestantism to Catholicism, offers an excellent framework in his book *Filling Our Father's House: What Converts Can Teach Us about Evangelization* (Sophia Institute Press, 2015). He suggests a four-part outline. "Your outline will include four elements: your theme, the details of why you're Catholic, your life after being a Catholic and the great benefits of your decision, and your offer to your listeners." The rest of his book explains those parts in detail.

You may be wondering, though, what if I just don't have an exciting story? What if I never had a crippling dark point in my life or a transformative "come to Jesus" moment? McAfee emphasizes that your testimony doesn't have to be based on a difficult or flabbergasting experience:

All people of God have a unique story to tell. For example, if you're a cradle Catholic and think you have had a rather uneventful spiritual journey, you still might have a strong faith and have reasons for keeping that faith. Tell about why you hold on to the hope that is in you, why you're obedient to the Church's teaching, and what has helped you grow and maintain your faith for so long. Even if you've been Catholic your whole life, chances are good that there was a time when you decided to become a more serious and devout Catholic. Tell *that* story!

If you want more examples to use as guidance while compiling your own story, check out the stories at WhyImCatholic.com. There you'll find stories from converts to Catholicism from all sorts of backgrounds—Protestant, Hindu, Jewish, atheist, and even some self-described pagans. The stories are short but moving, describing how people were drawn into, or back to, the Catholic Church and how their lives dramatically changed for the better as a result.

Find a Partner

At this stage in your game plan, while equipping yourself for the rest of the mission, it's a good idea to pull someone else into your pursuit. It could be a friend, a spouse, a priest, or a spiritual mentor, but you want someone not so much to directly help your efforts to draw your child back to the Church, but to serve as an outlet for *you.*

You want a partner. A partner will help in a few ways. First, he'll ensure you're not alone. You need someone to encourage you and affirm you, especially when things stagnate and you don't seem to be making much progress. The journey will be smoother, and it will be easier to persevere, with a partner cheering you on from the sidelines.

Second, a partner can amplify your efforts. He can pray and fast *with* you. Jesus confirms that when "two or three are gathered together in my name, there am I in the midst of them" (Matt. 18:20). Our spiritual effectiveness becomes even stronger when friends join in.

Third, your partner can offer an objective view of your situation. You might need someone to bounce ideas off of and judge whether you're pushing too hard—or not moving firmly enough. An outside view of the situation is often helpful.

* * *

To recap, we've learned in this chapter that even before you begin dialoguing with your child, you first want to equip yourself. You need to have a solid familiarity with the Bible and the *Catechism of the Catholic Church*. You should absorb helpful Catholic books and websites, which will give you the answers and confidence you need. All of that is designed to help you answer the question "Why are you Catholic?", although the best answer will come through your own testimony. When you learn and practice your story and are able to situate it within God's greater story, you have the most powerful tool in your arsenal. You are then well-equipped.

At this point, your next step is to begin planting seeds of faith and trust into your child's life.

CHAPTER 7
Plant the Seeds

It was in college that Emily's faith began to crumble. "I was baptized in the Catholic Church, and always called myself a Catholic, but by freshman year of college my faith had been thoroughly defanged." She became "sexually active and spiritually passive . . . constantly starting the weekend feeling like I *should* go to church and constantly choosing sleep and a leisurely brunch when Sunday morning came."

Things probably wouldn't have changed if it weren't for her brother. A devout Catholic, he decided he didn't want to lose his sister to a lazy secularism. So he began planting seeds of faith in her life. He knew if he pushed too hard, she would resist. But he set out to slowly and gently begin turning her back to the Church.

"My brother planted little seeds of truth in me for a while before I was open to hearing the words," she remembered. "After several conversations, when I was finally open, he told me that I needed to turn around and return to the Church. . . . It was not a one-and-done thing; it was a continuing conversation that took several years. But you never know when something you say will stick in someone's craw and drive them to discover more on their own. About eleven months later, I made the choice to hand everything over to Christ and accept whatever he sent my way."

Emily's reversion offers an important lesson: even before you move into substantial conversations about God, you must first plant seeds in your child's life, seeds that will eventually grow into the fruit you hope to see.

Share Unconditional Love

I was once talking with a father of several wayward children, when the father asked me, "What do I do if our relationship is completely cut off? Some of my children, I haven't talked to in months. Either they cut me off because I didn't approve of their lifestyle, or I cut them off because they were disrespecting my wife and me and bleeding us dry of money. How do I help them come back to the Church if our relationship is totally severed?"

I told him, "You need to reestablish a bond of love. You need to commit, in your own heart, to forgiving them and loving them unconditionally, no matter what has happened in the past. You must apologize for your role in the damage and beg forgiveness. All of this is hard, but unless it happens you may be severely hobbling your efforts to help your child return to the Church. They simply won't listen to you."

If your child is like most, the first seed he needs, way before he's open to anything you say about God, is unconditional love. He needs to know that you love him and forgive him for any wrongs, without qualification. This gets back to the first spiritual threshold we covered in chapter 4, "Initial Trust." Your child needs to trust that you love and care for him, and only want what's best for him. But how do you get that message across? Here are some proven tips.

Make Your Love Unmistakable

"The great danger for any parent," says Rob Parsons in *Bringing Home the Prodigals*, "is that the desire to let a child know how strongly we disapprove will be greater than the impulse that lets him know, no matter what he has done, he is still loved."

Unconditional love is one of the most powerful forces on the face of the earth. But it can be very hard to express. And if your child doesn't *know* you love him unconditionally, it won't have much effect.

It's not enough just to say, "I love you." Though your child may appreciate that, especially if you didn't say it a lot during his childhood, sometimes it fails to carry much weight. You need to *show* him you love him unconditionally. It needs to be unmistakable so that he can't interpret your actions any other way. This is typically what he needs before he'll become vulnerable enough to have a serious, spiritual conversation with you.

So decide right now that you are going to love your child intentionally and openly. You might begin with a simple email, letter, or phone call that says, "Look, I know we disagree about some things like religion, but I want you to know that no matter what you believe or choose, I will always love you. That will never change, no matter what you do or don't do, or what you believe."

Expressing this no-strings-attached love does not validate your child's misguided choices or lower the moral bar. It's not to say, "I don't ever want you to change" or "I don't care whether you return to the Church." Love is, as St. Thomas Aquinas defined, to *will* the good of the other—to want what's best for your child. Your child needs to know that even if you disapprove of his religious or moral choices, you still want what's best for him. You *will* his good, even in situations with which you don't completely agree.

If you need some help in this area, I recommend Fr. Lawrence Lovasik's book, *The Hidden Power of Kindness* (Sophia Institute Press, 1999). It contains simple, step-by-step directions on how to overcome all unkindness and meanness and instead radiate love.

Ask for and Express Forgiveness

Every child longs for forgiveness. The great novelist Ernest Hemingway wrote a short story set in Spain titled "The Capital of the World." The main character, Paco, has a falling out with his father and runs away to Madrid. The father is desperate to find his son and bring him back home. He searches fruitlessly all over Madrid. Finally, with no other options, he decides to put a short ad in the local newspaper, which reads: "Paco, meet me at the Hotel Montana at noon on Tuesday. All is forgiven. Papa."

The problem is that Paco is a common name in Spain. When Paco's father arrives at the hotel plaza at noon on Tuesday, he cannot believe his eyes. A squadron of police officers has been dispatched there to control a crowd of eight hundred young men, all named Paco, all of them looking to reconcile with their fathers. They all want forgiveness.

Your child needs forgiveness too. Will it be hard to forgive him? Almost certainly. You know the deep hurts, dashed hopes, and broken promises that your child has delivered over the years. He's likely disappointed you several times.

Forgive him anyway. The more you harbor a grudge, the more unlikely his return.

I want to note that it's not necessary to *verbally* forgive him. It can backfire to forgive someone when they don't think they did anything wrong. But make sure that you've forgiven him in your own heart.

You should also take responsibility for anything *you've* done to hurt him. Don't just offer a general apology. Be specific and detail your wrongdoings. For instance, you might apologize for harsh words about his lifestyle. You might say you're sorry for the passive-aggressive barbs you've sent his way over the years. You might ask his pardon for pressuring him to attend Mass instead of trying to understand why he has left the Church. Don't require or expect him to accept your forgiveness immediately or reciprocate with apologies of his own. Simply ask forgiveness.

For many parents, this is one of the most difficult steps of the game plan. I won't pretend it's easy. But when parents do accomplish it, the only thing they regret is that they didn't heal the relationship earlier. The reconciliation lifts a huge weight from their shoulders, one so large they can't believe they suffered under it so long.

Take an Interest in His Hobbies

If you're like most parents, you're probably not thrilled with the music, hobbies, and activities your child prefers. Nevertheless, if you want to plant the seeds of reversion in your child, strive to find value in his interests and, to the extent you can, encourage them. When your child was young, you attended his sports games, school performances, and other events. Your presence communicated to your child, "I care about you. I support you. I'm interested in what interests you." What can you do today to show that same encouragement?

A friend of mine, Michael (not his real name), was getting discouraged as he saw his teenage son slowly drifting away from God. Even though Michael was a mega-successful Catholic author and speaker, selling thousands of books and keynoting huge conferences, he was losing his son. They seemed to have nothing in common and were constantly at odds.

Michael eventually reached a breaking point. He knew he could either pursue his son or risk losing him forever. So he made decision to learn more about his son's interests. Through many stilted discussions, he eventually discovered that his son was a huge fan of a small, hardcore metal band—not Michael's favorite type of music—and he also learned that the band was on tour and would be hosting a concert in their town in just a few weeks. Michael purchased tickets. The next day, when he gave the tickets to his son, the boy was stunned and overjoyed. Then Michael explained that one ticket was for his son, but the other was not for a friend or date. It was for Michael. If his son wanted to go, they had to go together. Though reluctant, his son agreed.

Before the event arrived, Michael researched the band on the internet. He bought a couple of their CDs to become familiar with their music. It was hard. Can you imagine a middle-aged father listening to hardcore metal throughout the day? But it was worth it. His son was incredulous when Michael spoke intelligently about his favorite band, mentioning specific songs and lyrics. When the big day arrived, Michael remembered, "To be honest, I wasn't looking forward to the concert. I couldn't stand hardcore metal—the loud, screaming lyrics. But I love my son, and that's what he liked. I had to do it for him. I wanted to recapture his heart and I knew this was a way in."

After the concert, the two went out for a late dinner, and his son opened up about many problems and issues he had been struggling with but never felt comfortable bringing to his father. That night revived their relationship and helped his son begin a slow journey back to God and the Church. His son is now a fully committed Catholic, studying at a Catholic college, and his relationship with his father has never been better.

Now, is this a typical story? Will *your* child reverse his drifting simply because you attend one event with him? Maybe not. But I can assure you that any sign you show that you are genuinely interested in what he's passionate about, simply because it's interesting to *him*, will warm your relationship, build more trust, and increase the possibility that he'll be open to discussions about faith.

So find an activity that your child likes that you can share together. Maybe it's tennis, fishing, or basketball. Maybe it's going to bookstores, movies, or concerts. Is there something that once upon a time, long before your child left the Church, you and he enjoyed doing together? Is there something your child currently enjoys that you might be able to join him in? Find something, anything, you can do with him to strengthen the bonds of love.

Cultivate a House of Hospitality

A wise man once said, "When the Father's house is filled with the Father's love, the prodigals will come home." The assertion of course has a double meaning. Prodigals need to experience the love of God in the Father's spiritual house—the Church—but they especially need love in their earthly father's house—your family home.

Rob Parsons tells of a young man who had drifted away from his faith and his family. His parents couldn't remember the last time he was home. But one day, after many years of selfish living and partying, he eventually decided to return. The driveway that led to his parents' house was over a mile long. Like the prodigal son in Jesus' story, he trudged up in trepidation, rehearsing what he would say to his father. As he passed the final bend in the road, he spotted a light on in the house. Suddenly he was overcome with emotion. He thought of all the good memories he had of this home—the birthday parties, the Christmas celebrations, the love his parents poured on him over the years. His spirits began to lift and finally he was at the front porch. His knocked on the door. His father opened it and gazed at him.

"Dad, I'm home," he said.

But his father replied, "I have no son," and closed the door in his face. They never saw each other again.

Would it be at all surprising to learn that the young man never returned to his faith? After reconsidering his lifestyle, and finally summoning the courage to come back, the last thing he needed was rebuke or rejection. He needed unconditional love. He needed to be welcomed like the prodigal son in Jesus' parable. He needed his father to spot him in the driveway, run to him, embrace him, and shout, "Let us celebrate with a feast, because this son of mine was dead, and has come to life again; he was lost, and has been found!"

Abraham Piper notes that, "Because your deepest concern is your son's heart, not his actions, don't create too many requirements for coming home. If he has any inkling to be with you, don't make it hard for him. God may use your love to call him back to Christ. Obviously, there are instances when parents must give ultimatums: 'Don't come to this house, if you are . . .' But these will be rare. Don't lessen the likelihood of an opportunity to be with your child by pushing him away with rules."

Piper offers some vivid examples:

If your daughter stinks like weed or an ashtray, spray her jacket with Febreze and change the sheets when she leaves, but let her come home. If you find out she's pregnant, then buy her folic acid, take her to her twenty-week ultrasound, protect her from Planned Parenthood, and by all means let her come home. If your son is broke because he spent all the money you lent him on loose women and ritzy liquor, then forgive his debt as you've been forgiven, don't give him any more money—and let him come home. If he hasn't been around for a week and a half because he's been staying at his girlfriend's—or boyfriend's—apartment, urge him not to go back, and let him come home.

All of these strategies, from expressing forgiveness, to outward expressions of love, to joining your child's hobbies, to welcoming him in your home, are arranged around a single mission: to show your child that you love him without condition.

Plant "Seed Gifts" in His Life

My friend Josh grew up in a Catholic home, yet like many young students, he went off to college and left his faith behind. But his mom never gave up hope. She prayed for him and tried talking about the Church. When none of that worked, she needed some other strategy. Her solution? Slip good Catholic resources into his life.

She began covertly leaving CDs in his truck, and she dropped Catholic booklets on his desk. Josh became a little frustrated. In fact, he distinctly remembers throwing at least one CD out of his truck window. But over time, Josh became more open and curious. He listened to one or two of the CDs, and one of the booklets particularly caught his eye. It was on the Eucharist. Despite years of religion class, Josh had never developed a clear understanding of what the Eucharist is, or why it matters. He certainly wasn't aware that it was the real Body and Blood of Jesus.

But after studying the booklet, he became convinced, and that conviction led him back to the Church. He later became a parish youth minister, then a Catholic entrepreneur, and now runs one of the largest Catholic website companies in the world—all because his mother planted a few "seed gifts" in his life.

There are many more stories of people who can point to a DVD, book, or CD that led them back to the faith. One mother says, "My son was given a copy of Matthew Kelly's book *Rediscover Catholicism* on the way out of church last Christmas. He stopped going to church regularly about ten years ago. We were away on vacation, and I was amazed to see him reading it the next day. I was even more surprised the following week when he suggested we all go to church and then to brunch. . . . You don't know how happy it makes a mother to see her son return to church."

Chela, the mother of a teenage agnostic, shared with me, "One night, my daughter caught my husband and me watching Bishop Robert Barron's *CATHOLICISM* film series and for some reason she plopped down on the couch and started watching. She didn't give any indication that she *liked* what she was watching, but I'm confident we planted some seeds." Another mother, Kelly, wrote to Bishop Barron to say, "You are making a difference with young people. I 'caught' my 16-year old daughter watching one of your videos last week. She thinks you are a pretty cool priest."

I call these DVDs, books, and CDs "seed gifts" because they are seeds of truth and faith that you plant in your child's life. They're small gifts offered with unconditional love, and far from the nagging, "over-the-top religious and political e-mails" we talked about earlier. The great part is that they do almost all of the work for you. If you feel inadequate to answer your child's questions or objections, handing him a DVD, book, or CD can be a lot less intimidating than having to sit down and explain things yourself.

One of my favorite "seed gift" stories comes from a woman named Leila. Leila's mother-in-law, Carol, was in town visiting Leila's family. To say the two women were different is a dramatic understatement. Carol was a secular, Jewish, pro-choice, liberal mother-in-law; Leila was a conservative, devout Catholic and a stay-at-home mother. Carol could hardly be further from the Catholic Church, a fact that created tension ever since Leila's husband (Carol's son) decided to convert to Catholicism. Carol still didn't understand.

But one night after dinner, as Carol got up from the table, and as Leila thought about heading upstairs to spend time on the computer, Carol pointed to a boxed DVD set by the TV in the next room. She asked, "Can we watch that?"

Leila was stunned. Before Carol arrived, Leila had consciously debated whether to move the DVD set out of sight because she didn't want to be too "in your face" with all the Catholic items in their home. But for some reason, she left it where it was. It was Bishop Barron's *CATHOLICISM* DVD series.

Trying to keep her shock in check, she answered, "Sure! Do you want to watch it now?" Carol did, and they sat down together on the couch. Leila recalled, "I was almost apologetic as I chatted with her as it began, not fully believing that she really wanted to watch, and praying that she would stay awake." Sure enough, about ten minutes into the first episode of the series, she was sound asleep. Leila was worried she had missed her opportunity, but she decided to watch the rest of the episode, alone, just in case Carol woke up. Unfortunately, Carol slept through the whole thing. But when Leila moved to turn off the television, Carol suddenly awoke, looked at her, and said, "That was very interesting! Can we watch more?"

Leila quickly responded "Sure!" and they moved to episode two. Over the following week, they watched all ten episodes of the *CATHOLICISM* series together—almost ten hours of film. Before each session, Leila was sure that Carol would forget about their plan to view the next DVD, or decide she wasn't interested in continuing. But she never forgot, and she was always excited. Carol never fell asleep during the rest of the series.

When they got to the final episode, about the Last Things (death, judgment, heaven, and hell), Carol began asking questions. They had an excellent theological discussion. Leila's husband and daughter had joined the two ladies, watching the final episodes that night, and they were equally stunned with this strange and wonderful situation. Still, they all tried to remain nonchalant, not expressing surprise or exuberance.

With the series finally completed, Leila's husband went to bed while the ladies lingered a bit. Carol seemed to want to keep talking, as this was her last night visiting. As they stood in a hall area chatting, she finally said what Leila had been waiting for: "I can see the appeal of Catholicism . . ." Leila was stunned, and a bit tongue-tied. How should she reply? Leila didn't want to push her away, but she also didn't want to miss the opportunity. So she said a quick prayer to the Holy Spirit, asking him to give her the right words.

"Oh, yes," she muttered out loud, "now you can see the beauty of the faith that your son and I are drawn to! I know it was hard for you to understand back when he became Catholic. And he never felt he had to abandon his Jewish roots, but he was simply completing his Judaism. He discovered that Jesus is the Messiah, and the Church he founded is the New Jerusalem."

Leila later recalled that those few sentences were the most she had ever spoken to Carol about her son's conversion in the fifteen years since it happened.

Carol thought about Leila's reply. Then she asked, "How long does it take?"

Leila and her daughter looked at each other. What did Carol mean? Was she asking how long it takes to become Catholic? Leila assumed so and explained that it takes several months to go through the process and that she used to teach a class of new converts years ago, in case she had any questions.

Leila also mentioned that it was possible to have private lessons if you can't physically get to a regular class.

Carol didn't request anything more that night. After Carol headed off to bed, Leila and her daughter quietly marveled together. Did she really say that? Did she really ask that? Was this for real? Leila was grateful her daughter was there to witness everything to confirm the things Carol had said. "I knew exactly what had occurred, of course," Leila remembered. "Carol had watched the series with an open heart, sincerely seeking God. God can work with such a heart. Ten hours of Truth, Goodness, and Beauty streamed through her eyes and ears, and her soul responded in exactly the way a soul is *made* to respond to Truth, Goodness, and Beauty: it was drawn in, excited, enchanted. One of my favorite sayings, 'Truth comes with graces attached,' played out right in front of my eyes that week. I had the privilege of *seeing* it happen."

Carol flew home the next morning. Things moved slowly over the next few weeks. Leila and her husband prayed about what they should do next, but they were very sensitive about not wanting to push or manipulate. They kept second-guessing the whole situation, wondering whether Carol would persevere or drop the pursuit. They decided to take a wait-and-see approach.

That decision paid off. Carol took the next step, calling Leila's husband several weeks later and shocking him when she said, "I would really like to be baptized." Eventually, they made arrangements for Carol's baptism, where Carol was also confirmed and received her First Communion at age sixty-seven. It was the first of only three Masses she would ever attend as a Catholic. Just a few months after entering the Catholic Church, Carol became ill and passed away.

What's the point of sharing this long, beautiful story of conversion? The point is that it was triggered by one simple act: leaving a DVD set standing next to the TV. That "seed gift," though seemingly small and insignificant, changed the course of Carol's eternity.

Picture your own life right now. How can you slip "seed gifts" into your child's life? Maybe, like Leila, you'll leave a *CATHOLICISM* DVD set sitting next to the TV, hoping that your child will spot it and become interested (or maybe you openly suggest watching it next time your child is around, or just have it playing on the TV in the background). Perhaps you leave good Catholic books scattered on different shelves. Maybe you keep an icon on the wall or a crucifix in each bedroom. Perhaps you buy some good Catholic books and CDs and pass them out to your child—in the mail, in his Christmas stocking, or just for no reason at all. These "seed gifts" may seem innocent but, as Carol's story shows, you never know what will serve as a spiritual springboard to launch your child back into the Church.

Share Helpful Articles and Videos

A recent survey asked hundreds of young atheists to describe their journey to unbelief. From a Christian perspective, the results were troubling. Most of the atheist participants had been raised in a Christian church and most left their churches sometime during high school. Many left because they received superficial answers to life's big questions, or their doubts were belittled and dismissed. Maybe the most surprising finding was this: the internet factored heavily in many conversions to atheism.

The head researcher explained, "When our participants were asked to cite key influences in their conversion to atheism—people, books, seminars, etc.—we expected to hear frequent references to the names of the 'New Atheists.' We did not. Not once. Instead, we heard vague references to videos they had watched on YouTube or website forums."

Here's the good news, though. Just as online articles, videos, and discussion forums can lead young people *away* from faith, they can also push them in the other direction.

A few years ago, while Bishop Barron was still Father Barron, he received an email from Dan, a skeptic in his twenties. "Dear Father Barron," the skeptic wrote, "Growing up, my parents didn't really believe in God. In fact, they were quite against religion—especially Catholicism. They were disgusted by anything we saw or heard about the Catholic Church. Worst of all were Catholic priests. I thought priests were nothing other than despicable child abusers.

"But though I hated priests," he continued, "I've always loved Bob Dylan. One day, not too long ago, I was browsing YouTube for Bob Dylan music videos, when I stumbled across one of your video commentaries on Bob Dylan." (Bishop Barron is a huge Dylan fan himself and has recorded several YouTube videos about the biblical themes in Dylan's lyrics.)

Dan continued, "When I saw you were a Catholic priest, however, I wanted to exit the video immediately. I thought, 'What could a priest possibly have to say to me about Bob Dylan?' Yet something compelled me to watch.

"As it turns out, I enjoyed the video and thought your insights were interesting. Then, as YouTube does, the site suggested other videos I might like based on the one I finished. That led me to your other Bob Dylan videos; then to your movie commentaries; then to your videos on theology and philosophy; and eventually I found my way to your website, WordOnFire.org.

"Since then, I started browsing your articles and following you, and I've been quietly lurking for a few months now. But I felt it was time to reach out to you and let you know this, that through your helpful work, you've not only convinced me that God exists, but yesterday I signed up for the R.C.I.A. program at a nearby Catholic parish. I've decided to become Catholic."

Now, Bishop Barron will be the first to tell you: this story is *not* typical. It's not every day he gets an email that says, "I watched a YouTube video. Now where's the baptismal font?" But it exemplifies the extraordinary potential of these digital tools for connecting with people far from the Church and slowly, perhaps unwittingly, drawing them closer. If a simple YouTube video can change a young atheist like Dan, what do you think it could do for your child?

The Pew Research Center found that 92% of teens go online every day, and a quarter say they are online "almost constantly." The average American teenager spends over seven hours a day on screen media. Your child likely feels more at home in the world of Instagram, Facebook, Twitter, and texting than anywhere else.

If you want to connect with your child, and woo him back to the faith, use this to your advantage. Go where your child is. Consider sharing an uplifting article about the faith to your child's Facebook account, or texting a link about how Catholic Charities has served the local homeless population. Anything that will boost your child's impression of the Church, or improve his vision of God, will be helpful. It may help him cross the threshold of "initial trust" we've mentioned a few times in this chapter.

If your child has a specific objection or stumbling block regarding Catholicism, then consider finding and sharing a good online resource with him. It might be an article from Catholic.com, a video from WordOnFire. org, or a helpful post from a Catholic blog.

* * *

It's unlikely that any of these strategies—sharing unconditional love, planting seeds gifts, passing on helpful resources—will by themselves bring about huge changes in your child's life. In fact, they might not provoke any outward reaction at all. But what they'll do is plant the initial seeds of faith, trust, and love that your child needs in order to be open to the later steps in this game plan. Once the seeds are in place, then you're ready to move to the next step in the game plan, where you'll finally learn why, specifically, your child has drifted from the Church.

CHAPTER 8
Start the Conversation

A recent survey of Catholic teenagers revealed that the large majority of parents rarely or never speak to their kids about religion. Only 8% of the respondents said their parents talked about religion daily and just 20% said they did it once a week.

For most parents, it's hard to open conversations about religion. Patrick Madrid, one of the most effective Catholic apologists in the world, admits, "Although I can draw to Christ the souls of strangers, I sometimes find myself unable even to get a hearing from some of those I love the most. I'm not alone." Indeed, Christ himself observed, "Amen, I say to you, no prophet is accepted in his own native place" (Luke 4:24). Even Jesus himself found it difficult to get through to those nearest to him.

Many parents believe it's impossible to talk with their children about God or religion or faith. But while it's true some children are more closed off than others, it's always possible to start a good conversation, no matter the child, *if* you know what you're doing.

What you need are simple, practical strategies to initiate the conversation and then stay in control—in a good way—even if your knowledge is limited. That's what you'll learn over the next two chapters.

The approach we'll use is grounded not on confrontation but on friendly curiosity, a kind of relaxed diplomacy. These tactics are not manipulative tricks. They are not designed to embarrass your child or coerce him into your point of view. Instead, they will help you gracefully discover his main objections, complaints, and accusations against Catholicism, and then effectively work through them.

Now, you might be nervous moving into such conversations with your child. That's normal—most parents are, at least at first. But once you learn the tips below, you'll feel extremely confident and prepared.

One final word of caution before we start: you should only begin these sorts of conversations *after* you've spent considerable time fasting and praying for your child and equipping yourself, and *after* your child has expressed some openness or curiosity toward returning to the Church. It often takes several months for a young person to reach that stage. So don't rush into these conversations. But when you sense your child is ready, the tips below will help tremendously.

So let's dive in by starting with a question you're probably asking yourself: "How do I even *open up* a conversation about God or the Church?"

Create Opportunities to Chat

Here's the first key to generating good conversations about faith: don't start with faith. Once your child has moved past the "initial trust" threshold and has become spiritually curious and open, you may discern it's time to start discussing these things with him.

But don't immediately begin with religious topics. This is a common mistake. Start by asking normal questions about his daily life. Show that you care about him—all of him, and not just his religious or moral dimensions. Sometimes this is where a conversation ends. You may not have time to get to any religious questions, or the atmosphere just isn't right. That's fine. Your purpose in this beginning stage is just to generate dialogue about *anything*.

Some former Catholics need lots of lead time before discussing heavy issues. They might be somewhat open to faith conversations, but they won't handle it well if you just switch from light chat about the weather to serious issues about God and eternity. You may need to test the waters before diving in.

Abraham Piper recommends another, slightly bolder way to open a meaningful conversation: "Just ask about his soul. You don't know how he'll respond. Will he roll his eyes like you're a moron? Will he get mad and leave? Or has God been working in him since you talked last? You don't know until you risk asking. God will give you the gumption."

At some point in the conversation, when it feels opportune, take a risk and ask a straight question: "Can I ask you something? I wonder if you'd be

up for talking about spiritual things some time. I know y
lationship with the Church, but would you be open to ta
me? I just want to listen and hear what's going on in your

Besides showing that you're not just trying to force yo
this shows your child that you respect him and his sensitiv
that, the question also gives room for your child to say, "I ɯ open, but just
not right now." Chances are, that's an answer you'd gladly take, for it's still
one step closer to a later, more meaningful discussion.

Now, again, I know—you're probably not comfortable with questions
like that right now. I know they're difficult and forward, and I know you're
probably skeptical about how your child will respond. That's all fine.

But once you've spent enough time on the preceding tasks—you've
prayed, fasted, made small sacrifices, equipped yourself, and planted the
seeds—your child is likely ready. Before the conversation begins, steel your
resolve to fight through the awkwardness. That resistance you feel is not
coming from God; it's coming from other powers bent on *preventing* you
from talking with your child about religious matters. Those powers want
nothing more than your silence. So take heart and push through. If it makes
things easier, you might start these conversations via email rather than
phone or face-to-face. You'll eventually want to move into face-to-face conversations, but if email seems more doable, then start there.

Also, if you're still a bit nervous, consider this question: What's the
worst that could happen? Maybe your child will brush you off. Perhaps he
might sigh or express frustration for a couple moments, or he might respond
negatively to your question. But even if all of that happens, let it roll off you.
Don't give up. Remember, you're in it for the long run—this isn't a convert-
your-child-quick scheme. If you can handle the worst-case scenario, which
basically involves a few uncomfortable moments, then these questions are
more than worth the effort.

When you do sense it's time to ask the questions and get the conversation going, stand confidently behind them. Don't worry about whether there
will an awkward pause after your query—there will be; expect it. Don't interrupt any silence that follows. Give your child time to think and respond.

And then what happens when he responds? That's when you begin to listen.

Listen First, Then Listen Some More

Theologian Francis Schaeffer was once asked what he would do if he had an hour with a non-Christian. He replied by saying he would listen for fifty-five minutes. Then, in those last five minutes, he would have something to say.

That's a great strategy for discussions with your child. Listening should be your first, second, and third move. Make it clear from the beginning of each conversation that your primary mission is to understand your child, that you're simply *interested in him*. At least initially, you shouldn't set out to get your point across or try to change his view on things. You just need to listen.

Listening to your child has at least three advantages. First, you immediately come across as agreeable. This can disarm your child and make it easier for you to persuade him later on.

Second, you get to hear your child's actual feelings and doubts, which may be far different than what you guessed.

Third, you give your child a chance to vocalize and clarify the reasons why he has drifted away from the Church. It may be the first time he's given serious thought to these, and he might surprise himself by what he says.

Marcel LeJeune, founder of Catholic Missionary Disciples, offers a list of helpful questions to ask during this listening phase. Review them carefully and choose a few that you can ask your child. They are perfect questions to pull out your child's thoughts and will make listening much easier.

- Tell me about what kind of role faith played while growing up, if any?
- How would you describe your idea of Catholicism (or Christianity)?
- Who do you look up to? What personality traits are most attractive?
- How do you handle the rough parts of life?
- What are you passionate about?
- What brings meaning to your life?
- What makes you happy?

- Would you like to continue our conversation?
- Would you be interested in learning more about God, Jesus, the Bible, the Catholic Church, etc.?
- Do you pray? If so, would you mind describing it for me? If not, have you ever prayed in the past?
- Do you believe a relationship with God is possible?
- Can you describe what it means to be Catholic, in your experience?
- Do you have a personal prayer life? If so, how do you pray?
- Is God someone you would say you have a personal relationship with?
- Have you had any kind of moment when you felt particularly close to Jesus? If so, can you tell me about it? If not, have you ever wanted to?

As you listen carefully to your child's answers, try hard not to think about what *you're* going to say next. That's a mistake most of us make in most conversations. Instead, think about what *your child* is saying. Ponder each of his words, and read between the words to discern what he's *not* saying too.

Once he's completely finished, then it's time for an important task: repeat his thoughts back to him in your own words.

This is critical. Begin your reply with, "Very interesting. So, if I understand you correctly . . ." and then narrate back to him what he thinks. This is not a time for judgment or commentary. Your aim is simply to reflect back to him, fairly, what you believe his comments represent. Show him that you get it, that you listened, that you have a good grasp of his thoughts and beliefs.

That will set the stage for everything that follows. By this point, you will have opened up one or more conversations about faith, and begun to understand what your child thinks about the topic.

The Five Most Powerful Questions You Can Ask

Talking with your child about the faith doesn't always require having the right arguments or answers. Often, you just need the right questions.

Questions are largely neutral, or at least seem that way to most people, and they ensure you don't come across as preachy, rude, or pushy. When you ask a question, you aren't actually stating your own view. Many times, you're helping your child see that his beliefs are not as firmly supported as he might think, causing him to reassess why he's drifted away from the Church.

Evangelist Gregory Koukl calls this the "Columbo tactic" in which you "go on the offensive in an inoffensive way by using carefully selected questions to productively advance the conversation." Koukl recommends that you should "never make a statement, at least at first, when a question will do the job."

Questions are engaging and interactive. Most importantly, they keep you in the driver's seat of the conversation, while your child does all the work. (By the way, this "Columbo" tactic was one of Jesus' favorite methods. Notice how Jesus begins almost all of his conversations with a question, and whenever someone asks *him* a question, he typically answers with a question of his own. It's a powerful tactic.)

My friend Trent Horn, staff apologist for Catholic Answers, offers five specific questions to use in conversations:

1. "What do you believe about _____?"
It's easy to assume what your child believes about Jesus, God, the Church, morality, or faith. You might guess, for instance, that since your child has been to Mass many times over the years, he fully comprehends what Catholics believe about the Eucharist. But this is unlikely. If he's drifted away from Catholicism, his views probably don't align with the Church's teachings, so it's important to figure out what exactly he believes. This gets his cards on the table. It will also cause your child to reflect on this question personally. Maybe he's never asked himself what he believes, so hearing you pose the question will allow him to identify and refine what he holds to be true.

2. "Why do you think that's true?"
We all have unquestioned assumptions, things we believe that haven't really been challenged. But for a belief to be justified, we should have good reasons

or evidence to support it. Asking this particular question will gently challenge your child's belief and cause him to search for the real reasons he holds it. Sometimes when you ask, "Why do you think that's true?", your child will discover that he doesn't really have *any* reasons to support his view. He just picked up his views at school, or casually through his friends or the media, and he accepted them without serious consideration. That's a good thing for him to realize, because it makes it far easier for you to change his mind. If his beliefs about God or the Church are unsupported, and if you're able to help him see that, you're in a much better place to show him the truth.

3. "How did you come to believe that?"

One of the most common logical mistakes is something called the "genetic fallacy." This involves rejecting a particular belief someone has shared simply because of where they got that belief from. For example, my friend Matt Fradd was talking with his young son, and the boy said, "Did you know that you can fit a million earths inside the sun?" Matt was surprised. "That doesn't sound right," he said. "Where did you learn that?" His son answered, "From a cartoon." Matt was skeptical and was inclined to reject the claim, mainly because it came from a cartoon. But that would have been a textbook case of the genetic fallacy, rejecting a belief simply because of where it originated—in this case, a cartoon. (And in this case, as it turns out, the cartoon was correct, and the statistic was true.) So we shouldn't reject a belief *solely* because of where it came from.

That said, sometimes *where* your child got his beliefs from is important. For instance, suppose your child said, "When I found out that the Church persecuted scientists and killed Galileo for his discoveries, I knew I could believe in science or religion, and I chose science." You might ask, "Well, where did you hear that from?" And your son may answer, "From the internet. I read it in an atheist discussion forum." Now again, dismissing his belief simply because it stems from an atheist discussion forum would be inappropriate—that's the genetic fallacy. Perhaps the forum was correct. But in this case, alarm bells should be going off in your mind. Chances are, the atheist discussion forum is highly biased and probably offered a very distorted view of the complicated Galileo episode. That should make you reexamine your child's belief from a different perspective and invite him to do the same as well. For instance, you might instead point him to a good book on the topic from a Catholic or neutral perspective. (Later, you'll learn exactly how to respond to this Galileo objection.)

4. "What do you mean by _____?"

If I told you that "my wife is a Seminole," you may assume, especially if you're not a sports person, that she is a Native American, part of the Seminole tribe of Indians. But what I really mean by the term is that, like me, she graduated from Florida State University, whose mascot is the Seminole. If we're not clear on that meaning though, almost any conversation regarding my wife will be unproductive—we'll just be talking past each other.

Defining terms is a critical step in any serious discussion. One of the most commonly misunderstood terms is "God." If your child has trouble with God, or no longer believes in him, you first want to ask, "Well, when you say that you doubt God exists, what do you mean by 'God'? Can you describe the God you don't believe in?"

Odds are high that the God they find problematic is one you would too. That God is probably like the one behind "moralistic therapeutic deism," which we explored earlier. He's usually some sort of cosmic moral policeman who literally lives in the clouds, brooding over the world and suppressing all joy, freedom, and fulfillment. But that's not the Catholic view of God. Catholics see him revealed in the person of Jesus Christ as a sheer act of love who wants us to "have life and have it to the full" (John 10:10, NIV). He exists in heaven, but heaven isn't a physical place in our universe. Yet until you and your child are both clear on who God is, you can't proceed to discuss his existence or nature. The same holds for other terms such as faith, religion, church, goodness, and belief. Before discussing those topics with your child, you should ask how he understands each term.

5. "What would you say to someone who says _____?"

The more your conversation becomes a personal showdown—me versus

you—the less successful you'll be at changing your child's mind. It's important that he not feel like you're personally challenging or attacking him, so
don't try to "win" the conversation. One way to do this is by pulling yourself
out of the dialogue and making your points through a hypothetical third
person. You do this by prefacing your responses by asking, "What would
you say to someone who says . . ." This makes your child respond to the hypothetical third person instead of you, diffusing the chance that he'll see the
conversation as a two-way sparring match.

For example, if your child says, "I just don't think the Mass is relevant to
my life," you might respond, "What would you say to someone who goes to
Mass every day and is convinced the Mass is deeply relevant because it offers something you can't find anywhere else in the world: a direct encounter
with God?" By using a question from a hypothetical inquirer, instead of an
assertion directly from yourself, your child is less likely to become defensive
or take the challenge personally.

Gregory Koukl offers a similar approach. He recommends saying, "Let
me suggest an alternative, and tell me if you think it's an improvement. If
not, you can tell me why you think your option is better." If you want more
tips like these on how to master the art of difficult conversations, I highly
recommend Koukl's book *Tactics: A Game Plan for Discussing Your Christian
Convictions* (Zondervan, 2009).

Identify the Big Roadblocks

We could add many more questions to those above, but these will suffice to
open a dialogue and get it going. Once you've begun listening to your child's
responses, the next step is to diagnose what's holding him back from the
Church. One really effective way I've found is to just ask directly:

"What's the biggest thing keeping you away from the Church?"
It's important to phrase it this way instead of asking "What happened to your
Catholic faith?" or "Why aren't you Catholic anymore?" or "Why have you
stopped going to Mass?" because, as we learned earlier, your child may still

identify as "Catholic" even if he isn't attending Mass or doesn't hold to many Catholic beliefs. By phrasing it this way you invite your child to home in on his biggest, most troubling roadblock to returning.

Another way to ask the same question, or perhaps to follow the one above, is:

"What's the one thing that bugs you most about the Catholic Church?" This question is particularly helpful at drawing out major *emotional* roadblocks your child has in regard to the faith. Phrased this way, in terms of "bugging," it gets at the barrier that most boils his blood or triggers his disgust. It may not be an intellectual objection, but if it bugs him, it's significant and you must engage it.

Absorb the Criticisms

Finally, in this initial phase of listening, you should be ready to absorb any frustrations your child has with the Church. There's a good chance that once you give your child permission to speak honestly, he may respond with anger, sarcasm, or dismissiveness—all toward the faith that you hold dear. Assume that will happen.

But welcome his venting. Let him know that you won't be offended, and you won't interrupt, no matter his criticism. If he's been hurt in the past by the Church, give him time to describe his pain. If he doesn't think faith is relevant to his life, invite him to explain why. If he finds the Church's teachings morally repugnant, allow him to voice those concerns. Through both your words and your body language, make it clear that you just want to know what he thinks. Don't be defensive or threatened—just hear him out.

Absorbing his criticisms will accomplish a few things. First, it will give you clarity about his main points of resistance to the Church. Diagnosing this will allow you to focus your energies on those issues rather than on topics that aren't really a problem for him.

Second, the venting will force him to clarify his own criticisms. Often a critique can sound reasonable in our heads—until we get it out in the open.

Once your child verbalizes his critique, he may discover it wasn't quite as strong as he first thought. Therefore, inviting his criticisms can itself be a subtle way of defusing their strength.

Finally, by listening you'll convey that you genuinely care for him and his concerns. This will help your child see that instead of adversaries on either side of a religious debate, you're really standing together on a shared search for truth.

Especially in this phase, patience is the name of the game. You need to patiently listen to your child's thoughts, and patiently absorb his pain and criticism. It's no accident that St. Paul began his famous catalogue of love in 1 Corinthians 13 with "patient" at the head of the list (1 Cor. 13:4–8)—love is patient.

* * *

After getting the conversation off the ground, and hearing your child's concerns, you're then ready to start actively moving the dialogue forward. That's what we'll learn in the next chapter.

CHAPTER 9
Move the Dialogue Forward

Gregory Koukl has a good rule: "If anyone in the discussion gets angry, you lose." When you get angry, you come across as a bully whose ideas are not as good as you thought they were. You'll seem belligerent and unpersuasive. If your child gets angry, he'll get defensive, and defensive people are not in a position to rationally consider ideas that contradict their own.

Few discussions between a parent and child are more prone to angry words than those about religion. If you've tried to bring up God or faith with your child, you've probably experienced this. The volume escalates. Sentences are interrupted and smashed. You and your child both know which buttons to push and what to say to elicit a heated reaction. Eventually, no one is speaking *with* each other, but only *at* each other, and often loudly.

Thankfully, after you've opened up a discussion about faith, there are several ways to keep it moving in a positive direction, producing more light than heat. Here are a handful of practical tips:

Stay humble: The sixteenth-century preacher John Bradford watched as criminals were led to their execution, saying, "There but for the grace of God, goes John Bradford." His point was that were it not for God's providential care, he could have easily been in their position. Try to have a similar attitude when talking with your child. Consider that you too have made bad moral decisions in your life, and you too have turned your back on God, whether in small or large ways. Don't talk down to your child or insult him. Don't speak from a privileged position. As the evangelist D.T. Niles said, "Christianity is one beggar telling another beggar where he found bread." Remember that were it not for the sheer grace of God, you could have easily drifted away from the Church too.

Use open body language: The psychologist Albert Mehrabian found that in common conversations, 55% of communication is body language, 38%

depends on the tone of voice, and 7% concerns the actual words spoken. When you talk with your child, be conscious of your facial expressions. Make sure you're not furrowing your eyebrows or pursing your lips. Be aware of your hands and body—lean forward to express interest and use open-hand gestures to communicate warmth and openness. And use calm, slow tones—don't be stern, rash, or aggressive.

Express empathy: As your child shares his thoughts, respond in ways that show you're not only listening, but that you also *feel* some of what he is feeling. You might offer replies such as "That make a lot of sense" or "That must be confusing" or "I can imagine how frustrated that must have made you." This is not just a restatement of his words but goes a step further and shows that you grasp the impact his thoughts and feelings have on him.

Restate your child's thoughts: One of the biggest frustrations in any conversation is when someone misinterprets your view. For instance, if your child says, "Mass is just so boring and I don't get anything out of it," it would be unhelpful to reply, "So you basically just want to be entertained at church? Is that it? You want lights and guitars and loud music?" Of course, that's not what your child said, and responding that way will only upset him. Before responding to anything your child says you should first make sure you fully understand his thoughts. Restating them, perhaps in your own words, is helpful. (A suggestion you may recall from the previous chapter but one that bears restating here.) For example, a better response in the above scenario would be, "Okay, I want to make sure I understand you because sometimes I hear what I want to hear instead of what you actually say. Tell me if I'm getting this right: you don't see any reason to go to Mass because it's boring, you're not learning anything, and it's not having any noticeable, positive effect on your life. Did I get that right, or did I misunderstand?" Notice how we phrased that last question, which puts the burden on *you*, not your child. You accept the blame for any misunderstanding, even if it wasn't really your fault. This simple but strategic language puts your child in a no-lose position and makes it more likely the dialogue will move forward.

Share your feelings: After listening to your child, try prefacing your thoughts with "I feel. . ." Doing so makes it impossible for you to come across as preaching or moralizing. A feeling is not a command, just an observation. Your child will be less likely to see it as an attack. You might say, "You know, if I'm being completely honest, I feel so devastated that you've stopped going to church. It hurts me not seeing you at Mass, knowing that you're missing out on many of the gifts God wants to give you. I'm sure you probably have reasons for drifting away, but it still pains me to see it." This will diffuse the tension far more than a demanding, "Get back to Mass!" This isn't about guilt-tripping them back to Mass, but it will help your child to process how devastating their decisions have been for you.

Don't be afraid to press pause: If you find the dialogue is grinding to a halt, don't be afraid to say, "Well, I'm not sure we're really getting anywhere, but I do really enjoy discussing these things with you. How about we take a break and pick it back up another time?" Remember, this is a long process. It usually takes many discussions before you'll notice any fruit. So don't be afraid to cut a discussion short. In fact, doing so may help your child feel less pressured and thus more likely, in the long run, to change his mind about Catholicism.

Clear Up Misconceptions

While writing this book, I emailed thousands of my online followers to ask whether they had children who left the Church, and if they did, why their children left.

One poor father wrote to me saying, "One of my daughters went off to college and was given a pamphlet explaining '10 Reasons the Catholic Church is Wrong.' She read it and left the Church forever. That was it."

Another woman, Kathy, had left the Church as a teenager but later returned. Now in her twenties, she said, "It was actually me who drifted away. My falling away from the Church was due to not really understanding what it was that I was falling away from. I never really understood the Real Presence in the Eucharist. I never understood why the Church taught certain things. I accepted what others had to say about the Church, but never let her speak for herself. Once I allowed her to speak, I was so captivated and could never imagine being anything but Catholic."

The biggest problem for many young people who drift away is misunderstanding the faith. Anglican theologian N.T. Wright offers a telling anecdote. Wright served for many years as a chaplain at Oxford University. Part of his role involved reaching out to first-year undergraduates to welcome them individually to the college and establish a connection. He would go from dorm room to dorm room, and most were happy to meet him. But many commented, often with slight embarrassment, "You won't be seeing much of me; you see, I don't believe in god."

After hearing this comment several times, Wright developed his own response: "Oh, that's interesting; which god is it that you don't believe in?" This usually surprised the students. Most of them would mumble a few phrases about the god they said they did not believe in, usually a being who lives up in the sky, brooding over the world, who occasionally dips in to perform a miracle or send bad people to hell. Again, Wright developed a stock response to what he calls this "spy-in-the-sky" theology: "Well, I'm not surprised you don't believe in that god. I don't believe in that god either."

At this point the undergraduates would look startled. They might wonder, "Am I really talking with a chaplain who doesn't believe in god?" Then, some might display a faint look of recognition: after all, it was sometimes rumored that half the chaplains at Oxford were atheists! But Wright would clear up the confusion: "No, I don't believe in that god. I believe in the God I see revealed in Jesus of Nazareth."

In today's world, it's not uncommon to find significant misunderstandings about God, faith, Jesus, and the Catholic Church. Archbishop Fulton J. Sheen famously observed, "There are not over a hundred people in the United States who hate the Catholic Church. There are millions, however, who hate what they wrongly believe to be the Catholic Church—which is, of course, quite a different thing."

Whenever I talk with people who have left the Church, and ask about why they left, it quickly becomes evident that they rejected not the Catholic Church but some strange, distorted vision of the Church. For example, here are the some of the most commons objections you'll encounter, and I've personally heard all of these before. We'll answer many of them in the final part of this book. Chances are, your child holds at least one:

- "Being Christian is just about being a good person. I don't need to go to Mass for that."
- "Catholics are responsible for so much violence and hate!"
- "The Catholic Church is so anti-science."
- "Catholics hate gay people and deny their humanity."
- "The Church thinks everyone who isn't Catholic is going to hell."
- "The Church condemns anyone who gets divorced."
- "Catholics worship Mary and the saints."
- "Catholicism is all about guilt and man-made rules. Catholics don't focus enough on Jesus or the Bible."

Now, of course, each of these stumbling blocks is a warped depiction of what the Catholic Church *actually* teaches. But as long as you've equipped yourself, as we learned how to do in the last chapter, it's not too hard to set the record straight, turning stumbling blocks into stepping-stones.

However, suppose your child shares an objection that stumps you. You're pretty sure it's based on a misunderstanding, but you're unsure how to articulate why. In that case, don't hesitate to say, "Hmm. That's interesting. I hadn't heard that before. Let me do some research on that, and I'll get back to you." Don't just try to wing it. Do your homework by researching the objection—remember the helpful Catholic.com search box we covered earlier—and then once you have the facts, gently share them with your child.

Be confident that the answers to *every* criticism and misperception are available *somewhere*. The Catholic Church has the fullness of truth and has weathered every challenge over the last two thousand years. So even if you don't know how to correct a misunderstanding in the moment, you can easily find out.

Stay Calm and Find the Positive Intention

When Pope Benedict XVI planned a visit to the United Kingdom in 2010, protests began months in advance. Critics condemned the pope for the sexual abuse crisis and the Church's positions on birth control and same-sex marriage. Leading atheists, such as Richard Dawkins, even called for British police to arrest the pope for crimes against humanity.

With the papal visit approaching, a small handful of local, ordinary Catholics decided to act. They wanted to change the narrative about the Catholic Church *before* the pope arrived, so that when he did, people would be far more receptive to his message. The group began meeting with communication experts, theologians, and media leaders, and eventually launched a ministry called Catholic Voices. Their mission? To understand criticisms against the Church and then to calmly reframe each issue by posing the Church's teaching in a positive, winsome way.

Their efforts proved tremendously successful. Catholic Voices team members participated in dozens of debates and news programs on radio and TV, appearing on all the major British channels. They helped to change both the coverage of the papal trip as well as the perception of the Church in the media.

One key to their success was their commitment to remaining calm. Most of us, when explaining or defending our deeply held beliefs, tend to blow up or raise our voice. That's the normal human response when we feel threatened. But of course, this doesn't make our beliefs any more persuasive—usually the opposite happens.

Remaining calm while discussing faith with your child is key to moving the conversation forward. But how do we do it? One strategy used by Catholic Voices is to always look for the "positive intention" behind any criticism your child levels against God or the Church. "Rather than be put on the defensive by the charge, we look for the positive moral value behind it," explain two leaders of Catholic Voices. "We try to begin our response by *agreeing with that value*, rather than seeking to defend ourselves from the unjust attack. . . . This makes it possible to communicate, to be heard, and to have a proper dialogue."

So, if your child is critical of the Church, don't immediately jump to the defensive. Focus instead on the value to which the criticism appeals. For example, if your child angrily references the sexual abuse crisis, you can acknowledge to them that as a parent, you, too, are outraged and disheartened by abuse. You can affirm that abuse is always and everywhere evil because it's an assault on human dignity, which your child should agree with.

When you identify this shared value—in this example, the inviolable dignity of every human person—you can diffuse the tension of the conversation and begin to make real headway. You and your child can then begin from a shared foundation, your mutual support of human dignity.

Here are some other "positive intentions" we can affirm:

- When someone disagrees with the Church's position on contraception or abortion, they often appeal to freedom or autonomy. These are good things, properly understood.
- Proponents of same-sex marriage typically appeal to love and equality.
- If your child insinuates that he prefers science to faith, he's appealing to the value of open and honest truth-seeking, and the objective, rational exploration of facts. Catholics agree with that completely.

All of these values are deeply rooted in Christianity. In fact, throughout Western history, the Catholic Church has been the strongest proponent of freedom, equality, love, and the open pursuit of truth. By identifying these values you share with your child, you can find common ground to move the discussion forward instead of getting stuck in conflict.

Look for the Seeds of the Word

Another strategy for moving the dialogue forward is to identify "seeds of the Word." We see this modeled in the seventeenth chapter of Acts, where St. Paul visits the Areopagus. It was a large hill in ancient Greece where the greatest thinkers of the day sat around and "used their time for nothing else but telling or hearing something new" (Acts 17:21).

The philosophers invited Paul to share his strange new message about this man named Jesus of Nazareth, whom Paul claimed had risen from the dead. With great excitement, Paul accepted their invitation. But he also knew that to convince these intelligent skeptics, he would have to speak in a way they would understand. He had to convey his message using references, symbols, and allusions from their own culture.

So while laying out his case for Jesus, he quoted Aratus of Soli, a famous Greek poet. He referenced a saying from Epimenides of Knossos, another Greek thinker. He even used Greek piety as a bridge to the true God, saying, "You Athenians, I see that in every respect you are very religious. For as I walked around looking carefully at your shrines, I even discovered an altar inscribed, 'To an Unknown God.' What therefore you unknowingly worship, I proclaim to you" (Acts 17:22–23). Once his listeners connected their own Greek poetry, ideas, and piety to Paul's message, they were much more receptive to his claims. They made sense of what he was explaining.

The early Church Fathers described this approach as identifying *semina verbi*—"seeds of the Word." The Fathers advised that before sowing the Word of God, we should always look for seeds of that Word already present among the people we hope to evangelize. The hope is that, once these seeds are uncovered, the Word of God will not seem so strange or alien.

What does this look like today? And how can you use this as a parent? Well, ask yourself: What kind of music does my child listen to? What shows does he watch? What hobbies or passions interest him? Consider ways that you can mimic Paul in using these things as bridges to the true God.

For example, the Irish rock group U2 is one of the most popular bands of all time, and one of their hit songs, "I Still Haven't Found What I'm Looking For," exhibits the same longing and dissatisfaction we find in the Psalms or the writings of St. Augustine. U2 sings, "I have run, I have crawled, I have scaled these city walls. . . . But I still haven't found what I'm looking for." Similarly, the Psalmist pants, "As the deer longs for streams of water, so my soul longs for you, O God" (Ps. 42:2), and St. Augustine writes, "You have made us for yourself, O Lord, and our hearts are restless until they rest in you." In each case, we see a similar longing for something that seems just out of reach—something that we crave *even after* attaining all that the world offers—all the money, power, pleasure, or honor we can grasp. Yet we still want more.

Bishop Barron is a master at this strategy and has written a whole book titled *Seeds of the Word: Finding God in the Culture* (Word on Fire, 2015), which is filled with essays identifying the *semina verbi* in popular movies, books, TV shows, and current events. You might consider using one of those essays as a launching pad with your child.

Introduce "Shoe Pebble" Questions

Have you ever found yourself walking, and then noticed somehow a small pebble has worked its way into your shoe? At first you just might be aware of its presence. It might not hurt. It might be more uncomfortable than painful. But the longer it stays in your shoe, the more the pebble rubs and works against your foot. Leave it there long enough and pretty soon you'll have a nice-sized blister or cut.

"Shoe pebble" questions work in a similar way. What pebbles do to shoes, these questions do to your child's mind. They won't hurt your child, of course, but they'll stick in your child's head. They will rub, poke, and work on his mind, bugging him until he resolves the question. Each "shoe pebble" question is meant to provoke your child to reexamine an assumption he has about God or the Church and perhaps see it from a different angle.

For example, if your child has left the Church and has become an atheist, he might boldly proclaim, "There is simply no evidence for God." A good "shoe pebble" question for him would be, "What do you think the strongest argument for God is, and what's wrong with it?" That may give your child pause because it puts him in a tough place: if he gives a poor argument in response, one that can easily be dismissed, then he'll come across as not being familiar with the *best* arguments for God. But if he gives a really *good* argument, one he might not know how to answer, he's in an equally uncomfortable position. Again, I want to emphasize that you shouldn't aim to "trap" your child with a "shoe pebble" question—your goal isn't to manipulate him or make him look foolish. The question is simply designed to bother him and cause him to reconsider whether he really does have a good grasp on the issue.

What about some other good "shoe pebble" questions? Another favorite is this: "What do you think is the best reason to be Catholic and why don't you agree with it?"

Or if your child has drifted into an Evangelical or nondenominational church, he likely places high value on the Bible, probably more so than he did as a Catholic. In that case, a good "shoe pebble" question would be, "How do we know which books belong in the Bible, and which don't? How can we be sure?" In my experience, few Protestant Christians have ever considered this question. They know the Bible is the Word of God, but they never really wonder how it came to be. They're not aware that the biblical canon, or the list of books that make up the Bible, wasn't finally approved until the late fourth century at a gathering of Catholic bishops, and only then because it was ratified by the pope. They're also typically unaware that Protestant leaders, such as Martin Luther, wanted to re-move several books from the Bible. (Luther wanted to discard Hebrews, James, Jude, and Revelation, among others.) On what basis can we say Luther was wrong? In reality, the only way Christians can be sure of what books make up the Bible is by trusting the authority of the Catholic Church to decide on the canon. So ironically, even a Protestant, such as an Evangelical or nondenominational Christian, must trust the Catholic Church. Of course, you don't have to lay out this whole argument to your child. Simply asking the "shoe pebble" question above will start turning the gears in his head and have him rethink positions that he may not have thought all the way through.

Speak with Positivity and Joy

To paraphrase St. Teresa of Avila, "A sad saint is a bad saint." It's also been held that "joy is the infallible presence of God." When we talk with our child about God, faith, or the Church, sometimes our attitude says more than our words. You may have incredibly strong arguments or the most astounding conversion story, but if you come across as melancholy or stern, your child will want nothing to do with what you're offering.

You need to speak with joy! As Pope Francis says, "The Christian message is called the 'Gospel'; i.e. 'good news,' an announcement of joy for all people; the Church is not a haven for sad people, the Church is a joyful home!"

Joy is especially compelling since there is so little of it today. Look around at the symptoms of our joyless culture: worry, anger, rage, sarcasm, cynicism, mockery, being offended. So when people encounter real joy—not superficial happiness, but true joy, deep in the bones—it is very attractive. People naturally want to know where that joy comes from and how they can get it.

Mike, a college friend of mine, exemplified this. He's still the most joyous person I've ever met. He always smiled, no matter whether he received a horrible grade on a test or a good one; no matter if the weather was terrible or an anticipated event was canceled. And it wasn't a fake, goofy smile. It was a natural extension of a deep, inner peace. I remember several times, when we were hanging around with non-Christians friends, they would ask, unprovoked, "Mike, why are you always so ridiculously happy? What makes you like that?" And without missing a beat, Mike always replied, "It's because I know Jesus Christ, and he fills me with joy." Again, it wasn't corny—he really meant that. And Mike led more than one person in our circle to faith.

We evangelize best by attracting others to Jesus, and we do that by radiating his joy in our lives. Here are a few practical ways to do that with your child:

Smile often: Mother Teresa liked to say that "peace begins with a smile," and so does joyful communication. Next time you talk with your child, try intentionally smiling. It doesn't need to be exaggerated or fake—smile too big, or too often, and you'll just come across as creepy. But maintain a subtle smile, especially while talking about your faith, and you'll lift the tenor of your conversation.

Emphasize the Church's "Yes!": Bishop Barron once taught me a helpful principle: "Anytime the Church says 'No' to something, she's really saying 'Yes!' to something else." In other words, when the Church says "No" to premarital sex, she's really saying "Yes!" to the proper home of sex within marriage. When the Church says "No" to abortion, she's really saying "Yes!" to the dignity of unborn children. Your child probably sees the Church as an endless stream of "Nos," but next time your child brings up such a prohibition, ask yourself quietly, "What is the Church saying 'Yes!' to in this case? And how can I communicate that 'Yes!' joyfully?" Then reframe the prohibition and share the affirmation with your child.

Share joyful stories: Reveal to your child the joy and peace that your faith brings you. Share an experience when you felt lost or depressed, or hurt or ashamed, until Christ liberated you through his mercy and love. The best part about stories like these is that, unlike arguments, they are unassailable. Nobody can contend that your faith didn't bring you joy—the evidence is personal and irrefutable.

Let your passion shine: The Scottish philosopher and atheist David Hume was once in a crowd, listening to the famous preacher George Whitefield. Someone recognized Hume and said, "I thought you didn't believe in the Gospel." Hume responded, "I do not." Then, with a nod toward Whitefield, Hume added, "But he does." Just as flies are attracted to a glowing light, your child will be attracted to your message if it burns with conviction and passion. If you're passionate about your faith, let it out! It will be attractive to others. (Just be careful that your passion doesn't become too aggressive or overbearing. There is such a thing as being *too* zealous about your faith.)

"The glory of God is man fully alive," wrote St. Irenaeus, and he got that idea from Christ himself: "I have come that you might have life and have it to the full" (John 10:10, NIV). When you dialogue with your child, keep reminding yourself that Catholicism is a joyful faith and that you're inviting your child to return not to a religious prison but to a path of human flourishing.

* * *

At this point in the game plan, you've prayed and fasted for your child. You've equipped yourself, planted seeds, and opened good conversations. Now it's time to lead your child from curiosity and openness to a more intentional phase of exploration. That happens when we reconnect him with a local parish and others who can help.

CHAPTER 10
Invite and Connect

Like many young people, I set off for college unsure about whether I would keep going to church. I grew up attending each Sunday and being involved in the youth group, but it never really took hold. I looked forward to college and the freedom it offered. Away from home, nobody would pressure me to wake up early on Sunday mornings. I could sleep in, do my own thing, and have more free time during the week.

However, I knew my family wouldn't be too happy—especially my mom. I dreaded telling her that I had quit going to church. So if for only that reason, I decided that I would at least attend church once a week. That's it. I wouldn't get involved; I wouldn't join activities; I wouldn't show interest. But I would at least show up on Sunday mornings and put in my time.

That first Sunday, I rolled out of bed and—here's how lazy I was—I decided I would attend the nearest church to my dorm. It ended up being a Methodist church. At the time, I didn't know any of the differences between Christian denominations. I just knew it had a cross in front, which meant they were Christian, so I went in. Over the next several weeks, I repeated the pattern—wake up on Sunday, put in my hour, and then go back to my dorm. A few different times, people at the church would try to engage me after the service, asking my name and what I was majoring in, or inviting me to come to a Bible study. But I used every excuse I could muster to escape.

Eventually, though, I ran out of excuses. One day, a young man asked if I wanted to join him and a few other guys for lunch after the service. I figured that was pretty nonthreatening, and I couldn't come up with any good excuses, so I bumbled, "Uh, yeah, I guess. Sure." I joined them, and I had a surprisingly good time. I remember thinking, "These guys aren't too bad. They're not weird or overly zealous. They're actually pretty cool. I don't mind hanging out with them." The following week, they invited me again and I joined them. Pretty soon, I was joining them every week for lunch, and then for basketball and football, and then we started sharing meals in between classes. It wasn't long before they invited me to their small-group Bible study. The same guys I had already been hanging out with showed up for that, so I figured it wouldn't be too off-putting.

That small group changed my life. Over the following weeks, my friends taught me how to read and study the Bible—not just as a literary text but as the living Word of God. They showed me how to pray, how to move beyond just asking God for things and to begin cultivating a true relationship with him. They taught me how to worship, how to praise the Lord and thank him for all his good gifts. By the year's end, I had not only committed to following Jesus with my whole life, but I had even volunteered to lead new small groups the next year!

I did end up becoming Catholic during my senior year, after three wonderful years in that Methodist ministry, but those experiences were a vital stepping-stone in my journey with God. They moved me down the thresholds of conversion from "initial trust" all the way to "intentional discipleship."

However, that entire transition hinged on one experience: an invitation to community.

Invite

Multiple studies have affirmed that one of the strongest ways to ensure someone becomes an intentional Christian disciple is to draw him into a community of other disciples. Once your child has expressed openness and curiosity toward returning to the Church, and after you've had some productive dialogue about his hang-ups or points of resistance, you next want to invite him to communal events that will satisfy his new yearnings. Here are some popular examples.

Weekend Retreats

Craig remembers the weekend well. "It was in May 2012, and the priest announced after Mass that all men in the parish are invited to sign up for a weekend retreat called 'Christ Renews His Parish.' One of the leaders went up to the microphone and talked about how attending the retreat changed his life, and I was pretty intrigued. But I never thought I would actually attend. I had been going to Mass sporadically, basically only whenever I was home from college. But as I walked out of Mass, they had a table set up, promoting the retreat, and a couple guys stopped me. They asked my name and shook my hand. Before I knew it, they had convinced me to sign up! My only excuse was that I would be away at college, but when they explained the weekend would be held later that summer, I had no other excuse. So I put my name down, and that was that.

"When the weekend finally rolled around, I told myself I would just sit in the back and listen but not really participate. It's obvious they planned against that. When I walked in, the tables were all arranged in circles with four or five chairs at each table. We were clearly being arranged in small circles to talk. I picked a table and sat down, and within a few minutes a handful of other men joined, introducing themselves. The weekend kicked off with some passionate talks by men who discussed things like the Bible, the Holy Spirit, and personal transformation. You could tell these men were on fire for their faith. I had never seen anything like it. Most of the people I saw in the pews at Mass seemed despondent, like they were just going through the motions. But these men seemed alive and passionate.

"Some of the men shared incredible stories of being saved from addictions to drugs or pornography. One man had visited a prostitute several times but then felt so empty and lost that he knelt in an empty church to pray. He heard God tell him that his life was full of darkness; he needed to turn to the light. He sensed God speak his name and offer to heal him. The man completely turned his life around. He never visited a prostitute again and cleaned up his life.

"The best part of the weekend, though, was the relationships I made with the men in my small circle. For the first time in my life, I encountered men who had truly been transformed by the power of Christ and were living noble, holy lives. I wanted that. The more I talked with them, the more I wanted what they had. By the end of the retreat, I was sure I wanted to change, to start a new path and start living for Jesus. A handful of the men prayed over me and while nothing physical happened, I sensed a deep change within me. Afterward, it was like my whole being shifted. I wanted to be holy; I wanted to live for God. From that point forward I was no longer my own person—I was completely his."

Millions of other people have experienced what Craig did, a dramatic conversion experience at a parish retreat. These renewal events, such as Cursillo, Christ Renews His Parish, and Christ Renews Our Community, are typically held once or twice per year, and are typically gender-specific—one weekend for men, and one weekend for women. Splitting up the genders allows the conversation to be much more open.

Each retreat typically begins with people separating into small groups, either chosen beforehand or based on where people choose to sit. The participants then listen to a handful of witness talks. Some speakers share stories of conversion or struggle. Others reflect on the sacraments or the power of community. Each highlights how their lives have been changed by an encounter with Jesus Christ. After each talk, the small groups discuss what they just heard and, to the extent each person is willing, open up and share their own spiritual journey. Finally, after a weekend of testimonies, sharing, bonding, and prayer, the retreat usually closes with an opportunity for confession. Priests who have helped with these retreats tell me that huge numbers of people show up after not having been to confession in decades. Returning to the sacrament is a life-changing moment, one that liberates them and sets them on a new path.

It can be a powerful experience if you're able to get your child to attend a retreat like this. Why? First, your child will encounter people who have been changed by Jesus Christ. They don't just teach about the Catholic faith; they demonstrate its effects. Pope Paul VI wrote, "Modern man listens more willingly to witnesses than to teachers, and if he does listen to teachers, it is because they are witnesses." Second, as Craig did, your child will meet other people in the parish who will not only usher them into a deeper relationship with God but will sustain and grow that relationship after the retreat. This will help develop the seeds you've planted into a long and lasting faith.

This week, check to see if your parish offers a renewal retreat, like the ones described above, and do what you can to encourage your child to sign up.

Parish Study Programs

Many parishes offer ongoing small groups to learn and grow in faith. Among the best are Alpha for Catholics and Discovering Christ. Alpha originated in England as a program designed to appeal to secular men and women who were seeking answers to life's biggest questions. It took off, and soon after launching, millions of non-Christians found their way to Jesus through the program. Sometime later, Alpha created a specifically Catholic version of their program called Alpha for Catholics.

Discovering Christ is a similar evangelistic program developed by ChristLife, a ministry based in the Archdiocese of Baltimore.

Many parishes use Alpha for Catholics or Discovering Christ as a sort of "pre-evangelization" entry point, a way for seekers on the earliest thresholds of conversion to begin their search and get connected to the parish, even before they're ready to seek initiation into the Church.

Some parishes also host weekly or monthly programs to learn more about the Catholic faith. Some use study programs such as Bishop Barron's *CATHOLICISM* series. Others choose a spiritual book and read through it together. Some groups commit to studying a particular book of the Bible, the liturgical readings for the upcoming Sunday, or a certain theological topic.

Now, as a fair warning, your child might be leery of joining a study group like this until he's already crossed a few of the thresholds of conversion we covered earlier. He'll typically have to move into the phase of active spiritual seeking before he's willing to join such a group. But it's worth extending the offer. Joining a community of other serious-minded disciples will work on him and help him along the journey better than almost any other experience.

Parish Events

Many parishes host larges events that are open to the whole community and are fairly benign when it comes to religious pressure. For example, each fall, the country is lined with parish festivals that typically host rides, games, food booths, and attractions. Inviting your child to one of these events can be an easy way to rebuild his trust and familiarity with the parish. After all, you're not pulling him to Mass or inviting him to a prayer service. You're simply asking if he'd like to join you for some fun at the fall festival. For some young people who have nostalgic memories of attending the festival during childhood, visiting an event like this can become the first step back to the Church. Remember, your goal is just to help move them a little further down the path of discipleship, and maybe the next step is just developing positive feelings and trust toward religious people.

Parish Community

We saw in the first chapter how "lack of community" plays a role in many people drifting from the Church. In fact, CARA, the leading Catholic research group, found that "if there is anything that studies of Mass-attending Catholics can teach the Church, it is that parish community is the most important element of parish life. If parishioners do not feel welcome, you can expect to have fewer parishioners soon. Anything that is unwelcoming or judgmental is likely to turn people away from your parish and the Faith." Look for opportunities in your parish to invite your child into your parish community, even beyond retreats and study groups. Maybe your child has computer skills and the church office needs to update their website. Or perhaps you can invite him to the annual parish picnic on the Fourth of July to help cook food. Whatever the case, allow him to experience the community that your parish offers.

Connect

There are lots of opportunities to invite your child to an event at your parish—whether a retreat, study program, or parish celebration. But sometimes connecting them to the right *people* can be just as helpful. Here are some ideas to consider.

Campus Ministry

I wouldn't be Catholic if it wasn't for the Catholic campus ministry at Florida State University (FSU). The ministry at FSU was run by a religious community, the Brotherhood of Hope, which specializes in campus ministry. The brothers serve on college campuses up and down the East Coast, where they help hundreds of young people discover the beauty and brilliance of Catholicism. As a young senior struggling to learn more, I was connected to one of the FSU brothers who took me under his wing and met with me one-on-one to answer questions and relieve my concerns. His personal, patient guidance eventually led me into the Church.

If your child is in college or preparing for college, do a quick Google search to find out whether the school has a Catholic campus ministry. Almost every large university does, but they're even popping up at smaller schools. Such ministries often identify as CCM (Catholic Campus Ministry) or the Newman Center (named after St. John Henry Newman.)

In addition, you should determine whether the college has any student missionaries. FOCUS, which as we noted earlier stands for Fellowship of Catholic University Students, is one such group. They send teams of young, trained missionaries to college campuses in order to reach students with the Gospel. In partnership with the local parish or Newman Center, FOCUS missionaries host large-group outreach events, weekly Bible studies, and offer one-on-one mentoring with student leaders. St. Paul's Outreach (SPO) is another great apostolate that ministers to college students and is present on many campuses. The best part about FOCUS and SPO is that the missionaries are young and dynamic. They're typically only a year or two out of college themselves, which makes it likely your child will relate to them if he's in college.

There are several ways to connect your college-aged child with groups like this. You can reach out to the campus minister, or the student missionary, and ask if *they* could make first contact with your child. Or perhaps you move the other way around and propose that your child check out a specific event hosted by the campus ministry or connect with a specific person who can answer his religious questions. Using the "seed gift" approach, you might slip a flyer for the campus ministry in his room or in the mail, and hope he gets the hint. Some of these strategies will work better than others, depending on your child, but just persevere. If he doesn't respond to one overture, don't give up. That doesn't mean he's completely closed off to the idea. Just regroup, re-strategize, and find another way to connect him to faith-filled people.

Spiritual Director

As the "spiritual but not religious" label becomes more popular, many young people are attracted to the idea of studying under a religious guru. Books such as Elizabeth Gilbert's *Eat, Pray, Love* trace a religious search across the world, through several spiritual masters, in the pursuit of inner harmony. Few young people are programmed to see priests as religious gurus, but most priests have undergone years of training in the art of spiritual mentoring. They're soul doctors with lots of experience.

If your child is open to the idea, you might ask if he would like to be connected with a wise and insightful priest who could help him process his life and guide him in the way of the spirit. A good spiritual director will be able to answer his questions, address his doubts, and help him discern how God is moving and speaking in his life. This can be a fairly significant step for a young person, especially if he's been away from the Church for a while. He'll usually only accept if he already has a very positive view of priests. But if your child fits that description, it's worth extending the offer. It may make him feel better if the spiritual director is *not* a priest he's already familiar with. Just as with confession, young people often prize their anonymity and may be more comfortable opening up to a priest they don't see every Sunday.

Former Catholics Group

Many parishes have responded to the surge of people leaving the Church by creating new groups to welcome those same people back. Some of the most popular groups include Catholics Come Home, Catholics Returning Home, and Landings.

"It would have been hard to stick with the Mass without Landings," Laura Bendini explains. Laura had been baptized Catholic and received her First Communion but hadn't gone to church much since then. In her thirties, she felt called back to the Church. "I was barely there and barely going to come back if it weren't for people constantly reaching out to me in a nonjudgmental way." Landings offered her a community of support, a place where she could express her concerns, ask questions, and learn about the faith. After going through Landings in the fall, she enrolled in RCIA and eventually became a team leader for the next Landings session.

Most programs aimed at former Catholics are designed to repair emotional difficulties suffered over the years, answer simple doubts and questions, and provide a space for people to work through the various issues they may have with the Church.

Don't Move Too Fast

We've now discovered lots of ways to invite and connect your child with other disciples, but one word of caution: don't rush your child. Let him journey down the path of conversion at his own pace. Carol Barnier knows this from her experience as a young adult revert. "When I was again ready to believe in God," she writes, "I needed to proceed very, very slowly. Yes, I had come to a place where I now believed in God, but that didn't mean I was ready to take back the prepackaged God of my parents and put him in my own basket. In essence, I was back where I had been in high school, kicking the tires of faith, ready to test the premises and claims, and finding out what stood up to scrutiny, what had to be dismissed, and what had to be reshaped to line up with God as I was learning him to be."

Some parents are so overjoyed when their child expresses even the smallest inkling of returning that they spring into action and offer too much too fast. But your child needs to progress at his own pace. Pushing him too fast can have bad consequences and undo all of the progress you've made up to this point. Instead, continue serving your child with grace, patience, and encouragement. "Think of your own journey to Christ," writes Gregory

Koukl. "Chances are you didn't go from a standstill to total commitment. Instead, God dealt with you over a period of time. There was a period of reflection as you sorted out the details." The same will likely be true for your child.

* * *

At this point in the game plan, your child has worked through many of his most difficult issues, and perhaps connected with some helpful, faith-filled people. But as wonderful as that is, you can't stop there. There remains one big step: you have to close the loop.

CHAPTER 11
Close the Loop

It had been several months since Susan began to evangelize her daughter, Teresa. She had prayed for Teresa every day, including several novenas. She had made small sacrifices. She had studied and prepared for their conversations, listening as Teresa explained why she was no longer Catholic. Slowly, over the course of several dialogues, Teresa let her guard down. The old barriers fell, and Susan felt like she was making real progress. In fact, it seemed like Teresa was on the verge of coming back to the Church.

But then, for some reason, the momentum stopped. For a few weeks, it seemed like nothing was changing, either for better or worse. Teresa just sat on the proverbial fence. She no longer resisted Jesus and the Church, but she wasn't pursuing them either.

What happened? Susan never closed the loop.

Gently Pursue a Commitment

Like a good car salesman who knows he must get the buyer to sign a contract, or a good math teacher who knows her instruction isn't over until the student can go all the way from problem to solution, you can't stop helping your child before he's made it *all the way* back. Even if he comes 95% of the way, there's a chance he might slide back and reverse all of the progress you've made. You need to lead him *all the way* to a relationship with Christ in the Church.

Prominent evangelist Marcel LeJeune notes that in his experience, "Catholics stop too soon when they evangelize. In fact, I might call it the fatal flaw." LeJeune suggests that after having several preliminary conversations with your child about God, you need to close the loop by asking a straightforward question, such as, "Would you like to make the choice to turn your heart over to God today?" or "Would you be willing to invite Jesus into your life right now?"

Shaun McAfee, a recent convert to Catholicism, recommends closing the loop by saying, "You might not be ready, but if you think you are up to it, why not turn your life over to God right now? Say a prayer with me that asks Jesus to guide your life and be your Lord. What do you have to lose?" Saying "you might not be ready" issues a sort of challenge, and it can motivate your child to make a positive decision, if only to prove he isn't afraid of the challenge! You don't have to be forceful, and you don't want to manipulate or coerce him. But subtly hinting that this is a difficult and weighty decision (which it is) can raise the stakes and lift your child out of apathy.

After asking a question like these, pause and wait for your child to respond—even if the question elicits awkward silence. Don't feel pressured to move the conversation forward. Don't break the silence with humor or by changing the topic. Give your child space to reflect and let the Holy Spirit work on his heart.

Now, I know. You're probably thinking you could *never* ask questions like this—they're too pushy or brash. Or perhaps you think they sound too "Protestant." You may have encountered a manipulative street evangelist who used the same tactics to try to lead you to pray the "sinner's prayer" so you would know where you would go after dying.

But this doesn't need to be the case. First, this isn't a "Protestant" technique. It's the same strategy Jesus used throughout the Scriptures. Whenever Christ encountered a potential disciple, his invitation was stark and immediate. Consider his first words to Peter and Andrew: "Come after me, and I will make you fishers of men" (Matt. 4:19). Or look at his direct words to Levi, the tax collector: "'Follow me'" (Luke 5:27). Levi got up, left everything, and followed him. Jesus didn't hope that his disciples would meet him and then, after a while and on their own accord, conclude that the natural next step was to follow him. He knew they needed a direct invitation. Your child does too. Waffling around the issue might be more comfortable, but without a direct and urgent invitation, you won't close the loop.

You might also worry that if you ask a question like this, your child will respond negatively. But as we considered earlier, think about the worst-case scenario. The worst outcome is that your child might blow up, end the conversation, and walk away. If that happens, you simply regroup and start fresh next time. It's not the end of the world. You've sacrificed only a few seconds of discomfort for potentially closing the loop.

Suppose instead that your child just flatly answers "No"—he's just not ready to commit his life to God or invite Jesus into his life. That's fine too. Not everyone whom Jesus encounters in the Scriptures responds positively either. For example, the rich young man balks when Jesus suggests he must go and sell all of his positions (see Matt. 19:16–22). But Jesus doesn't berate him or haggle with him; he respects his freedom to say "No." Scripture is silent on the young man's future, but perhaps later in life he changed his mind. A "No" today doesn't mean a "No" forever.

If your child does answer "No," you can respond kindly by saying, "I totally understand. It's a lot to ask, and you might not be ready yet. But what do you think is holding you back?" This question will reorient the discussion to any barriers blocking your child's return path. He might just say, "I don't know. I'm just not ready to do that right now." Again, that's fine. At least you've extended the invitation, which will make it much easier to extend it again, in the future, when he's more ready.

Marcel LeJeune adds one more bit of advice. Even though these questions can help close the loop of your child's return journey, they aren't the final step. "Catholics don't believe that offering this choice to someone (and their acceptance of Jesus) is the end of their journey of justification/ salvation. We are not a people who believe in once-saved-always-saved. Rather, this choice is the first step (or another step) in continuing to choose God."

These questions will help lead your child to commit himself to Jesus Christ, to make an intentional decision to become his follower. But that decision opens up a whole new world of joys and challenges. As one loop closes, another one begins.

Four Key Steps to Reuniting with the Church

At some point in the life of every potential convert or revert to the Catholic Church, the person realizes that there is no serious reason why he should remain away from the Church. At the very least, the things pulling him toward it are finally stronger than the things pushing him away. Perhaps all of his questions have finally been answered (or at least sufficiently managed) and while he may still have difficulties, he is convinced that it's now time to return.

But the convert or revert always faces a natural question: How do I do that practically?

A priest friend once told me about his cousin Lisa. Lisa had left the Church at age eighteen and was now in her mid-forties. When my priest friend asked her why she had never come back, she paused, reflected, and then said, "Well, I guess I drifted away when I was young, and even though I've thought about coming back every now and then, I just wasn't sure how to do it." Here's someone who needlessly missed out on the sacraments for more than *two decades*, deprived of all the gifts God wanted to give her through the Church, simply because she didn't know the path to come home. That's heartbreaking.

Even after completing all the previous steps in this game plan, and helping your child decide to return to the Church, there's still one last thing you need to do. You need to guide him all the way back into full communion with the Church.

Not sure how to do that? Reuniting with the Church typically involves four key steps:

Step 1: Connect with a local priest
Of all the steps, this is most important. A priest will be able to talk with your child, assess the situation, and determine what needs to take place to formally reconcile him with the Church. It's important to note that many young people get nervous around priests, especially if they've been away for a while, and might be more comfortable talking to one through email or on the phone. That's fine. Get the contact information from both the priest

and your child, exchange it with the two of them, and then encourage them to connect with each other. But however you do it, you definitely want to connect your child with a priest at this stage.

Step 2: Make a good confession

If your child has been away for some time, chances are the first thing a priest will recommend is that he return to the sacrament of Confession (i.e., the sacrament of Reconciliation). Help your child see this as his gateway back home. As with the prodigal son in Jesus' story, it's one thing to *decide* to come back home. It's another thing to journey all the way back to the Father and once more walk through the door. That's what confession is for.

Chances are your child will be nervous about going to confession. He might not have been to the sacrament since he was a small child and might panic at the thought of recalling all the sins he's committed over the years. This is completely normal.

One commenter in a Catholic discussion forum voiced the same fears. He wrote: "I'm a 27-year old revert who is dreading going to confession next weekend for the first time in almost twenty years! Well, maybe not dreading it, but I have to admit I'm pretty nervous about it. I think the hardest part for me is that the priest will be hearing some incredibly heinous things about me in that confessional. After that, it's going to be pretty awkward seeing the guy at the grocery store! But I know it's necessary and in a way, I'm looking forward to being able to get some of the things I've done out in the open to someone."

Besides revealing their sins to a priest, many reverts also get nervous because they don't remember the mechanics of a good confession. That's also understandable. The commenter above had the same issue. "One thing I'm worried about is that I'm not really sure how specific I need to be. The last time I went to confession I was a little kid and would have confessed things like 'talking back to my mom' and easy stuff like that. After the teens and early twenties my sins are a bit more lurid. Is it enough to give the general name of the sins or should I plan to give some details? Thanks for any answers or advice you can offer!"

Thankfully, several people responded to the young man. They offered helpful advice, such as:

- "Just tell him it has been twenty years. He'll help you from there."
- "He'll lead you through it. Just imagine the enormous feeling of relief afterwards!"
- "There isn't anything you can confess that the priest hasn't heard before."

(The original man responded in jest, "He probably *has* heard it all before. But just to be on the safe side I'm going to go to the oldest priest I can find.")

If nothing else, you should accompany your child to confession and offer whatever support he needs (short of going in the confessional with them, of course, which is not allowed). Also, it would probably be best for one of you to make an appointment for his initial confession since it might take some time. If it would make your child more comfortable, schedule the appointment with a priest at a distant parish—any priest can hear his confession. You can even visit a local shrine or basilica, which typically have round-the-clock confession times.

Soothe your child's worries about what to say by encouraging him to simply enter the confessional and say, "Bless me Father, for I have sinned. It's been about [number] years since my last confession. To be honest, I think I'm going to need some help from you to walk me through this." Some people find it helpful to bring in a prayer card, or one printed out from the internet, which scripts out the entire process. But either way, the priest will be there to help. Most priests will be overjoyed to welcome him back and will gladly assist with the mechanics.

Step 3: Complete Any Missing Sacraments and Get Up to Speed

For many reverts, a simple confession is all that's necessary to return (a priest will help you determine this), and if that's the case, your child only needs steps one and two above. But the priest may determine that since your child has not received the necessary sacraments and catechesis, he should enroll in RCIA (Rite of Christian Initiation of Adults), a Confirmation preparation course, or another form of adult catechesis. RCIA is the Church's official process for adults seeking initiation into the Catholic Church, but may only be necessary for your child if he has not completed his sacraments of initiation (Baptism, First Communion, and Confirmation). In some cases, if your child is baptized and has received his First Communion, an adult Confirmation course is all that is needed. Even if your child has completed his sacraments, it is usually worthwhile to enroll in an adult catechesis program offered at a parish, whether it is a class on the basic teachings of the Catholic faith, a Bible study, a book club, or a discipleship group. This will allow your child to fill in the gaps in his knowledge of the faith, to discover opportunities for prayer and reflection, and to have a chance to ask questions, discuss doubts, and clear up confusions. It will also bring him into relationship with engaged and committed Catholics, who can act as role models in the faith.

As noted above in the first step, it is always wise to begin by connecting your child with a priest as soon as he expresses interest in returning, since the priest will be able to diagnose the situation and determine which of these paths would be most appropriate for the unique situation of your child.

Step 4: Find and join a parish community

Not all parishes are created equal. Some are warm and dynamic, with reverent and beautiful liturgies, dynamic homilies, active ministries, and plenty of eager disciples to draw your child deeper into his faith. Others are just trudging along in maintenance mode, with banal liturgies and little substance to offer your child. Although it's not the best idea for Catholics to jump from parish to parish looking for the "ideal" church home (none exist), it may be prudent for your child to "parish shop" in the period after returning to the faith. His first few months will be critical and you don't want a bad parish experience to undo all the progress he's made. So help your child find a parish that fits his temperament and don't allow his dislike of one parish to stop him from returning. He needs to find one where he feels welcome and at home.

Keep in mind that it's possible the first people your child encounters at a parish—the receptionist, the ushers, the director of religious education, etc.—may be less than welcoming. This isn't to say all parish staff are un-receptive, just that many parishes are short-handed and rely on sometimes weary staff and volunteers. Many parishes have teens answering their phones and while these young people may have a lot of enthusiasm, energy, and good intentions, they may not have developed a lot of judgment and dis-cretion. To be frank, they may have no clue how to facilitate someone's re-turn to the Church. So brace your child for the possibility that some people he meets won't be helpful or understanding. Remind him that he's returning to Jesus Christ and his Body, the Church, not to the person who answers the phone at the local parish.

Another problem converts and reverts often face is that they get lost in the shuffle of a huge mega-parish. Because of the lack of priests today, a parish may serve thousands of families. It's not uncommon to find a par-ish with six to eight weekend Masses, over one hundred ministries, and five thousand people on the register. To make matters worse, few parishes run with the smooth, efficient operations of a similarly sized corporation. Instead, as one author put it, parishes today are "more like big, ongoing, and continuous multifamily reunions that are held together by the good will and love shared among the family members." Once you break into that family and feel at home, things are smooth. But it can be difficult for someone like your child, coming in new. He might experience confusion, hostility, and numerous mistakes of judgment. The best solution is to take it slow, and to get your child involved with at least one ministry. Don't see the mega-parish as a huge, intimidating metropolis. See it as a collection of smaller neigh-borhoods. Encourage your child to find one in which he feels at home—a young-adult group, a weekly Bible study, a prayer group, a men's or women's group—and then grow closer to the few people in that group.

For help in this area, I recommend Patrick Madrid's book *Now What? A Guide for New (and Not-So-New) Catholics* (Servant Books, 2015). The book has helped many returning Catholics get up to speed, as Madrid offers practical advice on how to plug into the life of the Church—and stay plugged in. In fact, that book would be a great "congratulations" gift for your child after he takes the final step.

Special Hurdles

In some cases, your child might be in a situation that requires additional steps. Four roadblocks are especially prevalent today: cohabitation, abortion, divorce and remarriage, and near-death situations.

Cohabitation

Unfortunately, cohabitation is quickly becoming the norm for young couples today. Many unmarried couples move in with each other for financial reasons, since it's usually cheaper to share bills. Others cohabitate as a trial run for marriage, thinking it's the best way to gauge whether their relationship will last. Still others, to be blunt, simply want to enjoy the pleasures of sleeping with their significant other without the hassles of a wedding.

Whatever the reason, in almost every case, cohabitation involves a sexual relationship. And when it does, it falls short of the moral vision of Catholicism, which rejects any sexual act outside of marriage. In the next section, we'll understand how to dialogue about cohabitation with your child, but for now, let's explore how to navigate the pastoral waters so that this doesn't prevent your child from returning to the Church.

Cohabitation can be a major stumbling block. At first glance, it seems like the conflict forces a choice between their relationship (often with someone they love) and the Church. Or to put it another way, between their sex life and God. That's obviously a difficult and painful impasse.

But it can be overcome. If your child is living with a boyfriend or girlfriend, and he has already expressed interest in coming back to the Church, your next move should be to connect him with your local priest. Most priests are well-trained in responding to these situations. Some years back, the bishops of America released a document called *Faithful to Each Other Forever*, which lays out a pastoral approach for cohabiting couples. It calls for priests to avoid two extremes: 1) immediately condemning the couple and their behavior; and 2) ignoring the cohabitation. Priests are instead encouraged to try to find a middle way, one that integrates correction with understanding and compassion.

More specifically, a priest will work with your child to chart a path forward, one in which he'll move in a more chaste direction, albeit through small steps. Ideally, that would eventually include becoming married in the eyes of the Church or refraining from sexual activity until that happens. But cohabitation is not an insurmountable barrier to reconciling with the Church. Many couples have conquered it, and your child can too.

Don't let your child think that since he is currently cohabiting, there is no way he can ever return to the Church. The US bishops expressly note that "since cohabitation is not in itself a canonical impediment to marriage, the couple may not be refused marriage solely on the basis of cohabitation. Marriage preparation may continue even if the couple refuses to separate. Pastoral ministers can be assured that to assist couples in regularizing their situation is not to approve of cohabitation."

"Above all," the bishops conclude, "when cohabiting couples approach the Church for marriage, we encourage pastoral ministers to recognize this as a teachable moment. Here is a unique opportunity to help couples understand the Catholic vision of marriage. Here, too, is an opportunity for evangelization. By supporting the couple's plans for the future rather than chastising them for the past, the pastoral minister can draw a couple more deeply into the church community and the practice of their faith. Treated with sensitivity and respect, couples can be helped to understand and live the vocation of Christian marriage."

Past Abortion

"I wish I could come back to the Catholic Church," one woman complained, wiping tears from her eyes, "but I know I'm excommunicated and the Church cannot forgive me." The woman had been born and raised in a Catholic family but fell away as a teenager. She then became romantically involved with an older man and, at the age of seventeen, found herself alone, pregnant, and brokenhearted. After experiencing intense pressure from friends and family, she had an abortion.

Over the following years, the woman experienced tremendous guilt. But she could have avoided many years of guilt and suffering had she not been convinced that God could never forgive her for aborting her child.

There is no sin that God is incapable of forgiving. If you confess your sin with contrition, meaning you're truly sorry for your sin, and if you genuinely determine not to commit the sin again, then a priest can offer God's forgiveness through the sacrament of Confession. God is bigger than any sin, whether it be murder, torture, rape, theft, or abortion.

Whatever the case, if your child has been involved with an abortion, the best course of action is to connect him or her with a local priest to discuss the situation. The priest will be able to determine the necessary steps to acquire God's full forgiveness and reconciliation. But emphasize this with your child: having an abortion in the past, though gravely evil, is not a deal-breaker for reconciling with the Church. God can forgive anyone and provide your child tremendous joy and healing through the process.

Divorce and Remarriage

Of the all the impediments that keep people away from the Church, this is probably the most common. I can't tell you how many people I've met who are convinced that since they've been divorced and remarried, there is simply no hope for them—they're forever banished from the Church.

Christopher is one example. After moving to Illinois, he met a nice couple who lived next door, and during one of their conversations, they mentioned they were very involved at a nearby Catholic parish. The kids attended school there and both parents were active in several ministries. Christopher was intrigued and said that he used to be Catholic himself. He had been away from the Church for almost twenty years. During that time, his first wife left him, despite the couple having children, and he eventually remarried another woman who helped raise the kids. Christopher admitted that while he found great joy in his new marriage, he was sad that he could no longer be Catholic, since he had remarried outside the Church. He loved his Catholic faith and remarked that the burden of not being able to be part of his Church was a constant source of sorrow and pain.

During their next visit, his neighbors gave Christopher a flyer for a Catholics Returning Home program at their parish. His neighbors encouraged him to check it out and reiterated that if he really wanted it, there was a path back to the Church. He decided to attend. After a few meetings, the ministry leader connected him with a pastoral associate who helped him through the annulment process, and eventually his first marriage was determined to be invalid and his current marriage became recognized by the Church. He was then fully reconciled.

The annulment process isn't new in the Church, but it has become more prevalent in America, especially since Vatican II. Despite a common misconception, it's not akin to "Catholic divorce." An annulment confirms, after rigorous reflection and many conversations, that a true, sacramental marriage never really occurred in the first place—that there was some impediment to matrimony. That impediment could have been a quick decision to get married simply because a couple got pregnant, even if they were not in love. Or perhaps the couple was too young or naïve to accept the responsibility of family life. Or maybe they were not fully committed to having and raising children or staying married for life. If a marriage is pronounced "null" by the Church, it means that neither party entered into a true marital bond and is thus free to marry any unmarried person.

Lorene Hanley Duquin debunks some popular myths about annulments:

- Receiving an annulment does not mean that a loving marital relationship never existed.
- Annulments do not have to proceed in Rome.
- Annulments do not cost thousands of dollars.
- A person does not need "influence" to get an annulment.
- The annulment process does not take "forever."

Your child may be hesitant to pursue an annulment for fear that any children he has might become "illegitimate." But it's important to note that even if a marriage is annulled, the marriage was still legal and any children it produced are legitimate. It just means the marriage was not sacramental in the eyes of God, and therefore not recognized by the Church.

The annulment process typically begins with one or both spouses meeting with a local priest to discuss the situation. The priest then connects them with a special tribunal in their diocese that examines all the elements of the marriage, interviewing friends and family, and makes a judgment about the marriage based on its findings. It's true that the process can sometimes be long, difficult, and somewhat intrusive. Some couples choose not to go through the annulment process simply because they don't want to open old wounds that caused such pain and despair. But for most people, the process is worth it, especially if it means being reconciled with the Church and entering a true sacramental marriage with a person they love.

Near Death

If your child is on the verge of death, or suffering from a terminal disease, you naturally face last-minute questions such as:

- Does your child want to see a priest?
- Which priest should you call? Your parish priest or the hospital chaplain?
- What if your child is not registered in the parish? Would a priest still come?
- What if your child *doesn't* want to see a priest? Should you call for one anyway?

The *Catechism of the Catholic Church* insists that a family in this situation "should encourage the sick to call for a priest to receive this sacrament [Anointing of the Sick]. The sick should prepare themselves to receive it with good dispositions, assisted by their pastor and the whole ecclesial community, which is invited to surround the sick in a special way through their prayers and fraternal attention" (CCC 1516).

If it's too difficult for you to raise the subject of calling a priest, you might ask a friend, nurse, or another family member if they will pose the question to your child ("Can we call a priest for you?") But it needs to be asked. The moments before death can be pivotal in reconciling your child with Christ and the Church. In many cases, a person's resistance to the Church sinks lower than ever before.

However, sometimes people still belligerently reject the Church, even on their deathbed. A ninety-two-year-old priest friend of mine loves to tell the story of a man he once visited in the hospital. The man had been away from the Catholic Church for over forty years, but as he neared death, one of his family members called the priest anyway. The man saw the priest walk into his hospital room and balked. "What the hell are you doing here?" he mumbled. The priest gently explained that he was there to get the man right with God, to help save his soul. The man asked the priest to lean in so he could whisper something in his ear. When the priest leaned in, the man spit in the priest's face and shouted, "Get out of here!"

The old priest gently pulled out a handkerchief and wiped the spittle away. He then walked to the corner of the hospital room and sat down quietly in a chair. "What are you doing?" the sick man demanded. "I told you to leave!"

"Well," the priest said, "I would actually like to stay. I've never seen a man die and go to hell. I thought I'd watch you."

The two men stared at each other for a few moments. Then, like a bursting dam, the man unleashed a stream of tears, filled with decades of pent up shame, regret, and sorrow. When his tears dried up, the man said he actually did want to be forgiven but was too ashamed to ask for it. The priest walked over and asked the man if he would like to go to confession. The man agreed. Afterward, the priest administered the Anointing of the Sick and prayed with the man. He died the next day, in a perfect state of grace.

Perhaps your child's experience won't be nearly as dramatic as that man's (hopefully not!) but his story illustrates something that priests will tell you: many people on their deathbeds want to be forgiven, and they want to receive the Anointing of the Sick, but they're too proud or scared to ask for it. They need help. They need you. So, if your child is on the verge of dying, gently push through any discomfort or shame he may feel and do everything you can to arrange a meeting with a priest. Ensure that your child receives the sacraments he needs in order to die in full communion with Jesus in his Church.

* * *

To recap, we've now journeyed from start to finish through the whole game plan. You've seen how to begin with prayer and fasting, equip yourself, plant seeds, and start productive conversations about God. In the last two chapters you've learned how to connect your child with a community of other disciples and help him close the loop with the Church.

In the final part of this book, we'll break down over twenty specific objections young people commonly give to explain why they're not Catholic. Arming yourself with helpful responses will make you ready to tackle even the most difficult challenges.

PART III
The Big Objections

"There are not over a hundred people in the United States who hate the Catholic Church. There are millions, however, who hate what they wrongly believe to be the Catholic Church—which is, of course, quite a different thing."

— VENERABLE FULTON SHEEN

CHAPTER 12
Personal Objections

It may be easy to assume that when your child drifted away from the Church, it was a careful and thoughtful decision. He must have had good, rational reasons for leaving. But in my experience, this usually isn't the case. Often "intellectual objections" are personal objections in disguise.

For example, one young man claimed he left the Church because he realized the Church's harsh sexual teachings were incompatible with a good and loving God (an intellectual objection). But the real reason he left was because he was living with his girlfriend and didn't want to change his lifestyle (a personal/moral objection). That's why in earlier chapters we focused on asking questions in order to drill down to the *real* objections your child has instead of settling for surface-level issues. When you ask why he doesn't go to Mass any more, his initial reasons may not be the *actual* reasons keeping him away.

(Of course, not *everyone* is masking deep emotional problems or guilt. Some young people have genuine theological problems, and we'll get to those in the last chapter. But in my experience, the personal and moral are far more often the culprits.)

In this chapter, we'll look at several common personal objections and then use the next two chapters to handle the moral and theological. For each objection, you'll find a simple response followed by a deeper explanation that supports it. The goal isn't to just parrot the response to your child, verbatim—this could actually hurt your witness significantly—but it's there to help frame the issue in your own mind as you formulate a reply. I've also included at least one book recommendation for each objection, which you may read yourself or pick up for your child.

"I just don't have time for church right now. I'm too busy."
Response: Mass becomes the highest priority only when
you realize it offers a direct encounter with God.

Today, people work more hours, sign up for more activities, spend more time online, and take less vacation than ever before. Free time is hard to come by. So it's understandable when people point to their tightly packed schedules when explaining why they don't attend Mass.

The problem, however, is that this only makes sense if the Mass is just one activity among many, with the same value as the other items on their schedule. But the Mass is something different. The Mass offers what nothing else can: a true, bodily encounter with the living God. The Eucharist, which is at the heart of the Mass, is not just a sign or symbol. (The novelist Flannery O'Connor famously said, "If it's a symbol, to hell with it.") For Catholics, the Eucharist is the true Body and Blood, Soul and Divinity of Jesus Christ. When the priest consecrates the bread and wine, they still retain the external qualities of those things—they still taste, feel, and smell like bread and wine—but their substance changes into the Body and Blood of Christ. At the level of substance, the level of what something essentially *is*, they take on the substance of God.

Few Catholics today realize this is what actually happens. For example, Catholic researcher Mark Gray discovered, "Fewer than two-thirds of Catholics believe that the bread and wine used for Communion really become the body and blood of Jesus Christ. How can so many disagree with this central teaching of the faith? Surprisingly, it is because many are unaware that this is what the Church teaches! Only 46% of Catholics are aware of what the Church teaches about the real presence and agree with that teaching. An additional 17% agree, but do not know this is what the Church teaches. A third do not agree with the teaching but are unaware of the teaching. Finally, only 4% of Catholics know what the Church teaches about the real presence and do not believe it."

So, if your child claims to be too busy for Mass, the key is to help him understand how the Mass is different than the rest of his activities, and ultimately more significant. It's different and significant because it offers a real, direct encounter with Jesus Christ.

One way to do this is to pose a thought experiment to your child: "Suppose you were watching TV when a breaking news story splashed across the screen. Miraculously, Jesus Christ has returned to the earth, in the flesh, and tomorrow morning he will be appearing at a nearby building. Of all the places and times he could have chosen in the world, he decided to return not just tomorrow, but *to your own neighborhood*. Wouldn't you do anything to make sure you were there? Wouldn't you clear your calendar, summon the energy to get up early, and make sure you arrived well before he did?"

Wait for your child to answer, then assuming he says yes, reply, "That's exactly what happens at Mass. The Mass isn't just some casual gathering where we exchange pleasantries, sing songs, and listen to a nice talk. The Mass is the place where we encounter Jesus, in the flesh. That's what the Eucharist is: the Body and Blood, Soul and Divinity of Jesus."

Researchers from the Diocese of Trenton, New Jersey, found after interviewing hundreds of former Catholics that misunderstanding the Eucharist was key in many departures. They called for "a fresh explanation of the nature of the Eucharist. Underlying all the opinions expressed by the [former Catholic respondents] is the fact that they are, for the most part, willing to separate themselves from the celebration and reception of the Eucharist. This calls for a creative liturgical, pastoral, doctrinal and practical response." They also called for a clearer explanation of why it's necessary to attend Mass each Sunday, framing it as a chance to give thanks, through sacrament and sacrifice, rather than a weekly imposition.

In the end, the only way your child will make Mass a priority is by valuing it above his other activities—even above sleeping in. That will happen only when he sees Mass as it really is.

To help him do that, you might consider giving him a good book on the Mass such as *The Lamb's Supper* (Doubleday, 1999) by Scott Hahn, which vividly explains what's really going on behind all the prayers and gestures. Or you might invite your child to watch episode 7 of Bishop Barron's

CATHOLICISM film series titled "World Made Flesh, True Bread of Heaven: The Mystery of the Liturgy and the Eucharist."

"Mass is boring and irrelevant."
Response: Mass is exhilarating once you
learn to see what's really going on.

This objection is somewhat tied to the last one. Most parents have heard it. What's a bad response? "I don't care if you think Mass is boring; you're going anyway. Now get in the car!" Remember what we learned in the "big myths" section of this book: *forcing* your child to Mass when he has no desire to go can do more harm than good.

(Again, I have in mind here older teenagers and young adults. Obviously, parents have a duty to bring younger kids to Mass even if they don't feel like going.)

"The Mass is very long and tiresome unless one loves God," wrote G.K. Chesterton. When we drag our child to Mass and force him to sit idly without a clue about what's going on, or without even an inkling of devotion to God, it's not surprising that he finds the whole thing boring and irrelevant. Who could blame him? Imagine yourself sitting through an hour-long service for another religion to which you have zero attraction or connection. Wouldn't you have the same reaction? Or picture yourself attending a talk about the First Anglo-Mysore War from 1766–1769 without any historical or political background. Could you make it to the end without dozing off?

The cure for this problem isn't to spice up the Mass by adding louder and more contemporary music or incorporating lights and video. The answer, as Chesterton noted, is to help your child fall in love with God. This is why the Mass is the last piece of the puzzle, not the first. Your child has to move across all of the "thresholds of conversion" before he'll finally fall in love with the Mass.

It's unusual for the pattern to go the other way. It's not common for a young person to first fall in love with the Mass and *then* enter a loving relationship with God. It's almost always reversed. A young person first needs to have a conversion experience, where he returns to God or the practice of his faith, and then, with that foundation in place, he develops a renewed appreciation for the Mass, the privileged place to encounter the God he's already returned to.

This doesn't mean there aren't legitimate ways we can improve the Mass experience. For instance, Protestant communities are known for their engaging, relevant sermons that delve deep into the Scriptures and apply them to our lives. Unfortunately, many homilies in the Catholic Church fall short of that ideal. Quite frankly, many are banal and shallow. There's also space to improve our music, making it more reverent and resplendent. But for most of us, those two facets—the homilies and music—are out of our control. We can't really affect *how* the Mass is celebrated in our parish. Therefore, we should focus on what we can directly influence—namely, our child's understanding of the Mass.

If your child describes Mass as "boring" or "irrelevant," your first move, in line with what we've learned earlier, should be to ask a question: "Why do you think it's boring? What would make it more interesting to you?" Listen to your child's answers. After hearing him out, you should next acknowledge and validate his boredom. Don't dismiss it by pretending it doesn't exist. Say, "I totally understand where you're coming from. I can see how Mass would be boring if you don't understand what's going on and especially if you don't see its value. Frankly, I would be bored too if the Mass meant just showing up every week, reciting some meaningless lines, listening to a bad talk, and then snacking on a piece of bread. If that's all the Mass was, I'd be equally bored." Affirm that your child's intuition is right: the Mass is not meant to be dry, repetitive, and boring. It is meant be alive, life-giving, and powerful. This will make your child much more open to hearing what you say next—namely, what actually happens at Mass and why it matters.

As with the last objection, the key is revealing to your child the true purpose of the entire service: meeting God in Word and Sacrament. A recent survey found that only 61% of Catholic teens agree that "Jesus is really present in the bread and wine of the Eucharist." The other 39% agreed more with the statement, "Bread and wine are symbols of Jesus, but Jesus is not really present." And these were teens who identified as Catholics, ones who have not yet drifted from the Church! Odds are your child is probably not convinced that the Eucharist is really Jesus.

You need to help him see that reality, and when he does, he'll no longer consider the Mass boring or irrelevant. Through your efforts and the grace of God, the Mass may truly become the "source and summit" of his personal relationship with Jesus and the foundation of his Catholicism. The two resources mentioned in the previous response will help, as will Mark Hart's great book, *Blessed Are the Bored in Spirit: A Young Catholic's Search for Meaning* (Servant Books, 2006).

"The Church is too focused on rules and making people feel guilty."

Response: The Church doesn't add guilt; it takes away guilt.
Its mission involves forgiveness and healing.

When I converted to Catholicism, one of the biggest surprises was meeting people—many people—who associated the Catholic Church with guilt. Often, when someone found out I had just become Catholic, they would remark that they grew up Catholic too but had since left the faith, making a joke about escaping "all that Catholic guilt." But such guilt-driven faith has never been my experience, and it's not the Church's true approach.

Someone asked G.K. Chesterton why he became Catholic, and he replied, "To get rid of my sins." Catholicism is not the source of guilt; it's the answer to it. Through the Church's sacraments, especially Baptism and Confession, God forgives our sins and washes them away. Rather than making us feel guilty or shameful, the Church liberates us. Since becoming a Catholic, I have found that one of the most comforting experiences in my life is hearing God speaking to me through the priest when he says in the confessional, "I absolve you from your sins."

What about the Church's many rules and regulations? Many of these pertain to the liturgy and Church life, but many apply to the moral realm too. Yet these rules are not arbitrary, and they're not meant to keep you down. They exist to guide you along the path of joy. Like any good roadmap, they keep you from taking wrong turns, down paths that will ultimately lead to emptiness and misery. So the Church's rules don't constrain you; they ensure you flourish.

Chesterton offered a good analogy here. He described a group of children playing on an island with steep sides. He noted that if the children were left on their own, they would likely move toward the center and only play in a small circle, afraid of falling over the edge. But suppose you erected a high fence around the entire island. The children would then be free to run around play on every inch of its surface. Here's the point: the fence would not constrict their happiness; it would enlarge it. That's how the rules of the Church are. They aren't meant to constrict your spiritual life—they're meant to give it life and vigor and keep it moving in the right direction.

"How could anyone remain Catholic after the sexual abuse crisis?"

Response: The Church has always been full of sinners, but our faith is grounded in Christ, not the actions of wayward men.

The sexual abuse crisis has been one of the most deplorable episodes in the history of the Church—certainly the darkest moment in American Catholicism. The revelations of priests who manipulated and abused young children, and the bishops who covered it up, often transferring the priests to new parishes where they were free to abuse again, are almost inconceivable. For many people today, these actions have stripped the Church of any credibility or moral authority. And who could blame that reaction?

There is no defense for the abuse; we can't explain it away. If your child brings up this objection, your first response should be to share his outrage. Affirm his disappointment. He is right to be upset by it.

Then, only after you have articulated your own disgust, you might consider introducing a few follow-up facts that will soften the blow. First, not all priests are abusers. In fact, the overwhelming majority of priests are heroic, charitable, self-giving men who offer their lives in service to their flock. They would never think of intentionally abusing anyone, much less a child. Recent data has shown that about 2–4% of priests were responsible for all of the sexual abuse, and almost all of them during the 1960s–70s. Notably, the priestly abuse rate was significantly lower than the abuse rates of fathers, public school teachers, sports coaches, or Boy Scout leaders. This wasn't a problem unique to the Catholic Church—it was indicative of a whole culture that turned a blind eye to the suffering and abuse of children.

Second, we shouldn't be surprised that the Church is full of sinners (after all, you and I are part of it!). As the famous saying goes, the Church is a hospital for sinners, not a museum for saints. It will always contain liars, murderers, thieves, betrayers, and, yes, even abusers. Jesus said the Church is like a field that is mixed with wheat and weeds (see Matt. 13:24–30). Only at the end of time will the two be separated. For now, we must move forward in a mixed field, a Church where many people—including us, at times—fail to live up to the Church's teachings.

Third and finally, after the abuse crisis reached its peak in the mid-to-late twentieth century, the Church implemented a zero-tolerance abuse policy that is being used as a model for other institutions throughout the world. Dioceses now conduct thorough background checks on all clerics, educators, employees, and volunteers, especially those working with children. Since the early 2000s, the Catholic Church has gone further than any other institution in Western society in ensuring past mistakes can never be repeated. These reforms have made the Church transparent, accountable, and one of the safest places for young people today.

If your child is concerned about the abuse crisis, suggest he read Bishop Robert Barron's magnificent little book, *Letter to a Suffering Church* (Word on Fire, 2019), or *Pope Benedict XVI and the Sexual Abuse Crisis: Working for Reform and Renewal* (Our Sunday Visitor, 2010) by Gregory Erlandson and Matthew Bunson. Another helpful resource is chapter 8 of *How to Defend the Faith Without Raising Your Voice: Civil Responses to Catholic Hot Button Issues, Revised and Updated* by Austen Ivereigh and Kathryn Jean Lopez. That chapter is titled "Never Again: The Legacy of Clerical Sexual Abuse."

"I'm married to a non-Catholic.
Returning to the Church would really upset my spouse."

Response: Your marriage is extremely important. In this case,
you should still move forward into the Church,
but gradually rather than suddenly.

Jim had felt drawn to come back to Mass for several weeks, but he just couldn't do it. He knew it would upset his wife who had many bad experiences with the Church as a child. For her, the Church was a corrupt group of old men who had nothing to say but "No!" She didn't want anything to do with that. But as Jim slowly learned, she didn't want him participating either. Whenever he revealed signs up warming back up to Catholicism, his wife shot him down with a silent stare or dismissive quip. "Are you serious?" she would sneer, or at other times say, "How could you possibly agree with such misogyny?" Jim was torn. The more he inched toward the Church, the more tension it created in his marriage. What should he do?

Jim's story is increasingly common today. A recent Pew Forum survey found that nearly 40% of marriages since 2010 can be classified as "religiously mixed," which is more than double the rate in 1960 (19%). If you visit your average parish on a Saturday afternoon, chances are high you'll see a Catholic marrying an Evangelical, a Baptist, a Methodist, a Jew, or sometimes even an atheist.

I've talked to many people in this position and the first thing to recognize is that it's an extremely delicate situation. Usually, the best strategy is to take things slowly. A radical or sudden reversion can upend the marriage, but the resistant spouse may be able to handle a slower, more gradual transition.

If your child is married to a non-Catholic spouse who is resistant to your child's reversion, let the results speak for themselves over time. Gradually, the spouse will begin to see the positive ways Catholicism has changed your child, how it has transformed him to be more joyful, more compassionate, and more peaceful. You can't argue with results. If the fruit borne from this religious attraction is positive, then the spouse will be far more likely to approve of your child's decision.

A good book on this topic is *When Only One Converts* (Our Sunday Visitor, 2001), edited by Lynn Nordhagen. It includes first-person accounts of couples living in mixed-faith marriages and advice from professionals on how to manage those differences effectively.

"I had a bad experience with church and I can't see myself coming back."

Response: I'm so sorry that happened. But the Catholic Church is so much bigger than one local parish or one mean priest. Don't let this keep you away.

Elizabeth struggled with her faith for many years, but it all came apart one Sunday. "The last straw for me was Christmas Mass, 2014. It was standing room only, and families that came together were forced to spread all over church. Our new priest who clearly was not wanting to be torn from retirement, posted in the bulletin, 'If you are not a regular church goer, you are not welcome to take communion.' Can you believe that? Here is an opportunity to draw people back into the fold. These men have dug their heels into an antiquated reality, and I do not see them as having moral authority. The falling away from church causes my mother great pain and that makes me sad."

Now, was that exactly what the priest wrote in the bulletin? We don't know. And even though he was right about the Church's position on Communion for non-Catholics, could he have been more sensitive or offered a clearer explanation of the teaching? Probably. But how sad that this one experience drove Elizabeth from the Church.

Marisa offers another heartbreaking experience. She wrote to me saying, "I left the Catholic Church at the age of eighteen. I was out celebrating my birthday one weekend when I was forcibly raped by a friend of a friend. I decided to keep the child due to my belief that abortion was wrong, and I didn't want to give the baby up for adoption. But after I had the child, I wanted to get her baptized, so I went to the local church that I had been attending to talk with the priest. He got very close to my face and told me I was a huge disgrace for having a child so young and having a child without a father figure. I proceeded to tell the priest how I was raped, but he told me I was still a disgrace to the Church. I had my daughter baptized but I never ever went back to a Catholic church. I felt like these people in the congregation were the most judgmental people I have ever met!" Again, if that was how the situation went down, who could blame Marisa for leaving?

As a third example, a woman explains why her sister left the Church: "My sister says Catholics are hypocrites. That last time she went to Mass, she accidentally bumped into some woman on her way back from communion and the woman gave her the dirtiest look. That was the straw that broke the camel's back. She now goes to a Protestant church where she says people are friendly and really care about you."

Mother Teresa once said, "Often we Christians constitute the worst obstacle for those who try to become closer to Christ; we often preach a Gospel we do not live." I've heard countless stories of people being hurt by people in the Church. In fact, *most* people I know, Catholics and former Catholics, had at least one bad experience—the only difference is that the Catholics were able to move past it and stay in the Church, while the others left.

So how should you respond if this describes your child? The first thing to do is apologize on the Church's behalf, even if you had nothing to do with the incident. You might say, "I'm so sorry that happened to you. That should never have taken place, and they never should have reacted like that." If the incident was several years back, encourage your child to give the Church another chance. Tell them not to let one incident from the distant past determine his future religious path. If the incident happened at a particular parish, suggest he try another one. One woman offers a helpful analogy: "A few months ago, the guy at the local supermarket completely humiliated me, but I haven't stopped shopping at the supermarket chain, only at that particular location."

Second, help your child see that the Catholic Church is bigger than just one local parish or mean priest. Your child must separate the person that hurt him from the Church and her sacraments. Explain that it's not worthy cutting himself off from the source of spiritual nourishment because of something one human being said or did—he's hurting himself more than anyone else.

A helpful resource here is Stephen Mansfield's book, *Hurting in the Church: A Way Forward for Wounded Catholics* (Our Sunday Visitor, 2017).

"God can never forgive me for what I've done."
Response: God's mercy is unconstrained. He can
forgive anything and restore your soul.

Whenever people mention to Fr. Andrew Carrozza that they could never go to confession because they don't think God will ever forgive them, he likes to give this answer:

> Suppose Adolf Hitler, right after he shot himself but before he died, had a moment of regret and asked God to forgive him. Do you think God would forgive him? They always respond, "Of course!" (There would still be penance and Purgatory necessary, but God would forgive him.) . . .
>
> So, I tell them, if God could forgive Adolf Hitler . . . do you think he will forgive you your sin, no matter how serious it is?" They immediately see the logic and say, "Of course!"
>
> Remember that God is trying to get us into heaven, not to keep us out!

If your child doubts that God could ever forgive him, remind him that God is more merciful than any fault. As Pope Francis reiterates, God wants a "Church of mercy," one rich in forgiveness and slow to condemn.

That's why Jesus gave the authority to forgive sins to his Apostles, saying before he ascended to heaven, "Receive the Holy Spirit. Whose sins you forgive are forgiven them, and whose sins you retain are retained" (John 20:23). The Scriptures confirm that God can "wash away [your] guilt" and make you "pure" and "whiter than snow" (Ps. 51:4, 9).

There is no limit to God's forgiveness, no matter what your child has done. Murder, rape, abortion, drugs, contraception, sex outside of marriage—it can all be forgiven in one moment, in the sacrament of Confession.

If your child still doubts this, even after your reassurances, connect him with your local priest. The priest will not only help him grasp the truth of God's forgiveness. He can also help your child experience it through the sacrament of Reconciliation.

I would also recommend Vinny Flynn's book, *7 Secrets of Confession* (Ignatius Press, 2013) as a resource that will help your child grasp the liberating fact of God's forgiveness.

CHAPTER 13
Moral Objections

One lady who left the Church was quite blunt in explaining why: "My daughter came out to me as gay, and I went through a divorce after thirty-eight years of marriage. The Church doesn't want either of us."

Of course, the Church wants both of them, desperately, because God wants and loves both of them. The Church yearns to welcome them back so they can receive all the gifts that God wants to give them. But unfortunately, the poor lady's perception is that because she was divorced, and because her daughter is attracted to other women, neither one has a place in the Church.

This is an example of a moral objection, and these can often be more sensitive than personal or theological objections. Let's explore some of the most common examples.

"The Church is so judgmental.
Didn't Pope Francis say, 'Who am I to judge?'"

Response: We should never judge persons, but it's okay and sometimes necessary to judge actions.

If your fallen-away child knows nothing else about Pope Francis, he probably knows this famous quote—"Who am I to judge?" The impromptu line came during a news conference with reporters on a flight from Brazil back to Rome. A reporter asked the pope about a rumored "gay lobby" in the Vatican, a group of priests and bishops who purportedly work at the Vatican and protect each other.

Pope Francis replied, "So much is written about the gay lobby. I have yet to find anyone who can give me a Vatican identity card with 'gay' written on it. They say they are there. When I meet a gay person, I have to distinguish between his being gay and being part of a lobby. If a person is gay and seeks the Lord and has good will, who am I to judge them? They shouldn't be marginalized. They must be integrated into society. Their [homosexual] orientation isn't the problem. . . . They're our brothers."

The media quickly pounced on the comment. Shortly after, Barbara Walters celebrated the pope as one of her "10 Most Fascinating People of 2013," in large part because of this comment. She said the pope has now "embraced" homosexuals by telling the world, "What these people do in their private lives is none of my business."

But is that what Pope Francis really said? Should Catholics stop their opposition to homosexual activity, divorce, artificial contraception, and other immoral acts because, well, "who am I to judge"?

In order to understand Pope Francis' words, we have to recognize that there are at least two senses of the term *judge*. In Jesus' famous Sermon on the Mount, he clearly commands, "*Stop judging*, that you may not be judged" (Matt. 7:1, emphasis added). But elsewhere, in the Gospel of John, we find Jesus commanding the opposite: "Stop judging by appearance, *but judge justly*" (John 7:24, emphasis added). How can Jesus both prohibit and require judging? Isn't this a contradiction? It's only a problem until we realize that even Jesus refers to two forms of judgment.

The first type of judging, which Jesus discourages, refers to the judging of *souls*. We should be extremely hesitant to judge the state of individual souls, to speculate about their eternal destiny, decide about their inner motives, or determine if they deserve condemnation from God, for the obvious reason that we can't see into their souls. As St. Paul admits, we're hardly capable of passing judgment on our *own* souls, much less other people's: "I do not even pass judgment on myself. I am not conscious of anything against me, but I do not thereby stand acquitted; the one who judges me is the Lord" (1 Cor. 4:4). This means we should be wary of rash judgment, which is defined in the *Catechism of the Catholic Church* as "assum[ing] as true, without sufficient foundation, the moral fault of a neighbor." We just don't know what's going on in our neighbor's soul.

But what about the second sense of judging, the one Jesus encourages? This refers to the judgment of *actions*, assessing the moral value of a particular act. To use an extreme example, if we discover a man torturing a child for fun, we can offer judgment swiftly and with confidence: that action is deplorable and unquestionably wrong. That's an example of judgment in the second sense. But even while judging the immorality of torturing children, we *can't* judge the torturer's soul (in the first sense) because we're not in a position to determine how culpable the man is for his sin—whether he's suffering from mental illness, or whether someone else is forcing him to torture the child under duress.

The *Catechism* echoes this subtle distinction: "Human acts, that is, acts that are freely chosen in consequence of a judgment of conscience, can be morally evaluated. They are either good or evil. . . . Although we can judge that an act is in itself a grave offense, we must entrust judgment of persons to the justice and mercy of God."

How does all of this tie back to Pope Francis' comment? In his airplane interview, the pope was simply affirming what the *Catechism* teaches, that we should never judge people in the first sense, by assessing the state of their souls or their standing with God. With the supposed "gay lobbyist," he rightly acknowledged that no one should condemn the man simply for his attractions.

When Pope Francis asked, "Who am I to judge?" he did *not* mean to suggest, "Anyone can do anything he wants and we have no right to make any moral judgments" or "What these people do in their private lives is none of my business." He was simply affirming the commonsense fact that while we have the ability, and sometimes the obligation, to judge certain actions, only God can judge people's souls.

For more on this distinction about judging, see Edward Sri's book, *Who Am I to Judge? Responding to Relativism with Logic and Love* (Ignatius Press, 2017).

"The Church hates gay and lesbian people."

Response: The Church welcomes everyone and demands that Catholics treat all people with respect, compassion, and sensitivity.

A few years ago, a collection of national surveys revealed that the most common perception of present-day Christianity is "anti-homosexual." This means the first thing people think of when encountering a Christian is not what they're for but what they're against. And in the eyes of most people, they're against gays and lesbians.

This is a huge problem. Not only does this stand against Jesus' own teachings—he was never "anti-" anyone—it presents a serious barrier for those who have left the Church. Even if your child finds many other strong arguments in favor of returning to the Church, this one issue alone could keep him away. In fact, after meeting with hundreds of non-Catholics, I'd say the Church is not even a serious option for most young people today simply because they see the Church as anti-gay people.

So how should we respond? We must break the issue down into three elements: the teaching of the Catholic Church, how that teaching is perceived by those with same-sex attraction, and how that teaching is implemented on the ground by Catholics.

First, the teaching of the Church. In my experience, few people who disagree with the Catholic Church's position on homosexuality actually know what that teaching is. Most reject a caricature. They assume the Church has issued a blanket condemnation of all gay and lesbian people and that if you're attracted to people of the same sex, you're inevitably destined for hell. But that's not the Church's position. The *Catechism of the Catholic Church* offers a far more nuanced and compassionate response, which is worth reading in full:

> Homosexuality refers to relations between men or between women who experience an exclusive or predominant sexual attraction toward persons of the same sex. It has taken a great variety of forms through the centuries and in different cultures. Its psychological genesis remains largely unexplained. Basing itself on Sacred Scripture, which presents homosexual acts as acts of grave depravity, tradition has always declared that "homosexual acts are intrinsically disordered." They are contrary to the natural law. They close the sexual act to the gift of life. They do not proceed from a genuine affective and sexual complementarity. Under no circumstances can they be approved.

The number of men and women who have deep-seated homosexual tendencies is not negligible. This inclination, which is objectively disordered, constitutes for most of them a trial. They must be accepted with respect, compassion, and sensitivity. Every sign of unjust discrimination in their regard should be avoided. These persons are called to fulfill God's will in their lives and, if they are Christians, to unite to the sacrifice of the Lord's Cross the difficulties they may encounter from their condition. (CCC 2357–2358)

The Church makes an important distinction between homosexual *orientation* and homosexual *activity*. We'll look more at this in the next objection, but for now, know that the Church explicitly teaches that homosexual *orientation* is not sinful in itself. All of us experience wayward inclinations that we can't control and thus can't be responsible for. For example, you might experience a disordered appetite for alcohol, sex, food, or even exercise. That inclination only becomes sinful when you act on it—when, for instance, you give into your excessive desire for alcohol and become drunk. Only then, when the *orientation* is acted upon and becomes an *action,* can we judge, "That is wrong."

The second element worth noting is how the Church's teaching is perceived by those with same-sex attractions. While it's true most people who identify as LGBT (lesbian, gay, bisexual, or transgender) probably disagree with Catholic teaching on this issue, a major national Pew study found that more LGBT people identify as Catholic (17%) than any other religious tradition. They identify with Catholicism more than Evangelicalism (13%), mainline Protestantism (11%), agnosticism (9%), or atheism (8%). For all the rhetoric in the media about the Catholic Church being the greatest enemy of homosexuality, it appears actual LGBT people may disagree.

Finally, the third element worth examining is what the Church's teaching looks like in practice. A priest friend recently shared a story with me about a pastor he knew who served in a downtown area with a large population of gay people. There was a transgender person who would regularly visit his church and light candles at the various shrines. He would present himself with great drama, very theatrical, wearing over-the-top wigs and hats and dresses. He was never irreverent, but whenever he came in, he naturally captured everyone's attention.

The priest would always greet this man with a smile and kind words. Once, he found the man weeping at the shrine of Our Lady. The priest asked what was the matter, and the man revealed that his mother had died and the family had requested that he not attend the funeral, as they thought his presence would confuse and scandalize members of the close-knit Baptist congregation. He reluctantly complied, missing his own mother's funeral. While the funeral was taking place, he came to this Catholic church so that, gesturing to the statue of our Lady, he could be with his Mother. He then told the priest that all his life he had been the object of derision and mockery, and he had known very little kindness. But over the years, he discovered that the one place he could go where he knew someone would be kind to him was the Catholic Church. And even if someone wasn't kind to him there, he found that kindness in the faces of the plaster saints.

A few years passed, and the priest noticed that the man was not coming around as much, and when he did he looked like a shadow of his former self. The priest made inquiries and discovered the man was gravely ill. Before the man died, the priest visited him (in the man's disheveled apartment). The man was utterly despondent, sure that he would die alone and that no church would bury him. But through the priest's intervention and by the grace of God, the man became open to being received into the Catholic Church. Shortly before he died, he became Catholic, and the priest offered him a funeral Mass. Few people were in attendance, but those who came remembered the man from his theatrical visits—the daily Mass-goers and the Rosary ladies. After the funeral, they all stayed behind to light candles and pray for the repose of his soul.

This is precisely what Pope Francis means in his yearning for a "Church of mercy." No one had to do anything more to convince the man of his misery. What he needed was to be convinced that he mattered and that he could be loved. No moral teaching was compromised in letting the man know mercy. That's what saved him.

That's what the Church's teaching on homosexuality looks like, ideally: disagreement with homosexual activity, but a strong love for homosexuals. As the *Catechism* says, they must be treated with "respect, compassion, and sensitivity."

"I'm gay. How could I ever be Catholic?"
Response: Same-sex attraction isn't incompatible with Catholicism, but those who struggle with it need love, support, and guidance.

I recently messaged all my friends and followers online, looking for former Catholics who would be open to sharing why they left the Church. The most surprising result was the number of replies from people who left because of their sexual orientation. For example, Kat said, "I was baptized and raised Catholic. In my youth, I was very involved with our parish as an altar server, children's liturgy supervisor, and a dedicated member of the choir. But I officially left the Church when I discovered how unaccepting Catholics could be. After realizing I am bisexual, I felt I could not come out and still be involved in the Catholic Church. After telling only one person I was blatantly told that I was going to burn in hell. That was it for me." It took just one regrettable conversation.

Allys responded saying, "I no longer associate with being a Catholic or Christian due to the people I know from my former church. Most of them are so hate-filled it makes me uncomfortable. I'm a lesbian, and it hurts when so many lash out saying it's disgusting, offensive, etc. Even my own mother is in denial, rolling her eyes every time I even mention it."

We previously pointed out how rolling your eyes, or any other passive-aggressive behavior, will quickly get your child to ignore everything you say afterward. Should we be surprised by Allys' reaction?

As we noted earlier, it's important to point out that being attracted to someone of the same sex is not incompatible with Catholicism. In fact, there are thousands of holy, devout disciples of God who deal with such attractions every day. Often these attractions are unwanted, though sometimes, in a culture that increasingly celebrates them, the attractions are embraced.

When addressing same-sex attraction, the last thing you want is come across as uncaring or moralistic, more interested in your child's behavior than his heart. Compassion must be your operating principle; love must be your first and last word. Your child must know that you love him unconditionally before he'll hear anything you have to say about his same-sex tendencies.

Once you've established that trust, and only then, there are several helpful resources you can share with him. First, the Catholic ministry Courage International. Courage is a leader in ministering to people with same-sex attraction. As they note on their website, CourageRC.org, people with same-sex desires have always been with us. However, until recent times, there has been little, if any, formal outreach from the Church in the way of support groups or information for such people. Most were left to work out their path on their own. As a result, such people found themselves listening to and accepting the secular society's perspective and opting to act on their same-sex desires.

But on the Courage International website, you'll find resources for people experiencing these attractions, for the parents of those who struggle, and for priests and Church leaders who minister to each of those groups. The website includes testimonials from people who have escaped the homosexual lifestyle and have instead chosen a life of chastity and well-integrated sexuality. That doesn't mean they joined a monastery or "turned off" their sexual dimension. They are still real people, living real lives in the world, and in many cases still struggling with their sexual attractions. They just discovered the freedom of interior chastity, and in that freedom discovered the steps necessary to live a fully Christian life in communion with God and others.

Courage chapters meet throughout the country and the members help each other walk this journey. Courage also has a companion organization called Encourage, which supports family and friends of persons with same-sex attraction.

A second resource to share with your child is a film created by Courage called *Desire of the Everlasting Hills*. You can watch it free online at EverlastingHills.org. It's about an hour long and features three intimate and candid portraits of Catholics trying to navigate the waters of self-understanding, faith, and homosexuality. These are not tidy stories with easy morals, but rather tales of real human beings with complex and on-going struggles. (Another excellent film, similar in aim, is titled *The Third Way*, and you can watch it free online at BlackstoneFilms.co/thethirdway.)

One final resource, which will be especially useful to you as a parent, is a document written in 1997 by the US Catholic Bishops titled "Always Our Children: A Pastoral Message to Parents of Homosexual Children and Suggestions for Pastoral Ministers." It's full of sensitive, pastoral advice borne from many conversations and experiences working with families in difficult situations. The message is not a treatise on homosexuality. It is not a systematic presentation of the Church's moral teaching. And it does not break any new ground theologically. Rather, it speaks words of faith, hope, and love to parents who need the Church's merciful presence at a time that may be one of the most challenging in their lives.

I want to emphasize that no website, video, or book will automatically remove your child's same-sex attractions, or that these attractions are simply problems to fix. What your child needs are companions who welcome him, whatever his attractions, into a warm circle of loving family and friends. Only after he experiences your love, and usually only after a personal encounter with Christ, will he be open to reordering his lifestyle.

"Why is the Church against me living with my boyfriend/girl-friend? We love each other, so what's the problem?"

Response: True love leads to a lifelong commitment in marriage, not a temporary partnership through cohabitation.

Patricia is quite sure that since all of her young adult children live with their significant others, unmarried, they feel rejected by the Church. "I know it's why they stay away from the Church and their faith," Patricia explains. "They know living together before marriage is wrong, they just don't want to acknowledge it. Not to themselves, not to parents, and especially not to any priest by going to confession. They resist getting married in the Church simply because of the hassle (read: embarrassment) of going through the process of reconciliation and having to go through the Pre-Cana marriage preparation program."

We addressed this objection in chapter 10, but only from the perspective of reconciling your child with the Church. We'll engage it a little more here and discuss the actual reasons why cohabitation is a bad idea.

Cohabitation involves a relationship between an unmarried couple who live together and remain sexually active. Today, roughly two-thirds of couples cohabitate before marrying, a 900% increase in cohabitation over the last fifty years. A scenario that would have been scandalous in 1950 is exceedingly common today and is mostly accepted: only one in four Americans disapprove of cohabiting before marriage.

Even beyond the moral question, this is a huge problem since it seems to be causing massive numbers of young people to stay away from the Church. A Pew study found that the sharpest growth of people unaffiliated with any religion are those "who are living with a partner, never married." In 2007, 26% of those who lived with a partner were unaffiliated. Just seven years later, that percentage climbed to 35%.

If your child is cohabiting, he will likely not be open *at first* to the Church's moral argument against sex before marriage. You can't just say, "Cohabitation is wrong because the Bible (or the Church) says so." Therefore, you need solid, nonreligious reasons why cohabitation is a bad idea.

The US Bishops seem to agree, writing in a document, "For cohabiting couples, a specific goal may be added: To encourage the couple to reflect on their situation and why they decided to cohabit and to provide insights into possible consequences, factors that may present special challenges to them or put them at risk for later marital disruption." In other words, you should show why cohabitation is actually *bad* for the future of their relationship.

Here are a few specific facts to share with your child. First, the large majority of couples who cohabitate break up within ten years and are at a much higher risk for divorce down the line, if they eventually decided to marry. Many couples see cohabitation as a "test run" for marriage, a way to make sure the relationship is stable and primed for the long run. But studies show that cohabitation itself damages that relationship. Why?

Because it's not grounded on the permanent commitment marriage provides. Little disagreements that would be dealt with and solved by a married couple suddenly become deal-breakers for a cohabiting couple who have made no vows to each other. Many young people today have felt the effects of our divorce culture and would do anything not to go through a divorce themselves. So you might ask a question such as this: "Son, I know you love your girlfriend and want the best for her. So why put her through an experience that significantly increases your risk for break up or divorce down the line, and thus increases the odds of hurting her?"

Second, one out of every five women who cohabitate become pregnant within the first twelve months of moving in. If you have a daughter, this statistic should be particularly alarming to her. The risk of single motherhood is much higher for cohabiting women than married women because there is no marital vow to ensure the father stays in the picture. Sure, in some cases, if the cohabiting woman becomes pregnant the father will man up and marry her. But in most cases, that doesn't happen. Bradford Wilcox, the director of the National Marriage Project at the University of Virginia, observes, "Cohabitation fosters enough intimacy to facilitate childbearing but not enough commitment to make people deliberate about their choices to become parents. The result, an unplanned birth, can pose real problems to their relationship and to their future odds of successfully marrying."

And third, it's much harder to end a cohabiting relationship than a dating relationship. This is why many young people slide into marriages, even when it's not the greatest fit, because they think moving out would be more stressful than just getting married. Meg Jay, a clinical psychologist, explains, "I have clients who say, 'I spent years of my 20s living with someone who I wouldn't have dated a year if we had not been living together.' Once you buy dishes, share a lease, have a routine, and get a dog, it can be difficult to cut your losses and accept that the relationship isn't working."

So, if your child is in a cohabiting relationship, and that's his or her main resistance to becoming Catholic, how should you respond? As we've seen over and over, the best strategy is to lead with questions, ones that allow your child to consider his motives and plans, maybe for the first time.

Some good questions include:

- Why did you originally choose to live together?
- How do you think your family and community feels about your living together?
- How do these feelings affect you?
- Do you expect to get married in the near future?
- What does marriage mean to you?
- What do you think will be the largest barriers to a lifelong marriage for you?
- Does living together now increase or reduce those barriers?

As mentioned before, cohabitation is clearly a moral problem. It typically involves a sexual relationship detached from the bond of marriage, which is a serious sin. But if you want to help your child gradually move through and beyond the situation, you need to first help him fall in love with Christ in his Church—that's what the whole game plan section was about—and *then* he'll be ready to pursue a new moral framework. If you lead with morality, trying to first end his cohabiting relationship, you'll make no headway and will likely do serious damage to your relationship. Trust that if God moves first in his life, and he becomes a committed disciple, that God will help deal with this problem and regularize his relationship, either through marriage or separation.

"I'll come back when the Church stops oppressing women."
Response: Even though women can't be priests,
they overwhelmingly lead the work of the Church.
The Church praises women's "feminine genius."

Courtney, a former Catholic, explained to me why she left the Church: "As a woman in the Catholic Church, I was treated as a second-class citizen. Women are not allowed to say Mass. One day, I walked out on a homily about women being created solely to support their husbands. This is absurd. I face enough of this in daily life as an intelligent and hard-working woman and choose not to face it in religious life."

Some people look at the Church's features, especially the male-only priesthood, and conclude that the Church must be anti-woman. How else would you describe an organization led exclusively by men who make sweeping decisions about woman-related issues such as contraception, abortion, and sexuality? Women can't be priests, women can't be bishops, and by outlawing contraception and abortion, the Church won't even let women make decisions about their own bodies. We'll handle the contraception and abortion objections in a moment, but for now let's tackle the general criticism that the Church suppresses women. If this is a stumbling block for your child, you might offer three thoughts for consideration.

First, why can't women be priests? Most people who champion "female ordination" do so with good intentions. They passionately support gender equality and value the unique gifts women can offer the Church. However, unfortunately many have a warped idea of the priesthood. They presume the priesthood is merely a functional profession, a task-based job that involves showing up for Mass, reading prayers from the missal, lifting up a piece of bread and wine, offering a good homily, and so on. That's part of the priestly role, but if that's *all* it means to be a priest—to perform pious tasks—then sure, women can perform them just as well (often better). But the Catholic priesthood is not just functional; it also has a symbolic dimension. When a man is ordained a priest, he is commissioned to act *in persona Christi* (in the person of Christ). He represents Christ to his people in the heavenly wedding banquet, which is the Mass. Through the liturgy, Christ offers himself as a husband to his bride, with the moment of communion as an act of spiritual consummation. But to effect that sort of symbolic union, the priest must be male, representing Christ not just in his words and actions, but in the essential masculinity of his body. This is why Jesus only chose male Apostles—not because he was a male chauvinist (Jesus never sinned) or because he bowed to the social conventions of his time (Jesus routinely broke the conventions)—but because the "male-ness" of priests matters.

As the leaders behind Catholic Voices explain, "Reserving the priesthood to men is not a judgment on women's abilities or rights, any more than celibacy is a judgment on marriage, or marriage a judgment on single people. The teaching reflects the specific role of the priest in the Catholic understanding, which is to represent Jesus, to stand in his place."

Second, if the Church suppresses women, nobody told that to the millions of women who fill her pews and fuel her ministries every day. Women lead most of our Catholic parishes, schools, hospitals, and social service agencies. A large number of women are professional lay ministers and theologians, and many teach in Catholic seminaries. Notre Dame theologian Catherine Lacugna paints the statistical picture: "85% of those responsible for altar preparation are women. Over 80% of the CCD (religious formation) teachers and sponsors of the catechumenate are women. Over 75% of adult Bible study leaders or participants are women. Over 70% of those who are active in parish renewal and spiritual growth are women, and over 80% of those who join prayer groups are women. Nearly 60% of those involved with youth groups and recreational activities are women." If nothing else, the Church is dominated by women. It's true that women can't serve as priests, but in every other respect, they overwhelmingly lead the work of the Church.

A third and powerful response to this objection is to simply point to Mary, the Mother of God. Nobody can look at the Blessed Virgin and see someone oppressed. God chose her to literally bear him in her womb, the highest honor ever bestowed on any human being. For the last two thousand years, no human outside of Christ has received more love and veneration than Mary. The book of Revelation depicts her being crowned Queen of Heaven (Rev. 12), where she will reign with her son forever and ever. Mary is the ultimate response to anyone who suggests the Church denigrates women.

Now, your child still may not be convinced after these considerations. That's okay. Sometimes this issue—loaded with political and social implications—touches a nerve. But if he's open, you might point him to other resources for further reflection. On the issue of female ordination, the two best resources are both essays, available free online. First is Peter Kreeft's article titled "Gender and the Will of God", and second is an essay by C.S. Lewis titled "Priestesses in the Church?" Both lay out the philosophical and theological reasons why the Church has always embraced a male-only priesthood. If your child is hung up on what he perceives as Catholic chauvinism in general, get him a copy of *Breaking Through: Catholic Women Speak for Themselves* (Our Sunday Visitor, 2012), which features essays by nine smart, eloquent Catholic women who share personal stories of how they struggled toward the realization that the demands of their faith actually set them free.

The Catholic Church is not about putting women down. It's about lifting them up and recognizing, in the words of St. John Paul II, their full "feminine genius."

"The Church is behind the times on contraception and abortion."
Response: Contraception and abortion are harmful to women and children. Thankfully, the Church offers better alternatives.

Contraception and abortion may be the two most controversial issues within the Church. In response to a Pew Forum survey about why they left the Catholic Church, nearly six in ten former Catholics who are now unaffiliated say they left Catholicism due to dissatisfaction with Catholic teachings on abortion. Around 50% cited concerns about the Church's teachings on birth control.

The statistics don't improve much when surveying Catholics. The large majority of sexually active Catholic women have used contraception at some point, despite the Church's teaching against it, while huge numbers disagree on abortion.

There's a good chance your child thinks the Church is wrong about both contraception and abortion. So how can you prevent either topic from remaining a roadblock to your child returning? The solution requires a two-pronged approach, one that first shows why contraception and abortion are harmful in themselves, and then a second that offers positive alternatives.

First, why are contraception and abortion bad in themselves? In 1968, Pope Paul VI issued *Humanae Vitae*, a document that reiterated the Church's rejection of contraception, released at a time when most of the culture was enthusiastically embracing it. Reflecting philosophically on the contraceptive mindset, he predicted that if contraception became popular, our culture would suffer many grave consequences, including higher rates of infidelity and divorce (since contraception lowers the risk of extramarital pregnancy), an increase in pre-marital sex (for the same reason), and a growing disrespect for women (since contraception allows men to treat women as objects of selfish enjoyment). No one can doubt the fulfillment of these prophetic words. Our culture has been decimated by rampant divorce, affairs, cohabitation, pornography, and sexual violence, all of which flow from the contraceptive mindset, which envisions sex as essentially about pleasure, totally disconnected from children. So the first strike against contraception is that it directly contradicts a culture of fidelity and selfless love.

Added to that are the harmful health effects. Dr. Marguerite Duane, a family physician and professor at Georgetown University, affirms, "The pill is the only drug that was developed to be given to a woman who was healthy to create a diseased state." The nonreligious World Health Organization has placed the birth control pill on its list of Group 1 carcinogens, the most toxic rating it can impose—the same rating as cigarettes. Depending on the study you look at it, women who take the pill are somewhere between 20–40% more likely to have breast cancer than women who don't and are far more likely to have cervical and skin cancer than other women. They're also twice as likely to have a fatal heart attack and three to eleven times more likely to develop blood clots. Therefore, the health dangers offer a second strike against contraception.

But if contraception is bad for relational and health reasons, are there any viable alternatives? What if your child doesn't want to have a million children?

Thankfully, there is a better alternative to contraception. A diverse and growing movement—composed of atheists, secular environmentalists, Catholics, Protestants, and more—have promoted Natural Family Planning (NFP) as a healthier solution for women. NFP is a blanket term covering several medically approved methods of fertility awareness, but they typically follow the same principle: using natural signs to determine when a woman is fertile, a couple then chooses to have sex during fertile or infertile times, depending on whether they need to achieve or avoid pregnancy. Even though NFP and artificial contraception may achieve the same result—not getting pregnant—they do so by two very different means. NFP does not impede the procreative dimension of sex; it merely avoids sex when the woman is fertile. Contraception, on the other hand, actively prevents conception. It severs the procreative and unitive dimensions of sex. When used properly, some NFP methods have been measured to be over 98% effective in avoiding unintended pregnancy—as good as any artificial contraceptive. But even more, because NFP encourages dialogue and mutual respect between a husband and wife, those who practice NFP have far lower divorce rates than couples using artificial contraception.

What about abortion? Many support abortion in the name of freedom, trumpeting the rights of women to govern their own bodies. Freedom is generally praiseworthy, and the Catholic Church is the strongest proponent of human rights in world history. But freedom is not absolute. We don't have the freedom to destroy another person's property, or to damage his body. Which brings us to the main problem with abortion: it involves not just one body but *two*, the mother's body and the unborn child's body. Modern science, including most embryology textbooks, affirms that a new human life, distinct from its father and mother, begins at the moment of fertilization, when a sperm fertilizes an egg. But if this is true, then abortion isn't just a surgical procedure that vacuums away a clump of cells. It's a violent act that terminates the life of an innocent, unborn human being, small though it may be. While a woman does indeed have a right to "govern her own body," she has no right to destroy the body of the small child growing within her.

That's the moral case against abortion. But as with contraception, a case can also be made from the awful health effects. The abortion procedure itself, even if performed by professionals, has a surprisingly high rate of injuring or even killing the mother. Researchers have also identified a pattern of psychological problems known as Post-Abortion Syndrome (PAS). Women suffering PAS experience higher rates of drug and alcohol abuse, personal relationship disorders, sexual dysfunction, repeated abortions, communications difficulties, and damaged self-esteem. Many attempt suicide. Psychologists note that even men can suffer debilitating effects after facilitating or supporting an abortion.

But what if a woman becomes pregnant while young, or in school, and feels her only option is to abort? Well, any alternative would be better than killing an unborn child. Two better options are to either keep the child or give it up for adoption. Catholic organizations lead the way in both areas, equipping young mothers with the resources they need if they choose to keep the child, or helping them to facilitate an adoption. A simple online search can help you find a Catholic pregnancy center in your area—almost every diocese has one.

With all that said, it's important to note that contraception and abortion aren't just moral issues—they are personal and heartfelt. If your child strongly pushes against the Church's position on one (or both) of these two issues, chances are they are personally using contraception, or they've personally suffered from the guilt and anguish of abortion. In either case, objections they raise may be shields to protect them from confronting and dealing with their own pain.

If you have a daughter who has experienced an abortion, you should encourage her to find out more about Project Rachel (HopeAfterAbortion.com), a post-abortion healing ministry of the Catholic Church. Project Rachel hosts weekend retreats called "Rachel's Vineyard," which are designed to help abortion sufferers release repressed feelings of anger, shame, and guilt, and to experience God's total forgiveness. Many women (and men) have been healed through experiences like these. If abortion is a personal stumbling block for your child, consider pressing "pause" on the rest of the game plan until your child has had time to begin sorting through and addressing the difficulties associated with having had an abortion.

From an intellectual perspective, the two best resources to give your child on contraception and abortion are Patrick Coffin's book *The Contraception Deception* (Emmaus Road, 2018) and Trent Horn's book *Persuasive Pro-Life: How to Talk About Our Culture's Toughest Issue* (Catholic Answers, 2014). Those two resources will help you and your child understand the logic behind the

Church's position, showing why it falls on the right side of reason, dignity, and human flourishing. The US Bishops also feature a helpful website, ForYourMarriage.org, that answers frequently asked questions about dating, marriage, and family life.

"I'm divorced. The Church doesn't want me."
Response: Divorced people are most certainly welcome in the Church. They are vital parts of the Body of Christ.

Divorce is a trial that is unfortunately all too common today. Roughly half of marriages today end in divorce (the numbers for Catholics are almost identical to mainstream numbers). Divorce is hard enough when it happens to you, but it can be just as devastating when one of your children goes through it. One mother verbalized the thoughts that many parents share: "The biggest thing for me was, how can we have a child who is getting a divorce? How could this happen in a Catholic family?"

One of the biggest myths today among those who have left the Church is that a person who gets divorced is automatically excommunicated or can no longer receive the sacraments. This is simply untrue, and it's heartbreaking to hear stories of people staying away from Mass for decades because they thought they were somehow banned. "I was told that my divorce prevented me from being a Catholic," one man explained. "The best thing I ever did was go and talk to a priest who told me there was no reason that I couldn't come home."

The Church bases her teachings on the words of Jesus Christ, who clearly taught that marriage is a lifelong union between man and woman, which no one should break apart (Matt. 19:6). Marriage is permanent, ending only with the death of either spouse, which is why the Church does not recognize "second marriages" while both spouses are still alive. Even if a couple contracts a civil divorce, they are, in the eyes of the Church, still married. This may be surprising, but the Church believes that not even the government can sever what God has joined together. Therefore, so long as a divorced person has not attempted to remarry or enter into a sexual relationship with someone other than his spouse, that person remains a Catholic in good standing. He can receive Communion, go to confession, participate in the parish, and do everything that other Catholics can do. In fact, many divorced Catholics feel called to take on leadership roles in ministries that help other people who are going through divorces of their own.

In an earlier chapter on closing the loop, we learned about the Church's annulment process, which is commonly misinterpreted as "Catholic divorce." But unlike divorce, an annulment doesn't end a valid marriage; it affirms that a valid marriage never occurred. In that case, both the man and the women are free to marry someone else in what will essentially be their "first" (and only) valid marriage.

However, suppose your child has already been civilly divorced and remarried *without* an annulment, meaning their "second" marriage is not valid in the eyes of the Church. What then? Well, first, and most difficultly, it means that your child is indeed living in a serious state of sin. His culpability may be lessened if he doesn't quite grasp the significance of his decision, but it is nevertheless problematic. Few in our culture bat an eye when someone enters a second, third, or even fourth marriage. But the entire Christian tradition has unequivocally taught that this is a serious sin.

But with that difficult reality in mind, here's what is often not said: divorced and remarried people are most certainly still welcome in the Church. They cannot receive the Eucharist while living in a state of grave sin, but they are still invited to attend Mass. They can still go to confession, work with a spiritual director, and participate in the life of the parish. They will likely not be allowed to take a leadership position in the parish, but they will not be shunned or rejected. Like any other sinner, they are wayfarers on the journey to God, voyaging to a state of perfection they have not yet attained. We shouldn't endorse their second marriage as valid, but we shouldn't sever their connection to the faith either.

It's also important to note that many who have civilly divorced and remarried without an annulment have later been able to go through the annulment process and "convalidate" their marriage, making it a real sacramental marriage in the eyes of the Church. This isn't the case with every couple. It's possible your child's second marriage cannot be convalidated, and thus the only way forward is for him to separate from his partner, or to make the heroic decision to live a celibate marriage, as brother and sister. But this is why each case should be brought to a local priest as soon as possible. If your child is divorced and remarried, delicately suggest that he explore this process, and remind them that the Church doesn't condemn them forever, but wants to welcome them with mercy.

One recommended book on this issue is *Divorced. Catholic. Now What?* (Journey of Hope, 2007) by Lisa Duffy and Vince Frese. The two authors are both divorced but faithful Catholics, and they offer ways of navigating all the trials and tribulations of divorce while remaining true to the faith. The result is a clear, inspiring, and motivational resource.

CHAPTER 14
Theological Objections

We finally come to the last set of common objections. Unlike the personal objections, which primarily stem from emotions and lifestyles, or the moral objections that concern the "dos and don'ts" of Catholicism, theological objections focus on questions surrounding God, faith, worship, evil, and the Bible. As with the past two chapters, you'll find a simple response to each objection followed by a lengthier explanation and at least one book recommendation.

"There is simply no evidence for God."
Response: There is plenty of evidence for God,
including, strongest of all, the universe itself.

The great atheist philosopher Bertrand Russell was asked what he would say if he found himself standing before God on judgment day, and God asked him, "Why didn't you believe in me?" Russell replied, "I would say, 'Not enough evidence, God! Not enough evidence!'"

If your child no longer believes in God, especially if he's aligned himself with the so-called New Atheist movement, he might say the same thing: "There is no more evidence for God than there is for Santa or the Easter Bunny."

How should you respond? An important first step is to separate *subjective* reasons for believing in God from *objective* reasons. Perhaps you've sensed God's presence in prayer or at Mass. Maybe you've witnessed a miracle or two. Or perhaps God's existence is just something you've always intuited, something you've known unwaveringly to be true. Those are all good reasons for *you* to believe in God, but they won't mean much to your child. They are *subjective* and unique to you. Your child has no way of verifying whether they're true.

If your child raises the "no evidence" claim, he is looking for *objective* evidence for God, evidence not dependent on personal experience or emotion.

Your first reply, following advice offered in an earlier chapter, should be to inquire what he means by "evidence." If by that he means empirical or physical evidence, then he's asking for something that is illogical. Why? Because God is, by definition, immaterial. Therefore, we wouldn't expect to find *direct* empirical evidence for an invisible God. That would be like asking for evidence of a bachelor's wife. A bachelor, by definition, doesn't have a wife.

That said, we can find *indirect* empirical evidence for God. Many thinkers from Aristotle, to St. Paul, to St. Thomas Aquinas have seen the universe itself as evidence for God. Since the universe does not have to exist, we're forced to ask, *Why did it come into existence?* It didn't have to exist, but it does. And it can't explain its own existence since nothing causes itself to exist. It must have needed some reason for its existence beyond all space, time, energy, and matter, something spaceless, timeless, immaterial, and extraordinarily powerful—and that something is what most people call God. (This is a very abbreviated summary of one version of the "cosmological argument" for God.)

Perhaps by "evidence," though, your child does not mean empirical evidence but simply "good reasons to support a belief." In that case your job is much easier. There are plenty of good reasons to believe in God, ranging from philosophical proofs, to historical events (such as Jesus' Resurrection), to the presence of beauty and reason. In fact, philosophers who specialize in this field, often called the "philosophy of religion" or "natural theology," have identified dozens of reasons and arguments. (Many of these are detailed at StrangeNotions.com.)

None of these arguments is *compelling* in the sense of forcing your child to believe in God if he strongly wills otherwise. The French mathematician Blaise Pascal said God provides enough light for those who want to see, and enough darkness to hide in the shadows. But there is enough evidence for God if people are genuinely open to the evidence.

Whether or not that's true of your child, the best book on this subject is Trent Horn's *Answering Atheism: How to Make the Case for God with Logic and*

Charity (Catholic Answers, 2013). You might also point your child to an on-line article by Peter Kreeft titled "20 Arguments for God's Existence" (find it at StrangeNotions.com), or if he's a bit more sophisticated or scientifically inclined, give him a copy of Fr. Robert Spitzer's impressive book *New Proofs for the Existence of God: Contributions of Contemporary Physics and Philosophy* (Eerdmans, 2010).

"Faith and science are at odds, and I choose science."

Response: Faith and science are mutually supportive and do not conflict. Some of the most famous scientific pioneers were Catholic.

A recent Pew survey found that one-third of former Catholics agree that "science proves religion to be superstition." Similarly, around a quarter of young adults believe that "Christianity is anti-science."

These views have gained traction thanks to a surge of new books by vocal atheist scientists, such as Richard Dawkins, Daniel Dennett, Lawrence Krauss, and Stephen Hawking.

When responding to this charge, I find it helpful to push back gently with some questions. The first one to ask is, "How *specifically* are faith and science at odds?" In my experience, nine times out of ten, you'll hear something about either evolution or Galileo.

While evolution may be troubling to fundamentalist Protestants, it doesn't pose a problem for Catholics. The Catholic Church has declared that Catholics are free to either accept or reject evolutionary theory, within certain limits. For example, we cannot believe that *souls* have evolved into being. Souls are immaterial, so they can only be directly created by God. But since evolution only concerns the natural, material world, there isn't any conflict in believing that evolution played some role in the formation of the human body. So, with evolution, Catholics are free to follow the evidence where it leads. Evolution isn't a problem for Catholicism, and it doesn't conflict with faith.

The Galileo case is a bit more complicated. While it's true Galileo was placed under a mild form of house arrest (in a palace, with a servant), he was not imprisoned or tortured. And his punishment came not because the Church disagreed with his science but because he mocked the pope, betrayed his friendship, and demanded the Church change its theology in light of his scientific theories, which were yet unproven. In the end, both sides were to blame, Galileo for his belligerence and Church leaders for their overreaction. Years later, under the leadership of Pope St. John Paul II, the Catholic Church formally apologized for any injustices done to Galileo, calling the affair a "sad misunderstanding" and praising the otherwise brilliant work of the scientist. If your child uses the Galileo affair as an argument against the Church, it's important to note that the affair was one passage on one page of a much longer story of faith and science.

A second question to ask in response to this objection is, "Which scientist or experiment or discovery has disproved Catholicism?" This is somewhat of a trick question, because in reality there *isn't* (and can't be) a specific scientist, experiment, or discovery that has disproved faith, at least the Catholic faith. When your child is unable to come up with a specific answer, he may reexamine his assumption that faith and science are at odds.

After asking these questions and starting a back-and-forth with your child, you might also share four key points.

The first point is that science can't settle the God question. By its nature, science only concerns the natural, material world. But since God is, by definition, immaterial—meaning he has no body or physical properties—he is beyond the reach of science. It's not just that science hasn't *yet* discovered or disproved God. Science is incapable of *ever* doing so. As we saw in the previous section, science can produce evidence that indirectly points to God, such as the existence of a contingent universe or the incredible fine-tuning of the universe for life, but it can never directly answer the God question itself.

A second point is that we need other tools besides science to answer religious questions. Science has been unquestionably successful in fields like medicine and technology, which tempts us to think that science is the key to unlocking *all* of our questions and problems. But science has methodological limitations. As Trent Horn says, "The torch of science can't illuminate the answer to every question we have about the world." Some questions can only be answered through philosophical reflection or with the help of divine revelation, such as the Bible and Church Tradition. These questions include moral questions (is this behavior good?), questions concerning meaning and purpose (why am I here?), and questions concerning God and his nature (does he exist, and if so, what is he like?). Science can probe questions that fall within its jurisdiction, but outside it we need other tools such as philosophy and faith.

A third point, which may surprise your child, is that many scientists believe in God. Recent surveys show that roughly half of working scientists are theists, meaning they believe in a personal God, and only about 20% are atheist (the rest are unsure). This confirms that being a scientist doesn't require being an atheist. Historically, many of the greatest scientists have not only believed in God but have been committed Catholics. For example:

- **Roger Bacon (1214–1294)**—Credited with discovering the "scientific method," also a Franciscan friar
- **Nicolaus Copernicus (1473–1543)**—Developed the heliocentric theory of the universe and was a Catholic cleric
- **Nicolas Steno (1638–1686)**—A pioneer in anatomy and geology and a Danish bishop
- **Gregor Mendel (1822–1884)**—The founder of the modern science of genetics and an Augustinian monk
- **Father Georges Lemaître (1894–1966)**—The father of the "Big Bang theory" and a Catholic priest

If science and faith are really at odds, nobody told these heroes of scientific discovery.

A fourth and final point is that modern science supports belief in God. Instead of challenging Christianity, many recent scientific discoveries have provided a surge of support for the Christian worldview, especially in the field of cosmology. According to physicist and philosopher Fr. Robert Spitzer, "There is more evidence from physics for a beginning of the universe than ever before." A beginning to the universe supports the biblical account of creation rather than the common atheist view that the universe was uncreated and infinite, existing forever in the past. If the universe had a beginning, a point before which there was no time or space, then something timeless and immaterial must have caused it to come into existence from nothing. This sounds like what Christians call God. So rather than disproving God, or conflicting with faith, modern science provides strong corroboration.

With all of these facts in mind, the *Catechism of the Catholic Church* sums up the relationship between religion and science, or faith and reason, like so: "Though faith is above reason, there can never be any real discrepancy between faith and reason. Since the same God who reveals mysteries and infuses faith has bestowed the light of reason on the human mind, God cannot deny himself, nor can truth ever contradict truth."

For more on the faith-science relationship, read Trent Horn's short but enlightening booklet *20 Answers: Faith and Science* (Catholic Answers, 2015).

"I never found a personal relationship with Jesus in the Catholic Church."

Response: The Church exists to help people encounter Jesus Christ.

Jessica could barely contain her enthusiasm. She recently accompanied a friend to a local Evangelical megachurch, and it was unlike anything she experienced growing up as a Catholic. The pastor, who was young, hip, and energetic, preached a passionate sermon on the importance of intimately knowing Jesus. He spoke on Jesus' parable of the ten virgins in Matthew 25, who were preparing for a wedding. Five of the virgins were foolish, and five were wise. The wise virgins carried plenty of oil in their lamps and were well-prepared. The foolish versions, though, had no oil. When the bridegroom finally arrived, the foolish virgins ran out of oil. They begged the wise virgins to share their oil, but they refused, saying, "No, for there may not be enough for us and you. Go instead to the merchants and buy some for yourselves." The pastor explained that the oil represented intimacy with Christ. We can't borrow or buy that intimacy from someone else; we need it ourselves. We need a personal relationship with Jesus that will prepare us for the heavenly wedding feast. We can only enjoy God's banquet if we have a personal relationship with him now.

After the service, Jessica talked with her friend about the sermon. "That was amazing," she said. "I never understood God in that way. I guess I always thought of him as distant and unapproachable. How do you have a personal relationship with him?" Her friend replied, "Well, come to our Thirst group this Wednesday and you'll see." Jessica attended Thirst, the megachurch's small-group Bible study, and from that moment on, her faith life bloomed. She began reading the Gospels and praying every day. She continued attending the megachurch, and her soul soared during worship. After a couple months, she felt closer to Jesus than ever before in her life. She loved him, trusted him, and hungered to know him more.

A couple months later, she passed by her old childhood parish. Remembering all of the memories growing up there, she was forced to wonder: "Why didn't my parish teach me about this personal relationship with God? How come I never picked that up during all my years of Mass, religious education, and Catholic schools?"

Jessica isn't alone. This experience is shared by many young people who leave the Catholic Church, especially for Protestant communities. Pope St. John Paul II affirmed, "Sometimes even Catholics have lost or never had the chance to experience Christ personally: not Christ as a mere 'paradigm' or 'value,' but as the living Lord, the way, the truth, and the life."

They move through our institutions and receive the sacraments, yet they are never told about the importance of developing a personal faith life or shown how to do so. A recent Pew survey found that only 60% of Catholic adults even believe in a personal God. If hardly a majority believes it is possible to personally know God, is it any surprise so few have accomplished it?

Yet despite our general failure to help Catholics encounter God in a real and personal way, that deficiency runs counter to the Church's own mission. Everything the Church teaches and offers revolves around Jesus. Why do we go to Mass? To meet Jesus in the Eucharist. Why do we venerate Mary? Because she's the mother of Jesus. Why do we believe marriage is a lifelong, sacramental union? Because it symbolizes Christ's union with the Church. Why do Catholics confess their sins to God through a priest? Because Jesus commissioned priests to channel his forgiveness. Everything in the Catholic Church comes back to Christ; everything exists to help you know and love him more.

Now, it's likely your child hasn't yet discovered this—if they did, they probably wouldn't have left! It's likely your child doesn't know that all seven sacraments offer direct encounters with Christ. In an article titled "How I Led Catholics Out of the Church," Catholic convert Steve Wood says, "In my experience as a Protestant, all the Catholics who had a conversion in a Protestant setting lacked a firm grasp of their Catholic faith. In twenty years of Protestant ministry, I never met a Catholic who knew that John 3:3–8 describes the sacrament of Baptism. It wasn't hard to convince them to disregard the sacraments along with the Church that emphasized the sacraments."

In other words, if your child was never taught or shown how the sacraments fuel a personal relationship with Jesus Christ, we shouldn't be surprised when they look for that relationship elsewhere. But in my experience, I've found that once former Catholics are finally *shown* how the sacraments offer a special encounter with God, deeper and more personal than anything they'll find elsewhere, they become open to returning.

In the meantime, don't react as though your child is "lost" or has somehow betrayed you if they join a non-Catholic church community. Instead, be happy that your child has faith and has encountered Jesus personally, while still trying to lead him to the fullness of faith found in the Catholic Church. When the time is right, you might say something like, "I'm so sorry you never encountered Jesus personally in the Catholic Church. That's precisely why the Church exists! Let me tell you how *I've* encountered God in the sacraments . . ."

Some books that will help you in this regard are *Discover Christ: Developing a Personal Relationship with Jesus* (Our Sunday Visitor, 2011) by Catholic writers Bert Ghezzi and David Nodar. This book shows the "why" and "how" of building such a relationship within Catholicism. Other helpful books include Peter Kreeft's *Jesus Shock* (Beacon Publishing, 2012), Matthew Kelly's *Rediscover Jesus* (Beacon Publishing, 2015), and Sherry Weddell's

Forming Intentional Disciples (Our Sunday Visitor, 2012). Each resource shows how the Catholic Church offers an intimate relationship with Christ.

"Catholics don't value the Bible."
Response: Catholicism is a Bible-based faith that reveres Scripture as the Word of God.

This objection is common for people who have left the Catholic Church for a Protestant community, often either Baptist or Evangelical. The objection may take other forms such as "Catholics don't read the Bible" or "Catholicism is unbiblical" or "They don't have Bibles in their pews." Your child may even accuse the Church of chaining down Bibles in past centuries so people couldn't study them or, even worse, burning copies of the Bible.

Of course, all of these are misunderstandings or myths. The Catholic Church reveres the Bible. It was the Church who compiled, safeguarded, and delivered the Scriptures down through the ages. Without the Catholic Church, there would be no Bible for Protestants to use!

Henry Graham wrote an excellent book debunking many of these rumors titled *Where We Got the Bible: Our Debt to the Catholic Church*. Graham himself was Protestant until he was swayed by the historical facts supporting the Catholic Church. In his book, he debunks several myths such as the "Bible-chaining" claim. The Catholic Church indeed chained Bibles to churches and libraries, but it wasn't to keep people from reading it—it was to allow *more* people to read it! In the centuries before the printing press, Bibles were rare and precious. To prevent people from stealing or damaging them, the Church chained them down in secure locations, much as we do today with phone books, chained in booths. The chaining was a safeguard, not a prohibition.

Graham also deals with the "burning" myth. Again, this one is technically true. The Church indeed burned many copies of the Bible, but its reasons were just. After the fourteenth century when English became a mainstream language, dissident priest John Wycliffe translated the Bible into English. However, as a Protestant reformer, he also tacked on a heretical prologue to his translation, denouncing many Catholic doctrines. Later Protestant translations by men such as William Tyndale contained dubious renderings that gave certain passages a more Protestant spin along with anti-Catholic footnotes. The Catholic Church condemned these translations, but even the Anglican King Henry VIII said, "The translation of the Scripture corrupted by William Tyndale should be utterly expelled, rejected, and put away out of the hands of the people, and not be suffered to go abroad."

To protect the Catholic flock from confusion and heresy, the Church burned these faulty translations. Does this make the Catholic Church anti-Bible? No. Its strong appreciation for the Bible is why it went to great lengths to make sure it was translated accurately. (It's also worth noting that the Protestant founders could be liable to a similar charge. During the time of the Reformation, it was common to burn unapproved books. John Calvin, for instance, the leading Protestant Reformer after Martin Luther, had several copies of the Servetus Bible burned since he did not approve of its translation. Later, Calvin had Michael Servetus himself burned at the stake for professing a different theology. So the burning of Bibles was not unique to the Catholic Church, nor was it a sign of disregarding the Scriptures.)

Suppose that when your child makes this criticism, however, he doesn't have chaining or burnings in mind. He simply thinks that today, in real-world cities and churches, Catholics just don't pay much attention to the Bible. There are two ways to respond.

First, refer to the liturgy. More Scripture is heard during a single Mass than in almost any Protestant service. Catholics hear three substantive readings during every liturgy for Sundays and major feast days: one from the Old Testament, one from New Testament letters or writings, and one from the Gospels. (Weekday Masses have one reading from the Old Testament or New Testament, and one from the Gospels.) The second half of Mass, the Liturgy of the Eucharist, uses words taken from, and based on, Scripture. This means it's not unusual for Catholics to hear hundreds of words from Scripture at each Mass.

The Catholic lectionary, which lists the Bible passages read at Mass, follows a three-year cycle of readings for Sundays and a two-year cycle for weekdays. A Catholic who goes to church faithfully will, over three years, hear a large portion of the Bible read. On the other hand, the typical Protestant community usually reads only a very small passage of Scripture during the service, and almost always from the New Testament. It's not uncommon for Protestant pastors to preach exclusively on passages they prefer or feel more comfortable with. So Catholics generally receive *more* Scripture and hear from a greater *range* of the Bible.

A second response to this objection concerns the Church's official teaching on the Bible. The Catholic Church encourages its faithful to read, study, and learn the Scriptures. *Dei Verbum*, a document from the Second Vatican Council, says that "all the clergy must hold fast to the Sacred Scriptures through diligent sacred reading and careful study. . . . The sacred synod also earnestly and especially urges all the Christian faithful . . . to learn by frequent reading of the divine Scriptures the 'excellent knowledge of Jesus Christ' (Phil. 3:8). 'For ignorance of the Scriptures is ignorance of Christ' [St. Jerome, Commentary on Isaiah]."

If the Church's relationship to the Bible presents a stumbling block for your child, you might point them to the work of respected Catholic biblical scholars such as Pope Benedict XVI, Scott Hahn, Brant Pitre, John Bergsma, or Michael Barber. Or you can lead them to great Catholic Scripture experts of the past such as St. Augustine or St. Jerome.

In terms of books, you might want to get your child a good Catholic study Bible. I highly recommend *The Word on Fire Bible* series. Another great option is the *Ignatius Study New Testament*, which offers notes and commentary from many saints and scholars. Other helpful books include Patrick Madrid's *Where Is That in the Bible?* (Our Sunday Visitor, 2001), Scott Hahn's *Signs of Life: 40 Catholic Customs and Their Biblical Roots* (Image Books, 2009), George Martin's *Reading God's Word Today* (Our Sunday Visitor, 2009), and Fr. Peter Stravinskas' *The Catholic Church and the Bible* (Ignatius Press, 1996). And, as previously mentioned, there's Henry Graham's *Where We Got the Bible*: *Our Debt to the Catholic Church*, which can be found free online.

"I just wasn't being fed in my parish. I've found another church that is more vibrant and fulfilling."

Response: Nothing can replace the Eucharist, which offers a direct encounter with God that no song, sermon, or experience can match.

When former Catholics who join a Protestant denomination are asked why they made the transition, fully eight in ten (81%) cite enjoyment of the religious service and the style of worship as a main reason. Many of these people reflect back and say, "I just never got anything out of Catholic Mass."

One serious but perhaps snarky response is, "Well, what did you expect to get?" If the answer is "warm feelings" or "peace and comfort" or "positive experiences," these are all things you can just as easily find in a movie theater or a concert. You don't need religion for that, much less the Mass. Usually, people who expect to "get something" out of Mass don't know what the Mass is *for*.

Jesus didn't establish the Mass to give us good feelings, though those may come. He created the Mass to give us *himself*, and to allow us to participate in his sacrifice to God the Father. The Eucharist is the source and summit of the Catholic faith because it *is* Jesus, Body and Blood, Soul and Divinity. Powerful music, relevant homilies, reverent liturgies, and warm hospitality all amplify the experience of communion with God. But they're secondary, not primary, to encountering Jesus in the Eucharist; they're the icing, not the cake.

Your child may have found another Christian community with better music. He may have found a megachurch preacher who delivers better messages than old Fr. Joe, who seems to ramble on with vague aphorisms and bad jokes. He may have found a community with several dynamic small groups, an active youth ministry, and plenty of outreach ministries. But none of this can replace receiving Jesus in the Eucharist.

This is why the best response to the "I wasn't being fed" objection is threefold. First, you need to convince your child that Jesus is uniquely present in the Eucharist and that no music, preaching, or activity can replace this. We've covered this in our responses to some of the other objections.

Second, you need to help your child find a parish or ministry that actually *does* fulfill his need for warm feelings, peace and comfort, and positive experiences. If your child is bored by the preaching in your local parish, is there another nearby parish with better homilies? If he doesn't like the music, is there another Mass at your parish, or a nearby one, with more appealing music? If he can't find a small study group that he likes, can you plug him into another parish or help him find community online? You might think it's enough to convince him that the Eucharist is irreplaceable, but usually that's just one part of the puzzle. You also need to respond to his spiritual hunger, which at least right now he doesn't think can be satisfied in the Catholic Church.

One helpful book in this regard is actually a biblical book—the Gospel of John. Invite your child to slowly read through John 6 with you and reflect on its meaning. In this chapter, Jesus clearly defines what "being fed" spiritually means: eating Christ's Body and drinking his Blood. Some may see those statements as mere metaphor, but Jesus reiterates the claim and even ratchets up his language throughout the chapter, refusing to identify it as metaphorical even when many of his disciples leave over his statements. The sixth chapter of John affirms that the true Bread of Life is found only in the Eucharist, not in vibrant lights, music, or experiences. That's how we're fed.

"How could God possibly have let that evil thing happen to me?"
Response: Although pain and suffering are often difficult to understand, God doesn't abandon us—he suffers with us.

Susan keenly remembers when she lost her faith in God. "It was the death of my great-grandfather. I had prayed so hard for so long that God would heal him and restore him to my family. When he finally died, I felt like God had ignored my cries to him and that was when I decided that I couldn't have anything to do with a God that would allow that kind of pain in my heart."

It's not uncommon for people to drift away from the Church after witnessing or experiencing deep suffering. Watching a relative slowly die of cancer, losing a child during pregnancy, seeing addiction wreck a friend's life—events like these compel us to wonder why God doesn't step in. If God is all-loving and all-powerful, surely he would fix these problems, and since he doesn't appear to help, we can only assume he's either not all-loving or not all-powerful—or that he just doesn't exist.

This conundrum, traditionally called the "problem of evil," is an ancient difficulty, one that people have wrestled with for centuries. St. Thomas Aquinas, the thirteenth-century philosopher and theologian whom many consider the brightest mind in Church history, identified the "problem of evil" as one of only two formidable arguments against God's existence.

So it's a real problem, not something to gloss over. If your child has experienced deep suffering that has caused him to stay away from the Church, how should you respond? How should you answer his desperate plea to know why God allowed the suffering to occur?

The first and honest reply should be, "We don't know." We're not in a position to know God's reasons for permitting certain acts of suffering. God, by definition, transcends space and time, which means only he is in the privileged position to see the long-term effects of every action on earth. With that knowledge, he permits certain acts, even evil acts, and he is able to bring about greater goods from them.

Most of us have seen this dynamic play out on a smaller scale in our own lives. For example, when I bring my young children to the dentist, they look at me with terror as the dentist scrapes his metal tools over their teeth. I know they're thinking, "Ow! Dad! How could you let him do this to me?" They're too young to understand that I permit the dentist to cause this temporary pain because the long-term effects—healthy teeth and gums—are undoubtedly worth it. I permit incomprehensible suffering in that case to bring about a greater good. The analogy isn't perfect since I *cause* my children to go to the dentist while God never *causes* suffering—he only permits it. But the example shows how someone can be incapable of fully understanding why he is permitted to suffer, even if extraordinary goods may result.

But even with that logical explanation, the "problem of evil" is still difficult to swallow. It doesn't solve the emotional turmoil most people feel after experiencing serious pain. The more fulfilling answer, and the ultimate response for Catholics, is Christ crucified. On the cross we see God, in the flesh, not offering a trite answer to the mystery of suffering but instead choosing to embrace our humanity and *suffer with us*. He experienced the worst evil that the world could throw at him—betrayal, mockery, intense pain, torture, and execution. And he took it all upon himself for our sake.

So, if your child is suffering, you can affirm that God knows his suffering firsthand. He's not a distant force, watching your child suffer from beyond the clouds. He shares our hurt and disappointment and has already begun bringing good out of it.

Peter Kreeft has a remarkably helpful book on this topic titled *Making Sense Out of Suffering* (Servant Books, 1986). Or, for a headier response, you might point your child to C.S. Lewis' classic *The Problem of Pain* (HarperOne, [1940] 2015).

CONCLUSION
One Step Forward

We've all been there. You have a pivotal moment of inspiration and decide it's time to make a serious change in your life. Maybe you want to lose fifteen pounds, pay off some debt, or heal a particular relationship. You start planning and scheming. You research the best ways to accomplish it. You set specific goals with firm deadlines. You feel that rush that comes with believing your life is about to change for the better.

And then you hit a wall.

Some small, unexpected disturbance throws you off course, and before you know it your fiery ambition is extinguished. You eat a whole pizza and feel horrible. You receive a large and unexpected bill in the mail. A family member or friend takes yet another potshot at you, and you return fire.

You're not just back to square one. You feel even worse than when you decided to turn over that new leaf because now you're not just overweight, in debt, or mishandling your relationship with a difficult person; now you realize you tried to fix the problem and came up short. On top of everything, you feel like a failure.

Does that roller coaster sound familiar?

We've all ridden it. We know what it's like to rise, and we know what it's like to fall.

But we realize through experience that the key is *never* to give up (or, to continue the roller coaster analogy, not to throw up).

Drawing your child back to the Church will be a bumpy ride, full of twists and turns. I can promise you that. And as we've learned throughout this book, there's no quick and easy way to bring him home.

You have to buckle up and commit to the long, bumpy ride.

The good news is that you now have all the tips, tools, and strategies you need—a complete game plan. But chances are, if you're like most people, there's still a small, quiet voice holding you back, telling you, "Ah, this will probably never work."

For many parents, the voice suggests, "My child is just too far away. It's too big of a shift for them to come back." Indeed, focusing on the whole goal at once will almost certainly leave you paralyzed with inaction. Climbers standing at the base of Mount Everest don't think about the whole awe-inspiring challenge they must conquer. It takes six to nine weeks to go up and down the mountain! Instead, they simply focus on that day's journey. "All I have to do is just complete today's climb. That's it. I'll deal with tomorrow's challenge tomorrow."

Look at your mission with your child the same way. Just focus on the next step. Take the small, slow view. With each prayer, each "seed gift," each conversation, each invitation, your goal is simply to help your child take one step closer to God and back to the Church. That's it—just one step at a time. He doesn't have to come all the way back after one dialogue. He doesn't have to return to Mass, confession, and regular prayer within the next week. All he needs is to take one step closer to Jesus Christ in his Church.

To put it another way, just focus on helping your child become 1% closer to God each day than the day before. Don't try to move him 100% in a day—be thrilled with 1%. Over time, that 1% will build and compound, and you'll be surprised at how far he's come. The other benefit of this mindset is that the small, 1% successes you experience will feed on each other and start building momentum, which will encourage you to move forward with even more energy.

Of course, you'll encounter setbacks. Some days your child may move 1% *away* from God—or more! That's okay. Like the Everest climbers, forget about yesterday and concentrate on today. Get back on track and shoot for 1% in the right direction.

Another common resistance you'll likely experience is inner despair. You've discovered all of these strategies, and maybe you've even imagined yourself using them with your child. But then something snatches away the daydream. "I don't know," you think. "This sounds promising, but it probably won't work for me. I just can't see my child returning."

Don't think like that. Don't give into feelings of doubt and hopelessness. Those were your old feelings, the ones you had *before* starting this book, but they're in the past. You're starting a new path today, one rooted in hope—not hope in your *own* abilities, but in God's power. If your child's reversion was only up to you, there might be good cause for doubt. But God, the all-powerful Creator of the cosmos, is already moving in your child's life, and the Holy Spirit is already preparing the way. Trust that with God, nothing is impossible (see Luke 1:37). Even if you can't see the path of your child's return, God can, and he's eagerly awaiting the moment when he can rush toward your child and embrace him.

You now have everything you need. You have the tips, you have the tools, and you have the game plan.

The next step is to take action. Start at the beginning of the game plan, which begins with prayer and sacrifice. That's the bedrock you need to ensure the later steps are successful. Right now, after you finish these final pages, don't just close the book, set it aside, and move on with your day. Instead, close your eyes and pray for your child. Commit, right now, to offering some small sacrifice today for your child's return to the faith. Then do it again tomorrow—pray and sacrifice.

After laying that foundation, begin planting seeds, and when the time is right, open a dialogue. Then another dialogue, and another. Keep it moving.

But unless you do something with this newfound knowledge, it's mostly worthless. You need to decide to act. You need to take that first step.

So fight the urge to procrastinate. Don't make excuses and say, "I'll get to this tomorrow or someday." There may not be a someday. Your child's eternal future hangs in the balance right now, so don't wave the white flag of complacency.

Be the parent who moves and acts and activates your child's return.

One mother I know described her fallen-away son to me as an "Augustine-in-training." I love that. Remember Augustine, the wild young man who rejected his mother's faith? The one who partied all night, took a mistress, and had a child out of wedlock? That same prodigal eventually became *Saint* Augustine, the holy hero who helped shape the Church and changed the world.

Imagine your child as the next "Augustine-in-training." No matter how far he's spiraled away, don't lose sight of the fact that God yearns for your child to become a great saint.

For that to happen, your child doesn't need an earth-shattering experience or conversation that transforms him overnight. Like the prodigal son, he just needs to take that first, small step back toward his Father's home.

And he doesn't have to complete that journey in a single day. He just needs—day by day, and step by step—to continue drawing closer to the God who loves him even more than you do.

Make that your prayer today. Ask God to move in your child's life, to prepare his heart, and to give him the grace he needs. If you ask, God will give it to you. He promised, "Ask and it will be given to you; seek and you will find; knock and the door will be opened to you" (Matt. 7:7).

So pray, ask, and be confident. God deeply loves your child and he desperately wants the same thing you do: to help him return.

"For thus says the Lord GOD:

Look! I myself will search for
my sheep and examine them. . . .

I will deliver them from every place where they
were scattered on the day of dark clouds.

I will lead them out from among the
peoples and gather them from the lands;

I will bring them back to their
own country and pasture them. . . .

I myself will pasture my sheep;

I myself will give them rest. . . .

The lost I will search out,
the strays I will bring back,

the injured I will bind up,
and the sick I will heal. . . .

I will shepherd them."

—EZEKIEL 34:11–16

ACKNOWLEDGMENTS

So many family members, friends, and mentors contributed to this book. It definitely wasn't a solo effort.

My first thanks go to Bishop Robert Barron and Fr. Steve Grunow, my two spiritual fathers. You've taught me more about the priority of Christ and the urgency of evangelization than anyone else. You're my heroes.

Thanks also to the brilliant, innovative team at Word on Fire. You are more than coworkers and more than friends; you're family. It's such a privilege to herald the Gospel with you. This book is borne of our work together. I'm particularly grateful to Matt Becklo and Dan Seseske for masterfully editing and improving this book, Cassie Pease for her spectacular cover, and Peggy Pandaleon for writing two helpful companion guides.

Much gratitude to Bert Ghezzi, my editor and dear brother. You deserve credit for every clear sentence in this book. Also, if it wasn't for you, the passive voice would have been used a lot more often.

Special thanks to Stephen Bullivant, Marcel LeJeune, Leah Libresco, Matt Nelson, and Josh Simmons for reading early versions of the book and offering valuable feedback. This book is far better because of your input.

I want to thank the hundreds of people who discussed this topic with me over the last few years—parents, young people, those who left, and those who have returned. You made this book more than a collection of dry stats and advice. Your stories added color and depth. I'm grateful for you sharing them with me.

Finally, thanks to my extraordinary wife, Kathleen, who sacrificed much for this project and carefully pored over the text. I also must thank our wonderful children, Isaiah, Teresa, Augustine, Gianna, Zelie, Gilbert, and Maria. You are the lights that make my life shine. I love you all so much.

REFERENCES

While working on this project, I read dozens of books, and these proved especially helpful:

Forming Intentional Disciples: The Path to Knowing and Following Jesus (Our Sunday Visitor, 2012) by Sherry Weddell

Generation Ex-Christian: Why Young Adults Are Leaving the Faith . . . and How to Bring Them Back (Moody Publishers, 2010) by Drew Dyck

How to Defend the Faith Without Raising Your Voice, Revised and Updated (Our Sunday Visitor, 2015) by Austen Ivereigh and Kathryn Lopez

Mass Exodus: Catholic Disaffiliation in Britain and America Since Vatican II (Oxford University Press, 2019) by Stephen Bullivant

The Prodigal You Love: Inviting Loved Ones Back to the Church (Pauline Books and Media, 2014) by Theresa Aletheia Noble, FSP

The Rise of the Nones: Understanding and Reaching the Religiously Unaffiliated (Baker Books, 2014) by James Emery White

Search and Rescue: How to Bring Your Family and Friends Into—Or Back Into—the Catholic Church (Sophia Institute Press, 2001) by Patrick Madrid

Tactics: A Game Plan for Discussing Your Christian Convictions (Zondervan, 2009) by Gregory Koukl

unChristian: What a New Generation Thinks About Christianity . . . and Why It Matters (Baker Books, 2007) by David Kinnaman

When a Loved One Leaves the Church (Our Sunday Visitor, 2001) by Lorene Hanley Duquin

Young Catholic America: Emerging Adults In, Out of, and Gone from the Church (Oxford University Press, 2014) by Christian Smith, Kyle Longest, Jonathan Hill, and Kari Christoffersen

Find more specific references and citations below.

Introduction

xiv   Half of young Americans who were raised Catholic no longer identify as Catholic today: "America's Changing Religious Landscape," Pew Research Center, Washington, DC, May 12, 2015, https://www.pewforum.org/2015/05/12/americas-changing-religious-landscape/.

xiv   Roughly eight in ten (79%) who shed their faith leave before age twenty-three: "Faith in Flux," Pew Research Center, Washington, DC, April 27, 2009, https://www.pewforum.org/2009/04/27/faith-in-flux/.

xv   "It has driven a wedge through the core of our family": Quoted in Lorene Hanley Duquin, *When a Loved One Leaves the Church* (Huntington, IN: Our Sunday Visitor, 2001), 45.

xv   "I guess they weren't as good as we thought they were": Quoted in Lorene Hanley Duquin, *When a Loved One Leaves the Church* (Huntington, IN: Our Sunday Visitor, 2001), 46.

Chapter 1 – Why Are They Leaving?

3   half (50% exactly) of young Americans who were raised Catholic no longer call themselves Catholic today: "America's Changing Religious Landscape," Pew Research Center, Washington, DC, May 12, 2015, https://www.pewforum.org/2015/05/12/americas-changing-religious-landscape/.

3   just 7% of young people raised in the Church still actively practice their faith today: Christian Smith, Kyle Longest, Jonathan Hill, and Kari Christoffersen, *Young Catholic America: Emerging Adults In, Out Of, and Gone from the Church* (New York: Oxford University Press, 2014), 202.

3   eight-in-ten (79%) who drift away from faith leave before age twenty-three: "Faith in Flux," Pew Research Center, Washington, DC, April 27, 2009, https://www.pewforum.org/2009/04/27/faith-in-flux/.

3   one in four Hispanics in America are now *former* Catholics: Cited in "The Shifting Religious Identity of Latinos in the United States," Pew Research Center, Washington, DC, May 7, 2014, https://www.pewforum.org/2014/05/07/the-shifting-religious-identity-of-latinos-in-the-united-states/.

4   "As many as there are people": Pope Benedict XVI and Peter Seewald, *Salt of the Earth: Christianity and the Catholic Church at the End of the Millennium* (San Francisco: Ignatius Press, 1997), 8.

4 "The Church is a house with a hundred gates and people are rushing out of each one": G.K. Chesterton, *The Catholic Church and Conversion* (San Francisco: Ignatius Press, [1926] 2007), 38.

4 for every person who becomes Catholic, roughly 6.5 leave the Church: "America's Changing Religious Landscape," Pew Research Center, Washington, DC, May 12, 2015, https://www.pewforum.org/2015/05/12/americas-changing-religious-landscape/.

5 the diocese [of Springfield] partnered with researchers: Philip R. Hardy, Kelly L. Kandra, Brian G. Patterson, *Joy and Grievance in an American Diocese: Results from Online Surveys of Active and Inactive Catholics in Central Illinois* (Lisle, IL: Benedictine University, 2014), https://www.dio.org/uploads/files/Communications/Press_Releases/2014/Joy-and-Grievance-PUBLIC-FINAL-sep-11-2014.pdf.

6 Here were the most common reasons people gave: "Faith in Flux," Pew Research Center, Washington, DC, April 27, 2009, https://www.pewforum.org/2009/04/27/faith-in-flux/.

7 The Diocese of Trenton, New Jersey, found similar conclusions: Quoted in William J. Bryan, "Why They Left: Exit Interviews Shed Light on Empty Pews," *America*, April 30, 2012, http://americamagazine.org/issue/5138/article/why-they-left.

8 "I don't know what else to list": Sarah, "Christian Formation and the Cost of the Culture Wars", *A Queer Calling* (blog), May 1, 2014, http://aqueercalling.com/2014/05/01/christian-formation-and-the-cost-of-the-culture-wars/.

8 among former Catholics who are now unaffiliated with any religion: "U.S. Religious Landscape Survey," Pew Research Center, Washington, DC, June 1, 2008, https://www.pewforum.org/2008/06/01/u-s-religious-landscape-survey-religious-beliefs-and-practices/.

8 A group of University of Notre Dame researchers found: Quoted by Ann Carey, "Portrait of Young Catholics Sobering but Vital," *Our Sunday Visitor*, June 11, 2014.

9 what sociologists Christian Smith and Melinda Lundquist Denton have called "moralistic therapeutic deism": Christian Smith and Melinda Lundquist Denton, *Soul Searching: The Religious and Spiritual Lives of American Teenagers* (Oxford: Oxford University Press, 2009), 163.

9 **More than half (54%) of nominally Catholic young adults believe in God but think he is not personal:** Smith et al., *Young Catholic America*, 67.

10 **"What does it matter so long as they are contented?":** C.S. Lewis, *The Problem of Pain* (New York: Macmillan, 1962), 40.

10 **"We were not created for an easy life, but for great things, for goodness":** Pope Benedict XVI, "Address to the German Pilgrims Who Had Come to Rome for the Inauguration Ceremony of the Pontificate," April 25, 2005, http://www.vatican.va/content/benedict-xvi/en/speeches/2005/april/documents/hf_ben-xvi_spe_20050425_german-pilgrims.html.

Chapter 2 – Where Are They Going?

13 **From 2007 to 2014, the percentage of religiously unaffiliated Americans soared from 16% to 23%:** "America's Changing Religious Landscape," Pew Research Center, Washington, DC, May 12, 2015, https://www.pewforum.org/2015/05/12/americas-changing-religious-landscape/.

13 **21% were raised in an unaffiliated home while 28% were raised Catholic:** "America's Changing Religious Landscape," Pew Research Center.

13 **The median age of the unaffiliated? Just thirty-six:** "America's Changing Religious Landscape," Pew Research Center.

13 ***twice* as likely to say they have no religion than to identify as Catholic:** "America's Changing Religious Landscape," Pew Research Center.

14 **Some of their traits may surprise you:** "'Nones' on the Rise," Pew Research Center, Washington, DC, October 9, 2012, https://www.pewforum.org/2012/10/09/nones-on-the-rise/.

15 **"Believe it or not, that makes it easier to bring him back to the Church":** Patrick Madrid, *Search and Rescue: How to Bring Your Family and Friends Into or Back Into the Catholic Church* (Manchester, NH: Sophia Institute Press, 2001), 57.

16 **The share of mainline Protestant Americans dropped from 18% in 2007 to 14% in 2014:** "America's Changing Religious Landscape," Pew Research Center.

17 **"I believe in God and basically I celebrate Christmas":** Quoted in Anna Sutherland, "Young Catholic America," *Books and Culture: A Christian Review* (May/June 2014).

17   **"I simply don't practice anymore"**: Personal email correspondence.

18   **"see it as a positive source of family identity and togetherness"**: Christian Smith, Kyle Longest, Jonathan Hill, Kari Christoffersen, *Young Catholic America: Emerging Adults In, Out Of, and Gone from the Church* (New York: Oxford University Press, 2014), 107.

18   **"getting up early on Sunday is difficult"**: Personal email correspondence with the author.

18   **"deeper purpose in life wasn't a priority for them"**: Molly Oshatz, "From 'Meh' to 'Amen,'" *First Things*, June 8, 2015, http://www.firstthings.com/web-exclusives/2015/06/can-the-nones-go-from-meh-to-amen.

19   **"The object of opening the mind, as of opening the mouth, is to shut it again on something solid"**: G.K. Chesterton, *The Autobiography of G.K. Chesterton* (San Francisco: Ignatius Press, [1936] 2006), 217.

19   **"But a man who simply ignores the whole thing is acting like a fool"**: Frank Sheed and Maisie Ward, *Catholic Evidence Training Outlines* (Steubenville, OH; Franciscan University Press, [1948] 1993), 158.

19   **"The one thing it cannot be is moderately important"**: C.S. Lewis, *God in the Dock* (Grand Rapids, MI: Eerdmans, [1970] 2014), 102.

20   **"Nature to me is what God is all about. It's a renewal"**: Quoted in Lorene Hanley Duquin, *When a Loved One Leaves the Church* (Huntington, IN: Our Sunday Visitor, 2001), 38.

21   **"factors that contribute to a lot of switching"**: Christian Smith et al., *Young Catholic America*, 102.

22   **Their numbers have doubled over the last decade:** "America's Changing Religious Landscape," Pew Research Center.

22   **"12% of former Catholics identify as atheist and 16% as agnostic."** - Cited by Mark Gray, "Your Average American Catholic: A Model Citizen for a Diverse Church," *America*, May 18, 2015, https://www.americamagazine.org/issue/your-average-american-catholic.

Chapter 3 – The Five Big Myths About Fallen-Away Catholics

25   **"Some youth seem to *expect* to be religiously inactive during their pre-marriage, emerging adult years"**: Christian Smith, Kyle Longest, Jonathan

Hill, and Kari Christoffersen, *Young Catholic America: Emerging Adults In, Out Of, and Gone from the Church* (New York: Oxford University Press, 2014), 117.

25 **"rather than a foundation for launching into adulthood and parenthood":** Kay Hymowitz, Jason S. Carroll, W. Bradford Wilcox, and Kelleen Kaye, *Knot Yet: The Benefits and Costs of Delayed Marriage in America* (Charlottesville, VA: The National Marriage Project at the University of Virginia, 2013), 4, http://nationalmarriageproject.org/wp-content/uploads/2013/03/KnotYet-FinalForWeb.pdf.

26 **the lowest birthrate in recorded American history:** Quoted in Neil Shah, "Just How Much Did the Recession Make 20-Somethings Delay Children?", *Wall Street Journal*, April 28, 2015, https://blogs.wsj.com/economics/2015/04/28/just-how-much-did-the-recession-make-20-somethings-delay-children/.

26 **"The rituals without the relationship were not worth keeping":** Personal email correspondence with the author.

27 **"there is no significant direct effect of attending a Catholic school on increased religiousness in emerging adulthood":** Smith et al., *Young Catholic America*, 253.

27 **"little to no independent influence five years later on those who attended them":** Smith et al., *Young Catholic America*, 270.

27 **"have little to no effect on whether young people sustain their faith into adulthood."** "Faith in Flux," Pew Research Center, Washington, DC, April 27, 2009, https://www.pewforum.org/2009/04/27/faith-in-flux/.

27 **"a genuine preparation for a living faith and remain a support for it throughout one's life":** *Catechism of the Catholic Church*, 2nd ed., no. 2225 (Washington, DC: USCCB Publishing, 1997), 537.

28 **Ronda's son left the Church at age sixteen and didn't return until he was thirty-two:** Quoted in "To the Parent of a Prodigal," *Ronda's Resting Place* (blog), http://rondasrestingplace.net/subpage29.html (site discontinued).

29 **"we cannot legitimately be held responsible for that decision":** Bert Ghezzi, *When Someone You Love Leaves the Church* (Fort Wayne, IN: Our Sunday Visitor, 2009), pamphlet.

30 **"The one identity that is sound, true, and unshakable is that *you* are a**

precious child of God": Carol Barnier, *Engaging Today's Prodigal: Clear Thinking, New Approaches, and Reasons for Hope* (Chicago, IL: Moody Publishers, 2012), 111.

Chapter 4 – The Basics

35   "**the religious faith, commitments, and practices of their parents**": Christian Smith, Kyle Longest, Jonathan Hill, and Kari Christoffersen, *Young Catholic America: Emerging Adults In, Out Of, and Gone from the Church* (New York: Oxford University Press, 2014), 27.

35   "**most crucial are the commitment, intentionality, examples, and encouragement of Catholic *parents***": Smith et al., *Young Catholic America*, 268.

36   "**I wanted the peace that seemed to come from their faith in God**": Quoted in Lorene Hanley Duquin, *When a Loved One Leaves the Church* (Huntington, IN: Our Sunday Visitor, 2001), 89.

37   "**we're likely making them sicker, from a spiritual perspective**": Personal conversation with the author.

38   "**always be sure to focus more on his heart's sickness than its symptoms**": Abraham Piper, "Let Them Come Home," *Christianity.com*, July 19, 2013, http://www.christianity.com/theology/12-ways-to-love-your-wayward-child-11625957.html (article discontinued).

39   "**Today sometimes it seems that the opposite order is prevailing**": Pope Francis, "A Big Heart Open to God," interview by Antonio Spadaro, SJ, *America*, September 13, 2013, https://www.americamagazine.org/faith/2013/09/30/big-heart-open-god-interview-pope-francis.

40   "**said what she thought instead of pretending she was trying to help**": Personal email correspondence with the author.

40   "**if you're not careful, it can come across as aggressive proselytizing**": Personal email correspondence with the author.

40   "**The Church proposes; she imposes nothing**": John Paul II, *Redemptoris Missio*, 39, encyclical letter, Vatican website, December 7, 1990, http://www.vatican.va/content/john-paul-ii/en/encyclicals/documents/hf_jp-ii_enc_07121990_redemptoris-missio.html.

44   "**This is one of the most difficult transitions for a postmodern nonbeliever**": Sherry Weddell, *Forming Intentional Disciples: The Path to Knowing and Following Jesus* (Fort Wayne, IN: Our Sunday Visitor, 2015), 130.

46 **"only when he sees Jesus more as he actually is":** Abraham Piper, "Let Them Come Home," *Christianity.com*, July 19, 2013, http://www.christianity .com/theology/12-ways-to-love-your-wayward-child-11625957.html (article discontinued).

Chapter 5 – Pray, Fast, and Sacrifice

50 **"I prayed for St. Monica to intercede for our family members":** Quoted in Joseph Pronechen, "St. Monica, Pray for Our Wayward Children's Conversions," *National Catholic Register*, August 24, 2003, https://www.ncregister.com/features/ st-monica-pray-for-our-wayward-childrens-conversions.

51 **A recent survey asked Catholic parents:** Mary M. Gray, "The Catholic Family: 21st Century Challenges in the United States," The Center for Applied Research in the Apostolate (CARA), June 2015.

52 **[Bishop Robert Barron] was visiting a college campus:** This was a re-telling of the story in Bishop Robert Barron, "Bishop Barron on Evangelizing with the Heart of a Shepherd," YouTube video, September 25, 2014, 1:46, https://www. youtube.com/watch?v=dQBXwv-WCWU.

54 **"we'd never be able to get up off our knees again for the rest of our lives":** Peter Kreeft, *Before I Go: Letters to Our Children about What Really Matters* (Lanham, MD: Sheed & Ward, 2007), 231.

55 **"you can be sure you've already begun":** Josemaría Escrivá, *The Way*, ch. 3, no. 90, Josemaría Escrivá website, https://www.escrivaworks.org/book/the_way.

56 **"being at least like a dog at the master's door, ready in case he called me":** Fulton Sheen, *Treasure in Clay: The Autobiography of Fulton J. Sheen* (New York: Image Books, 2008, original 1980), 201–202.

56 **"this prayer is always heard and always answered":** St. Faustina Kowalska, *Divine Mercy in My Soul* (Stockbridge, MA: Marian Press, 1987), nos. 1209, 1397.

57 **"Prayer is a powerful gift":** Quoted in Marge Fenelon, "What to Do When Children Leave the Church," *National Catholic Register*, May 27, 2011, https://www. ncregister.com/features/what-to-do-when-children-leave-the-church.

61 **"only let my people be converted":** Quoted in Fr. Lance W. Harlow, "The Immolations of the Cure d'Ars," *Homiletic and Pastoral Review* (March 2011): 18–19.

Chapter 6 – Equip Yourself

74   **"that Catholicism is true":** G.K. Chesterton, "Why I Am a Catholic," in *The Collected Works of G.K. Chesterton*, vol. 3 (San Francisco: Ignatius Press, 1990), 127.

76   **"your offer to your listeners":** Shaun McAfee, *Filling Our Father's House: What Converts Can Teach Us About Evangelization* (Manchester, NH: Sophia Institute Press, 2015), 37–38.

77   **"Tell *that* story":** McAfee, *Filling Our Father's House*, 40.

Chapter 7 – Plant the Seeds

79   **"choosing sleep and a leisurely brunch when Sunday morning came":** Personal email correspondence with the author.

80   **"no matter what he has done, he is still loved":** Rob Parsons, *Bringing Home the Prodigals* (Colorado Springs, CO: Authentic Publishing, 2007), 34.

84   **"When the Father's house is filled with the Father's love, the prodigals will come home":** Quoted in Parsons, *Bringing Home the Prodigals*, 83.

84   **Rob Parsons tells of a young man:** Parsons, *Bringing Home the Prodigals*, 13.

85   **"Don't lessen the likelihood of an opportunity to be with your child by pushing him away with rules":** Abraham Piper, "Let Them Come Home," *Christianity.com*, July 19, 2013. Accessed online at http://www.christianity.com/theology/12-ways-to-love-your-wayward-child-11625957.html (article discontinued).

86   **"You don't know how happy it makes a mother to see her son return to church":** Quoted in Matthew Kelly, *The Four Signs of a Dynamic Catholic* (Hebron, KY: Beacon Press, 2013), 101.

86   **"I'm confident we planted some seeds":** Personal email correspondence with the author.

87   **One of my favorite "seed gift" stories comes from a woman named Leila:** Leila Miller, "Converted by the 'Catholicism' Series," Word on Fire, January 8, 2015, https://www.wordonfire.org/resources/blog/converted-by-the-catholicism-series/19987.

90   **A recent survey asked hundreds of young atheists to describe their journey to unbelief:** Larry Alex Taunton, "Listening to Young Atheists: Lessons for a Stronger Christianity," *The Atlantic*, June 6, 2013, http://www.

theatlantic.com/national/archive/2013/06/listening-to-young-atheists-lessons-for-a-stronger-christianity/276584.

91   **The Pew Research Center found that 92% of teens go online every day, and a quarter say they are online "almost constantly":** Amanda Lenhart, "Teens, Social Media & Technology Overview 2015," Pew Research Center, Washington, DC, April 9, 2015, https://www.pewresearch.org/internet/2015/04/09/teens-social-media-technology-2015/.

91   **The average American teenager spends over seven hours a day on screen media:** "Teen Social Media Statistics 2020 (What Parents Need to Know)," Smart Social: Learn How to Shine Online, February 25, 2020, https://smartsocial.com/social-media-statistics.

Chapter 8 – Start the Conversation

93   **A recent survey of Catholic teenagers revealed:** Mark Gray, "The Catholic Teenager: A Few Mysteries Solved," *1964* (blog), Center for Applied Research in the Apostolate (CARA), May 2, 2013, http://nineteensixty-four.blogspot.com/2013/05/the-catholic-teenager-few-mysteries.html.

93   **"I sometimes find myself unable even to get a hearing from some of those I love the most. I'm not alone":** Patrick Madrid, *Search and Rescue: How to Bring Your Family and Friends Into or Back Into the Catholic Church* (Manchester, NH: Sophia Institute Press, 2001), xix.

94   **"God will give you the gumption":** Abraham Piper, "Let Them Come Home," *Christianity.com*, July 19, 2013. Accessed online at http://www.christianity.com/theology/12-ways-to-love-your-wayward-child-11625957.html (article discontinued).

96   **Theologian Francis Schaeffer was once asked what he would do if he had an hour with a non-Christian:** Quoted in Jonathan K. Dodson, *The Unbelievable Gospel: Say Something Worth Believing* (Grand Rapids, MI: Zondervan, 2014), 51.

96   **Marcel LeJeune, founder of Catholic Missionary Disciples, offers a list of helpful questions to ask during this listening phase:** Marcel LeJeune, "Questions to Ask Others When Evangelizing," *St. Mary's Aggie Catholic Blog*, May 11, 2015, http://www.aggiecatholicblog.org/2015/05/questions-to-ask-others-when-evangelizing.

98   **"never make a statement, at least at first, when a question will do the job":** Gregory Koukl, *Tactics: A Game Plan for Discussing Your Christian Convictions* (Grand Rapids, MI: Zondervan, 2009), 47.

98   **My friend Trent Horn, staff apologist for Catholic Answers, offers five specific questions to use in conversations:** See Trent Horn, "The Apologist's Most Important Tool," Catholic Answers, July 10, 2013, https://www.catholic.com/magazine/online-edition/the-apologists-most-important-tool.

101   **"If not, you can tell me why you think your option is better":** Gregory Koukl, *Tactics: A Game Plan for Discussing Your Christian Convictions* (Grand Rapids, MI: Zondervan, 2009), 86.

Chapter 9 – Move the Dialogue Forward

104   **"If anyone in the discussion gets angry, you lose":** Gregory Koukl, *Tactics: A Game Plan for Discussing Your Christian Convictions* (Grand Rapids, MI: Zondervan, 2009), 30.

104   **55% of communication is body language, 38% depends on the tone of voice, and 7% concerns the actual words spoken:** Jeff Thompson, "Is Nonverbal Communication a Numbers Game?", *Psychology Today*, September 30, 2011, https://www.psychologytoday.com/blog/beyond-words/201109/is-nonverbal-communication-numbers-game.

107   **Anglican theologian N.T. Wright offers a telling anecdote:** N.T. Wright, "Jesus and the Identity of God," N.T. Wright Page, July 12, 2016, http://ntwright-page.com/Wright_JIG.htm.

107   **"There are millions, however, who hate what they wrongly believe to be the Catholic Church—which is, of course, quite a different thing":** Fulton Sheen, preface to *Radio Replies*, vol. 1, Catholic Apologetics Online: Radio Replies, http://www.radioreplies.info/vol-1-preface.php.

109   **"This makes it possible to communicate, to be heard, and to have a proper dialogue":** Austen Ivereigh and Kathryn Jean Lopez, *How to Defend the Faith Without Raising Your Voice: Civil Responses to Catholic Hot Button Issues, Revised and Updated* (Huntington, IN: Our Sunday Visitor, 2015), 15.

112   **"shoe pebble" questions:** Credit for the "shoe pebble" concept goes to Gregory Koukl; see Koukl, *Tactics*, 38.

114   "the Church is a joyful home": Pope Francis, "Angelus," December 15, 2013, http://www.vatican.va/content/francesco/en/angelus/2013/documents/pa-pa-francesco_angelus_20131215.html.

Chapter 10 – Invite and Connect

118   "So I put my name down, and that was that": Personal conversation with the author.

119   "if he does listen to teachers, it is because they are witnesses": Pope Paul VI, *Evangelii Nuntiandi*, 41, Vatican website, December 8, 1975, http://www.vatican.va/content/paul-vi/en/apost_exhortations/documents/hf_p-vi_exh_19751208_evangelii-nuntiandi.html.

121   "Anything that is unwelcoming or judgmental is likely to turn people away from your parish and the Faith": Quoted in Mark Gray, "Lapsed Catholics Weigh in on Why They Left the Church," *Our Sunday Visitor*, October 22, 2014, https://www.osvnews.com/2014/10/22/lapsed-catholics-weigh-in-on-why-they-left-church/.

124   "if it weren't for people constantly reaching out to me in a nonjudgmental way": Quoted in Kristin Peterson, "You Can Go Home Again: Catholics Return to the Church", *U.S. Catholic*, June 15, 2011, https://uscatholic.org/articles/201106/you-can-go-home-again-catholics-return-to-the-church/.

124   "what had to be reshaped to line up with God as I was learning him to be": Carol Barnier, *Engaging Today's Prodigal: Clear Thinking, New Approaches, and Reasons for Hope* (Chicago, IL: Moody Publishers, 2012), 111.

125   "There was a period of reflection as you sorted out the details": Gregory Koukl, *Tactics: A Game Plan for Discussing Your Christian Convictions* (Grand Rapids, MI: Zondervan, 2009), 39.

Chapter 11 – Close the Loop

127   "Would you be willing to invite Jesus into your life right now": Marcel LeJeune, "The Fatal Flaw of Catholics Who Evangelize," *St. Mary's Aggie Catholic Blog*, June 1, 2015, https://www.aggiecatholicblog.org/2015/06/the-fatal-flaw-of-catholics-who-evangelize/.

127   "Say a prayer with me that asks Jesus to guide your life and be your Lord. What do you have to lose": Shaun McAfee, *Filling Our Father's House: What*

Converts Can Teach Us About Evangelization (Manchester, NH: Sophia Institute Press, 2015), 45.

128   **"Marcel LeJeune adds one more bit of advice"**: Marcel LeJeune, "The Fatal Flaw of Catholics Who Evangelize."

133   **"the good will and love shared among the family members"**: Sally L. Mews, *Returning Home to Your Catholic Faith: An Invitation* (Liguori, MO: Liguori Publications, 2003), 25.

135   **"Pastoral ministers can be assured that to assist couples in regularizing their situation is not to approve of cohabitation"**: United States Conference of Catholic Bishops, "Marriage Preparation And Cohabiting Couples: An Information Report on New Realities and Pastoral Practices" (1999), United States Conference of Catholic Bishops website, http://www.usccb.org/issues-and-action/marriage-and-family/marriage/marriage-preparation/cohabiting.cfm.

135   **"I know I'm excommunicated and the Church cannot forgive me"**: Quoted in Pete Vere, "Strong Medicine," *Catholic Answers*, November 1, 2007, https://www.catholic.com/magazine/print-edition/strong-medicine.

137   **Lorene Hanley Duquin debunks some popular myths about annulments:** Lorene Hanley Duquin, *When a Loved One Leaves the Church* (Huntington, IN: Our Sunday Visitor, 2001), 198.

Chapter 12 – Personal Objections

144   **"know what the Church teaches about the real presence and do not believe it"**: Mark Gray, "Your Average American Catholic: A Model Citizen for a Diverse Church," *America*, May 18, 2015, https://www.americamagazine.org/issue/your-average-american-catholic.

145   **"This calls for a creative liturgical, pastoral, doctrinal and practical response"**: See William J. Bryan, "Why They Left: Exit Interviews Shed Light on Empty Pews," *America*, April 30, 2012, http://americamagazine.org/issue/5138/article/why-they-left.

147   **A recent survey found that only 61% of Catholic teens agree:** Mark M. Gray, "The Catholic Teenager: A Few Mysteries Solved," *1964* (blog), Center for Applied Research in the Apostolate (CARA), May 2, 2013, http://nineteensixty-four.blogspot.com/2013/05/the-catholic-teenager-few-mysteries.html.

148   **"To get rid of my sins"**: G.K. Chesterton, *The Autobiography of G.K.Chesterton* (San Francisco: Ignatius Press, [1936] 2006), 324.

151 **A recent Pew Forum survey found that nearly 40% of marriages since 2010 can be classified as "religiously mixed":** "America's Changing Religious Landscape," Pew Research Center, Washington, DC, May 12, 2015, https://www.pewforum.org/2015/05/12/americas-changing-religious-landscape/.

152 **"The falling away from church causes my mother great pain and that makes me sad":** Personal email correspondence with the author.

153 **"I felt like these people in the congregation were the most judgmental people I have ever met":** Personal email correspondence with the author.

153 **"She now goes to a Protestant church where she says people are friendly and really care about you":** Quoted in Lorene Hanley Duquin, *When a Loved One Leaves the Church* (Huntington, IN: Our Sunday Visitor, 2001), 22.

154 **"Remember that God is trying to get us into Heaven, not to keep us out":** Fr. Andrew Carrozza, "God would never forgive me THAT!" Rev. Andrew P. Carrozza: Being Catholic is Cool, April 24, 2012, http://fathercarrozza.com/2012/08/24/god-would-never-forgive-me-that.

Chapter 13 – Moral Objections

156 **"The Church doesn't want either of us":** Quoted in Mark Gray, "Lapsed Catholics Weigh in on Why They Left the Church," *Our Sunday Visitor*, October 22, 2014, https://www.osvnews.com/2014/10/22/lapsed-catholics-weigh-in-on-why-they-left-church/.

157 **"Their [homosexual] orientation isn't the problem. . . . They're our brothers":** Pope Francis, "Press Conference of Pope Francis during the Return Flight from Rio de Janeiro," July 28, 2013, http://www.vatican.va/content/francesco/en/speeches/2013/july/documents/papa-francesco_20130728_gmg-conferenza-stampa.html.

158 **A few years ago, a collection of national surveys revealed that the most common perception of present-day Christianity is "anti-homosexual":** See David Kinnaman, *unChristian: What a New Generation Really Thinks About Christianity . . . and Why It Matters* (Grand Rapids, MI: Baker Books, 2007), 27.

160 **a major national Pew study found that more LGBT people identify as Catholic (17%) than any other religious tradition:** "America's Changing Religious Landscape," Pew Research Center, Washington, DC, May 12, 2015, https://www.pewforum.org/2015/05/12/americas-changing-religious-landscape/.

162 "**After telling only one person I was blatantly told that I was going to burn in hell. That was it for me**": Personal email correspondence with the author.

165 "**having to go through the Pre-Cana marriage preparation program**": Personal email correspondence with the author.

165 **Today, roughly two thirds of couples cohabitate before marrying, a 900% increase in cohabitation over the last fifty years:** Lauren Fox, "The Science of Cohabitation: A Step Toward Marriage, Not a Rebellion," *The Atlantic*, March 20, 2014, http://www.theatlantic.com/health/archive/2014/03/the-science-of-cohabitation-a-step-toward-marriage-not-a-rebellion/284512.

165 **only one in four Americans disapprove of cohabiting before marriage:** Brandon Gaille, "43 Statistics on Cohabitation Before Marriage," Brandon Gaille website, May 20, 2017, http://brandongaille.com/43-statistics-on-cohabitation-before-marriage.

165 "**who are living with a partner, never married**": Quoted in Anne Hendershott, "Digging Deeper into the Pew Data about the Nones, Millennials, and Christians," *Catholic World Report*, May 25, 2015, https://www.catholicworldreport.com/2015/05/25/digging-deeper-into-the-pew-data-about-nones-millennials-and-christians/.

165 "**factors that may present special challenges to them or put them at risk for later marital disruption**": United States Conference of Catholic Bishops, "Marriage Preparation And Cohabiting Couples: An Information Report on New Realities and Pastoral Practices" (1999), United States Conference of Catholic Bishops website, http://www.usccb.org/issues-and-action/marriage-and-family/marriage/marriage-preparation/cohabiting.cfm.

166 **one out of every five women who cohabitate become pregnant within the first twelve months of moving in:** Fox, "The Science of Cohabitation."

166 "**can pose real problems to their relationship and to their future odds of successfully marrying**": Fox, "The Science of Cohabitation."

169 "**The teaching reflects the specific role of the priest in the Catholic understanding, which is to represent Jesus, to stand in his place**": Austen Ivereigh and Kathryn Jean Lopez, *How to Defend the Faith Without Raising Your Voice: Civil Responses to Catholic Hot Button Issues, Revised and Updated* (Huntington, IN: Our Sunday Visitor, 2015), 188.

169 "those involved with youth groups and recreational activities are women": Catherine Lacugna, "Catholic Women as Ministers and Theologians," *America*, October 10, 1992.

170 In response to a Pew Forum survey about why they left the Catholic Church: "Faith in Flux," Pew Research Center, Washington, DC, April 27, 2009, https://www.pewforum.org/2009/04/27/faith-in-flux/.

171 "The pill is the only drug that was developed to be given to a woman who was healthy to create a diseased state": Quoted in Matthew Bunson, "Pill's Pitfalls Create 'Contraceptive Conundrum,'" *Our Sunday Visitor*, August 12, 2015.

171 women who take the pill are somewhere between 20–40% more likely to have breast cancer than women who don't and are far more likely to have cervical and skin cancer than other women: Cited in Couple to Couple League, "The Pill: How Does It Work? Is it Safe?", EWTN, https://www.ewtn.com/catholicism/library/pill-how-does-it-work-is-it-safe-11232.

172 When used properly, some NFP methods have been measured to be over 98% effective in avoiding unintended pregnancy: See Joe Heschmeyer, "Just How Effective is Natural Family Planning, Anyway?", *Shameless Popery* (blog), September 11, 2013, http://shamelesspopery.com/just-how-effective-is-natural-family-planning-anyway/.

174 "How could this happen in a Catholic family": Quoted in Lorene Hanley Duquin, *When a Loved One Leaves the Church* (Huntington, IN: Our Sunday Visitor, 2001), 192.

174 "The best thing I ever did was go and talk to a priest who told me there was no reason that I couldn't come home": Quoted in Duquin, 193.

Chapter 14 – Theological Objections

178 God provides enough light for those who want to see, and enough darkness to hide in the shadows: Blaise Pascal, *Pensees* (New York: Penguin Classics, 1995), 50.

179 "science proves religion to be superstition": "Faith in Flux," Pew Research Center, Washington, DC, April 27, 2009, https://www.pewforum.org/2009/04/27/faith-in-flux/.

179 "Christianity is anti-science": "Six Reasons Young Christians Leave Church," Barna Group, September 27, 2011, https://www.barna.com/research/six-reasons-young-christians-leave-church/.

180 **"The torch of science can't illuminate the answer to every question we have about the world":** Trent Horn, *20 Answers: Faith and Science* (El Cajon, CA: Catholic Answers, 2015), 25.

181 **Recent surveys show that roughly half of working scientists are theists:** Cited in Fr. Robert Spitzer, "Jesuit Philosopher Works to Demonstrate Compatibility of Faith and Science," interview by Jim Graves, *Catholic World Report*, November 4, 2014, https://www.catholicworldreport.com/2014/11/04/jesuit-philosopher-works-to-demonstrate-compatibility-of-faith-and-science/.

181 **"There is more evidence from physics for a beginning of the universe than ever before":** Spitzer, "Jesuit Philosopher Works to Demonstrate Compatibility of Faith and Science."

183 **"as the living Lord, the way, the truth, and the life":** Pope John Paul II, *L'Osservatore Romano* (English Edition), March 24, 1993, 3.

183 **A recent Pew survey found that only 60% of Catholic adults even believe in a personal God:** Cited in Sherry Weddell, *Forming Intentional Disciples: The Path to Knowing and Following Jesus* (Fort Wayne, IN: Our Sunday Visitor, 2015), 35.

184 **"It wasn't hard to convince them to disregard the sacraments along with the Church that emphasized the sacraments":** Steve Wood, "How I Led Catholics Out of the Church," Catholic Education Research Center, https://www.catholiceducation.org/en/religion-and-philosophy/apologetics/how-i-led-catholics-out-of-the-church.html.

187 **"all the clergy must hold fast to the Sacred Scriptures"** – *Dei Verbum*, 25, Vatican website, November 18, 1965, https://www.vatican.va/archive/hist_councils/ii_vatican_council/documents/vat-ii_const_19651118_dei-verbum_en.html.

188 **eight in ten (81%) cite enjoyment of the religious service and the style of worship as a main reason:** "Faith in Flux," Pew Research Center.

189 **"I decided that I couldn't have anything to do with a God that would allow that kind of pain in my heart":** Personal email correspondence with the author.

Conclusion

193 **just focus on helping your child become 1% closer to God each day than the day before:** This idea is based on the concepts

214

discussed in Brett and Kate McKay, "Get 1% Better Every Day: The Kaizen Way to Self-Improvement," July 31, 2020, http://www.artofmanliness.com/2015/08/10/ get-1-better-every-day-the-kaizen-way-to-self-improvement.

ABOUT THE AUTHOR

Brandon Vogt is the Senior Content Director at Bishop Robert Barron's Word on Fire Catholic Ministries.

He's the author of ten books, several of which have been #1 Amazon bestsellers and have earned First Place awards from both the Catholic Press Association and the Association of Catholic Publishers.

Brandon hosts the weekly *Word on Fire Show* podcast with Bishop Barron, as well as *The Burrowshire Podcast* with Fr. Blake Britton. He also runs several websites, including StrangeNotions.com and ChurchFathers.org.

Brandon's work has been featured by NPR, FoxNews, CBS, EWTN, Vatican Radio, *Our Sunday Visitor*, *National Review*, and *Christianity Today*.

He is on the board of the Society of G.K. Chesterton and serves as President of the Central Florida Chesterton Society.

Brandon lives with his wife and seven children on Burrowshire, a small farm outside Orlando, Florida, with chickens, goats, pigs, rabbits, ducks, and a garden.

Download the individual reflection guide,
group discussion guide, and other resources at

https://WordonFire.org/Return